Surprise Cakes & Cupcakes

CANDICE CLAYTON

NEW
HOLLAND

Surprise Cakes
& Cupcakes

For my Mum,

Past the moon and stars and all the way back again.

Contents

Introduction

· ·

Welcome to Surprise Cakes and Cupcakes. This is a book that will show you how to bake, make and decorate cakes and cupcakes with a surprise hidden inside of them.

If your childhood was anything like mine, the birthday cake was eagerly anticipated when the big day finally rolled around. As a decorator who specialises in kids' novelty cakes there is nothing more rewarding than seeing the excitement on a child's face when they see their cake for the first time. The idea of continuing this surprise and excitement throughout the cake cutting and eating process is priceless. So, when I was asked to compile 50 of my favourite cakes and cupcakes, filled with secret surprises, my inner child was delighted at the opportunity to share how easy they are to create. And because cake surprises are not limited to children's celebrations, there are a few surprise options for the grown ups too!

From cakes baked inside cakes, cake-pop mixes, intriguing cake shapes, and cakes filled to the brim with lollies, to jelly and flavored chocolate ganaches that will deliver a surprising flavor burst upon first bite, I have tried to cover as many options as possible.

This book is intended to give you fun ideas and easy step-by-step instructions so that you can construct the cakes as they appear. Once you have the basic know-how, you can swap and change the cakes and their surprises—the colors, flavors and features of the decorations, and truly make it your own design. The best cake is the one that best suits the recipient.

Happy baking and creating cake-friends!

Candice X

TOOLS: (from top left): 1. Assorted shape cutters 2. Multiple sized Circle Cutters 3. Multiple sized Star Cutters 4. Measuring cups 5. Measuring spoon 6. whisk (or Mixer) 7. beater (for mixer) 8. white and gold dust and non-toxic glitter 9. Round Thermo Piping tip 10. Pastry cutters 11. Fondant Smoother 12. Piping Tip 1A 13. Piping Tip 2D 14. Piping Tip 1M 15. Piping Tip Rounded Size 3 16. Piping Tip 233, 17. Half moon Scraper 18. Cake Comb 19. Corn flour dust dispenser 20. Plunger Cutter – butterfly 21. Egg cup 22. Letter cutters – ClikStix/plunger 23. Sharp top edge smoother 24. small flower multi cutter 25. Oil based flavouring – Marshmallow 26. Colour and Flavour essence – Roberts Caramel 27. Sugar glue 28. Rose Spirit 29. Edible paint 30. Plaque Cutter 31. Plaque Cutter 32.Butterfly cutter 33. Bib cutter 34. Shamrock cutter 35. Coupler 36. Cloud cutter 37. Craft knife 38. Double sided rose petal and leaf cutters 39. Embroidery scissors 40. Wood grain embosser 41. Paint brushes 42. Piping bag – reusable (extra large) 43. Wooden rolling pin 44. Floral wire – white 45. floral tape – white 46. Multiple sized Square Cutters 47.Silicon mould – butterfly 48. Leaf veiners – slicon 49. Silicon mould – multiple bows 50. Large Number cutters 51. Large Letter cutters 52. Non-stick board & grip mat 53. small acrylic rolling pin 54. wheel tool cutter 55. dog bone tool 56. Dresden tool (Veining tool) 57. Frilling Tool 58. ball tool 59. ball & shell tool 60. edible ink pen (black) 61. Apple corer 62. crank handled spatula (small) 63. blossom cutter 64. Holly leaf cutter 65. Cutter – Christmas tree 66. Cutter – bunny 67. Cutter – Leaf 68. Wooden dowl 69. Wooden Skewer 70. Fondant Knife 71. Spatula 72. Crank-handled Spatula – large 73. Bread Knife 74. Fondant Smoother for rounded edges

Techniques

When you are making and decorating cakes for the first time allow yourself plenty of time and manage your expectations. There is no substitute for experience and even with years of it, I still get things wrong when I am trying out a skill. I am a big fan of YouTube tutorials in which cake-decorating skills can be viewed in online videos. It's like having someone in your kitchen with you demonstrating each stage, one-on-one, with the advantage that you can watch the tricky bits over and over again.

Also, remember that there is never 'only one way' or 'the right way' to do something. Every cake professional has their own preferred methods for making and decorating cakes and with experience you will find your own too. The end result is what matters, so do what feels right and easier for you, and that my cake-friends will be 'the right way'.

PLANNING YOUR CAKE

Wanting to make a cake yourself is always a great idea, and if you are like me, when you get the idea in your head you want to do it right now and see the results right away. With all of the cakes in this book, you need to allow time and planning. Break down the cake you want to make into steps and bake in advance. Here are some of my best tips for planning your cake:

- If you are busy and need the cake for an event, you can make it the week before and freeze it once it has cooled to room temperature, then when you thaw it out, it will still be as soft and moist as it would be if it were freshly baked.
- Determine what decorations you need on the cake, and assess which ones can be made in advance. If you are expanding on, or adapting a design from the book, do a rough drawing of it and make a list of what you need to make. You can be making decorations while the cake is baking, cooling and being refrigerated.
- Don't underestimate how long it takes to tint fondant. If you are coloring your own fondant, you can do this is in advance. Color it and wrap it in two layers of cling film (plastic wrap) and one layer of kitchen foil, then store it in an airtight container.
- Got lots to make? Making decorations and coloring fondant can be done while you sit and watch TV. Multitasking like this can make the production of 60 textured leaves for a forest floor, for example, seem less arduous.

Color me up! Coloring cake batter and buttercream (frosting)

Buttercream frosting and white cake batter are not white, but somewhere between yellow and cream. The yellow pigment, from the butter (and chocolate) will affect the tone of the gel food color you use.

If you are coloring the batter or cream using yellow, orange, red, green or dark/navy blue, the yellow base will not affect the outcome, as they are strong colors with a yellow base or strong enough pigment. However if you are aiming for a pastel hue—mint green, pink, or pale blue—the yellow will need to be neutralised before adding food coloring. You do this with white food coloring or batter whitener; I add whitener when my ingredients have just been combined.

White food coloring is great because it lets your batter reflect any color you desire, but because of the ingredients in it, the coloring won't emulsify as easily as standard colors, so you will need to be patient. Remember: you don't need the batter or buttercream to be as white as a sheet, but it needs to be predominately white, so when you look at it, you shouldn't see a yellow tone.

Once you have neutralised the color of the batter or buttercream and all of the ingredients have come together, add gel food coloring two drops at a time with your mixer on low speed until you reach the desired shade. You can then start mixing it on high speed for the set amount of time the idea is to the get the color in before mixing on a higher speed so that when the high speed mixing takes place, the water-based gel-color is emulsified into the fat-based ingredients of the batter and buttercream. Remember, you are using water based gel food coloring in recipes that contain a lot of fat based ingredients (butter, chocolate) so it takes a lot of mixing to get water and fat to emulsify.

For batter, because you have taken longer to mix the ingredients, you are likely to be developing the gluten in the flour a little more than usual. To avoid a tough, rubbery cake, let the cake batter sit in the tin on the bench for 5–10 minutes before baking, giving it time to 'relax' a little before baking.

You can't beat Royal: tips for coloring

If a light or sky blue is what you're after, use a small amount of royal blue coloring to achieve the desired shade. Royal blue has a darker pigment than lighter blue food colors so it will over take any residual yellow tones and still give a light effect—with no need for whitening color to be added at all!

A note on OMBRE

Traditionally, ombre cakes are made of three or more layers of cake, that are evenly colored and stacked in ascending or descending order of color or shade. If you choose to make each layer an even color, it is very important that you add the color as early as possible in the mixing process— I combine all of my ingredients in the mixer and follow the advice above for coloring batter.

Alternatively, one way to achieve a 'radiating ball effect' is to simply add color to the batter toward the end of the mixing time, so that it is mixed all the way through but is not completely emulsified. When the high temperature of the oven starts to bake the cake, the color at the edges will evaporate, leaving a darker concentration of color in the centre of the cake. An additional way to ensure this effect is to raise the oven temp by 5–10°C/41–50°F.

It's all about the flavor!

It is possible to flavor milk and dark chocolate cake batters to add extra flavors. The end result of the addition of these flavors tends to be 'Chocolate and ....' whatever you have put in there— Chocolate and Strawberry, Chocolate Cherry, Choc Mint, or Orange-flavored Chocolate.

White chocolate mud cake is the most popular choice as the cake tends to act like a vanilla or butter sponge in that it will take on the flavor that is added to it and that will become the overriding taste in the end product, for example, adding caramel flavoring into white chocolate mud cake turns the cake into a caramel mud cake with a subtle, white chocolate taste to it. Something more subtle, like a raspberry flavour, gives a white chocolate and raspberry taste to the end product. For this reason white chocolate mud cake is more versatile and is used most often throughout the book. Its creamy color allows it to be colored all sorts of shades which is in itself always a nice, unexpected surprise.

When using an oil-based flavor, add it to the oil/fat-based ingredients in the recipe. This helps to ensure the flavor is emulsified and even throughout the mix. Likewise, when using a water-based flavor, add the flavor when you add the milk and eggs. Remember, water likes water and oil like oil, match up your flavors and add them to their respective ingredient types and let the mixing process emulsify them together.

Prepare the tin

It is very important to prepare your cake tin because there is nothing worse than the cake sticking in the tin or only half of it coming out.

When using non-stick cookware I still lightly grease it. You can use a cake release spray (a commercially available mix of vegetable oils), or use cooking spray. Otherwise, you can grease it with butter or margarine and flour it—apply a thin even coat of margarine with a piece of paper towel, then shake half a handful of plain flour around inside the tin, over the sink or bin, to allow the flour to coat all of the greased surface.

For thin tins or tins without non-stick coating, it is best to grease the tin with butter/margarine or spray oil and line it with baking paper. If the tin is thin and you are baking a mud cake or any cake that requires a longer baking time, double line the tin for additional insulation to avoid the cake drying out.

Hemisphere and Dolly Varden tins

Baking in these tins requires them to be stabilised. You can stabilise the tin on an egg ring placed onto a baking tray or placed on top of a round cake tin. I like to place my hemisphere tin on top of a round cake tin and place a small amount of water in the round cake tin to make sure the top of the dome doesn't cook more thoroughly than its wider top (which will end up being the base of the cake.) If you decide to try this method ensure the top of the dome does not touch the base of the round tin, it should perch on top, enough to be stable but not cradled. Also, you don't want it sitting in the water otherwise you risk boiling the top of the cake.

Oven temperatures

Get to know your oven. Each oven is slightly different and requires adjustment. Don't think because your oven is old it won't be as good, sometimes older ovens cook the best cakes! Some ovens are fast and some are slow, this means some don't get as hot as the temp gauge says and some get more so. If you want to get technical you can buy a temperature gauge that goes inside of your oven and you can use that to regulate the temperature. However, I find that despite the temperature gauge, each oven regulates and conducts heat differently and you need to get to know it, like it has it's own personality! Be patient, check your cake is cooked and don't be alarmed if your cooking time varies from the recipe, just make a note for next time.

The science of baking is simply the ratio of ingredients and the conditions in which you bake it. The art of baking is knowing how your oven performs and what needs to be changed if anything, to bake the cake evenly.

Checking the cake is done

I check my cake with wooden cake skewers (you can also get metal) at three different points. The centre or core of the cake is the last to be completely cooked. You want to bake it evenly with a nice cooked centre without dry edges. I always check how cooked the edges are, as well as the centre of my cake by inserting the skewer in the dead centre directly downwards, and repeating this in the area around the centre at different angles. You know your cake is cooked when the skewer comes out clean.

After the cake has been baked, you need to invert it onto a wire rack to cool. It is very important that the cake has cooled completely to room temperature before you wrap it in cling film and/or refrigerate it, otherwise it will sweat.

Chilling cakes

When you read the recipes, it may seem as if I am obsessed with the refrigerator. Building in time to allow your cake to cool to refrigeration temperature definitely lengthens the cake-making process but it absolutely makes all the difference when you have to trim or carve a cake. A freshly baked, soft cake is very crumbly. If the cake is wrapped correctly, refrigeration doesn't reduce freshness, it only chills the butter and chocolate in the cake. This makes them harder, which makes the cake denser, so that when you cut it there is less crumb and more stability.

It's a wrap! Wrapping a cake for freezing

Any cakes to be frozen or refrigerated for a while should be wrapped carefully. I use two layers cling film (plastic wrap) and one layer of aluminum foil to seal in the freshness and protect against freezer burn.

An important note on cake balls

The balls need to be frozen when we bake them so that they don't dissolve and disappear into the mud cake batter (this can happen to cake balls at room temperature). The requirement to freeze means you can make the cake ball a couple of weeks in advance which always helps with a very detailed cake design. I use freezer wrap between each cake ball to ensure it doesn't stick to other cake balls and transfer colored crumbs. This also helps to avoid the icicle problem that can occur. Alternatively you can use freezer bags, either way—wrap them well before freezing them.

WHY? Why do we cook a mud cake with cake balls in it for the same time as a normal mud cake that size and not less? The cake balls do take up space and there is less raw cake batter to be cooked, but the cake batter is being heated by the oven and at the same time cooled by the frozen cake balls, this competition of temperatures slows baking time down and the balance must be just right to ensure the cake is cooked and your cake balls are not liquefied.

TRIMMING CAKES READY FOR DECORATION

Always trim a cold cake. Once cooked, refrigerate until cold, not frozen. A cold cake is denser, will lose fewer crumbs and will be more malleable under your hands and the knife you are using. Once your cake is baked, you should always trim the crust off the top and make it flat enough to be your base. Sometimes though (for friends and family), if you get slight doming and the whole top of the cake is moist and edible, you can choose to leave it, making it part of your design by turning over the top of the cake so that it becomes the base that is placed on the board and fill the gaps with your ganache or buttercream. It's a cheat's way to keep height, but remember when you cut it that the base of the cake won't look 'flat' all the way around.

There are several ways to trim a cake:

1 You can eyeball it. This is how I learned to trim and if you have a straight eye and steady hand this is definitely a viable option. I have neither of these and prefer options 2 and 3.

2 If you know you need a super flat cake top you can add a little extra cake batter to your tin, knowing it will rise above the depth of the cake tin sides. Once the cake is baked, and has cooled to refrigeration temperature, return the cake to the tin it was baked in and using a sharp bread knife set flush with the top of the cake tin, slice off the cake top using the sides of the tin as a guide. The trick to this is focusing on keeping the bread knife on top of the tin and using a small back and forth sawing motion. When I add extra batter to a tin on purpose, I line it with baking paper that comes up higher than the sides of my tin, so the excess I am cutting off rises straight up as it bakes, rather than mushrooming out like a muffin top, which would make it harder to level.

3 You can use a cake leveller. Unless you intend to do a lot of cake decorating or make a lot of torted cakes, buying one of these might be a waste of money—borrow one if you can and get a feel for it to see if you like it. Not all cake levellers are created equal and if you decide to invest in one, you need to know that you get what you pay for. Check online reviews, especially feedback from professionals before investing. Follow the instructions for the one you have purchased and go slowly.

   To use a standard cake leveller, with handle and metal blade, adjust the blade to the height you want your cake to be, and then being careful to keep the leveller upright and stable on the table, move the leveller in a side-to-side sawing motion through the cake. If you have a flimsy leveller and a round cake, do this for one-third of the cake and then change your approach. Leaving the cake leveller inside the cake, use the sawing motion side-to-side again without moving the leveller forward—instead, move the cake with your other hand in a circular motion. This method uses the stronger part of the blade at the edge to cut the cake. Once you have cut all the way around your cake, finish cutting the centre by moving the cake leveller forward in a sawing motion again, then gently remove the top of the cake.

What's with all the mud cakes?

You will notice that all of the cake balls and cakes that we cut shapes out of and bake again are mud cakes. We use a mud cake batter due to its density, which makes it more structurally sound, allowing for the double handling of cutting it out, freezing it, placing it and re-baking it. Mud cakes also withstand the re-bake a lot better than a sponge, both in terms of moisture (due to the high fat content) and in the retaining its form so it doesn't liquefy and disappear.

Waste not want not: What to do with leftovers and 'cake mistakes'

When you slice the domed top off a cake, you can eat it, or keep it. When I have cake off-cuts, I remove all traces of crust and crumb the cake into a bowl. I then tip the cake crumb into a plastic freezer bag, and put that inside an airtight container in the freezer to use at another time for pound cake recipes or cake pop-cake mix. These should last up to 3 months in the freezer and defrost fresh and moist.

If you bake a 'mistake cake', one that is cooked all the way through but is the wrong shape or you cut it incorrectly, freeze it whole and bring it out for a family dessert smothered in chocolate and ice cream (they will never know), or cut off the crust and 'crumb' it, freeze and use later.

How to crumb a cake: Cut away the outer crust. Holding the cake over a large mixing bowl start to break it into pieces with your hands. As the pieces fall away, pick them up and rub them between your fingers to form a fine crumb.

Ganache: Structure, crumb coat and pretty patterns

Chocolate ganache is a simple creation made of chocolate and cream however it is a wondrous ingredient that covers up a multitude of things! Once you get the hang of using it you will see why chocolate ganache is the cake decorators preferred icing to add to the cake surface to create both a glue for the fondant to stick to and a shape for the fondant to form around.

It is important to spend the time getting your chocolate ganache covering smooth and to the shape you wish your final cake to take. The ganache, once applied, needs time to set hard. Once set ,it provides a firm surface for which the fondant will rest upon and take the shape of, making the covering of the cake with fondant a lot easier.

If your cake design and schedule allows for it, let a ganached cake rest overnight before applying the fondant. If you are pressed for time, you can speed up the process by putting it into the fridge for 4 hours, allowing the chocolate to set hard. Bring it back out of the fridge and allow it to come to room temperature. The chocolate will go through a phase where it will 'sweat'—simply blot these beads of water off of your cake and when it has finished 'sweating' and is at/close to room temperature you can add your fondant. Be patient, this takes time but your end look and the ease of which you can add smooth fondant makes it worth it.

Because chocolate has a higher melting point than butter in buttercream and because the ganache has had time to set hard, the ganache will be able withstand the warmth of your hand through the fondant and the pressure applied by your fondant smoothing tools as you cover your cake. Coupled with the fact it has a thick consistency and malleability that allows it to cover a multitude of rough edges and divots in your cakes surface, it makes it the ideal icing to go under fondant.

It will, of course, still melt in the mouth when eaten. To achieve a firm texture (or 'under-fondant-ganache' as I like to call it) we use certain types of chocolate at certain ratios. See the recipe section for details.

Once you have made your ganache and have let it rest (or have purchased it) you can use it to cover your cake. At room temperature, ganache should be the consistency of hazelnut spread. If you have had it in the refrigerator you may need to heat it gently in the microwave to bring it back to the right consistency to use. Start with 10 seconds and stir vigorously, and then heat for 5 seconds at a time after that. If you ganache is still a bit stiff or difficult to work with you can mix it with beaters until it comes more malleable. You then apply this ganache to your room temperature cake (see next steps).

Got lots of crumb edges?

If I have carved a cake and have crumbly cake edges showing, or if I have stacked two or more cakes on top of one another with nice thick ganache between the layers, I apply my version of a ganache crumb coat to the outside of the cake before the real/proper ganache goes on later. This helps bind the cake layers together and secure the cake crumb sides so that they don't come loose when I apply the ganache properly in the next step.

First make sure your cake is secured to your cake board by following step 1 in the proper ganaching process on page 17. Allow at least half an hour for this to set.

For my crumb coat I heat a small amount of ganache in the microwave slowly until it becomes the consistency of soup. I then pour this over my cake, working quickly to smooth it over the top and down the sides of the cake evenly. It is very liquid so will pool at the base of the cake; once it sets this pooling excess can be cut way and discarded. Once the cake is coated with a thin, even layer, I refrigerate the cake and let the ganache set hard—it will look like a translucent shell coating. Once it is set I remove it from the refrigerator and let it come to room temperature before applying normal ganache (the consistency of hazelnut spread) using the proper methods as follows.

Applying ganache to a baked cake

Ganache under fondant shapes and smooths the cake so that when the fondant layer is added, there is less work needed to achieve a smooth, even finish. When applied well the ganache reduces the quantity of fondant needed to give a smooth finish to the cake. It may seem crazy to spend so much time perfecting a layer that will not be seen, but time spent on the foundation is time saved on fondant covering and patch jobs.

Tools

Crank-handled spatula
Ganache scraper
Hot water (to heat scraper/spatula)
Clean cloth (to wipe water and excess ganache form scraper/spatula)
1 or 2 cake boards

1   Apply a blob of ganache to the centre of the cake board and position the cake on top of it—to hold the board and cake together. If the side of the cake has been trimmed and has a crumb edge to it, ganache the entire board and put the cake onto it. Allow half an hour for the ganache to set so your cake doesn't move.
2   Using the cranked handle spatula, cover the entire cake with a thick layer of ganache. Don't worry if it looks messy. You are applying a thicker layer of ganache than you need.
3   With a clean spatula, smooth the ganache out and put the cake into the refrigerator to set for several hours. When you bring the cake out of the refrigerator, allow it to come to room temperature before continuing work.
4   You are now going to smooth the ganache. This involves removing and reapplying ganache to build the cake shape, and there are a zillion different ways to do it. My three preferred methods are as follows. Whichever method you choose, once you have smoothed your cake into shape it is best to allow the ganache to set overnight. If you do not have 12–24 hours, you can refrigerate it for 4–6 hours to help set the ganache, just make sure you allow it to come back to room temperature before applying the fondant.

The board method one

For this you will need two boards of the same size, and preferably the same size as the cake tin you used to bake the cake. You will have already used one board as the base for the cake. Place the second cake board on top of the cake like a lid. To avoid problems with it sticking later, you can either add a small amount of water to the ganache on top of the cake or cover the board with cling film (or go-between freezer wrap or baking paper). Have a bowl handy so that you can put any excess ganache into it. Using a ganache scraper that has been heated in a jug of hot water, line the top and bottom edges up so that they are parallel with both boards and scrape around the cake using the boards as a guide. Excess ganache will build up on the scraper; periodically scrape this into a bowl. Where there are gaps in the surface, fill these with the spare ganache until you have a perfectly smooth, round cake. Leave the top board in place and refrigerate to set for several hours. When you bring the cake out of the refrigerator, remove the top board by running a small knife underneath to loosen it and flip it off. The cake top will be very uneven compared to the sides, fill the gaps in the top and use a scraper to level it. Allow to set at room temperature overnight, or for several hours, at least, in the refrigerator.

The board method two

To save time, you can ganache the top of the cake and place the board on top of it before you apply the ganache to the sides of the cake—make sure you line up the boards as described above.

You then liberally apply the ganache to the sides of the cake, do not worry if the ganache sticks out further than your boards—this is preferable. Once you have liberally applied the ganache, give it half an hour to set. However, if you are short on time, smooth it immediately. To smooth, simply follow the steps in method one to scrap back the excess with the your ganache scraper and allow the perfectly smoothed cake to set before flipping off the lid and finishing the top.

The bench method

If you don't have two round boards that are the same size as the cake, but you do have a flat board, you can use as a work surface you can follow the above steps working upside down. First secure the cake base to the board and apply a thin layer of ganache tot he top of the cake. Then, place a layer of baking paper over your surface and turn the cake upside down. Apply the ganache as instructed in method one, using the work surface as the base board. Once you have applied and smoothed your ganache this way, and it has had time to set, turn the cake right way up and gently peel the baking paper from the top. Apply ganache to the top of the cake and allow it all to set overnight.

By eye

Lastly, you can follow all of the above described steps by eye instead of using boards. I learned how to apply ganache this way and still use this method when I am applying ganache as the only icing. For under fondant ganache I need to use boards.

Note: Never put fondant onto refrigerator-cold ganache. It must return to room temperature first, which will involve a period of 'sweating' which will look like beads of water over the cake. If you add fondant too soon the sweat will reduce the elasticity of the fondant and it will either show through or start to sag on the cake sides. Pat the cake with kitchen paper towel periodically to remove the excess moisture and allow the cake to come to room temperature before applying the fondant.

A note about buttercream (frosting)

I am often asked if it's possible to use buttercream under fondant instead of ganache and the technical answer is 'yes', but there are caveats. Buttercream is easy to make and we are often comfortable using it, but that doesn't mean it is easier to use under fondant than ganache. When making buttercream, you must use a 2:1 icing (confectioners') sugar to butter ratio, no milk (it will go off), and it must be stiff buttercream; you cannot cream the butter to be incredibly soft otherwise it simply won't perform.

You need to return the cake to the refrigerator more often too, as butter has a significantly lower melting point than chocolate and the weather or room temperature must be cool when you are working with it. When you apply a layer of fondant to cold buttercream, the buttercream will warm up very quickly under the heat of your hand on the fondant and movement of the fondant smoothing tools and may cause the fondant to rip or slide so you need to know you can work quickly.

If you are making a test cake, give it a go, but I wouldn't advise trying it for the first time when you have a party cake to produce. Ultimately, ganache will give a smoother finish and a better blank canvas under the fondant. That said, I do use buttercream under fondtant on kids' cakes as it's less rich.

Applying fondant: rolling out and covering up

Fondant brands vary and perform differently and it isn't always a matter of getting what you pay for. Choosing a fondant that you like to work with is subjective, some people like soft, other people prefer firm. Start by using a standard fondant rather than a super-soft fondant—even though the super-soft versions claim to never dry out or crack—since this fondant is also very soft and floppy, which makes it more difficult to handle in larger quantities. Never try to roll out and cover a cake with fondant when it is incredibly hot or humid, unless you have good air conditioning as the heat will make the fondant sticky.

Tools

non-stick mat
non-stick rolling pin (acrylic or wood)
Icing mixture, for dusting
fondant smoother, for finishing
fondant knife or kitchen knife, to cut away the excess

Before you start you need to measure the size of the fondant piece you will need. You do this by measuring the diameter of the cake (across the top of it) and also how tall the cake is. For example, if your round cake is 22 cm/9 inches across and 15 cm/6 inches tall your fondant piece needs to measure 52 cm/21 inches (15 cm/ 6 inches up onside + 22cm/9 inches across the top + 15cm/6 inches down the other side of the cake to cover it = 52cm/21 inches)

1 Make sure you have a clean and clear work space. Secure the non-stick mat to the work surface. If it isn't the type that adheres itself, use non-slip grip mats under each corner. Dust lightly with icing mixture. Have the ganache-coated cake to hand adhered to the board you intend to cover it on.

2 Knead the fondant so it is soft and pliable using your hands. Flatten it and pull it out into a round-ish or square-ish shape on the dusted mat.

3 Roll out the fondant using a non-stick rolling pin. You have two choices; you can roll over the entire length of the fondant, or roll from the centre outward working away from you (and turning the fondant more often). With both methods, after every third roll of the rolling pin, lift up the fondant and turn it 90 degrees. This achieves two things: it makes sure you are rolling the fondant evenly and checks that it isn't sticking to the mat. If the fondant is difficult to lift, or starts to feel tacky, dust underneath it with a light coat of icing mixture.

4 Continue rolling and turning until the fondant is the size and thickness required to cover the cake.

5 So, the fondant is rolled out and ready to go, and the cake is to hand. At this point, wash and dry your hands and dust them lightly with icing mixture. This allows you to handle the fondant without it sticking to you.

6 Lift the fondant off of the mat and onto the cake. There are two ways to do this: you can either roll it over the rolling pin and unfurl the fondant over the cake, or you can lift it up by putting both hands and forearms under the piece of fondant and lifting it up and placing it over the cake.

7 Once the fondant is on the cake, double check your hands and arms are clean of ganache, then start to smooth it down into place quickly. Make sure the top is smooth and the fondant

Fondant, in commercial baking terms, means a thick, gooey white substance that becomes liquefied when heated in a bowl set over a pot of hot water. When liquefied, it can be used as a quick setting glaze (like the icing on top of sweet buns and pastry scrolls) with a flat, gloss finish. The ready-to-roll version of this product is called ready-to-roll-fondant (RTR) and is often referred to as simply 'fondant' by cake decorators. They are both fondant, but commerical fondant has more glycerine in it than the other. For the purpose of this book and ease of reference throughout, I will refer to ready-to-roll (RTR) fondant as simply 'fondant'. Depending on the country of origin of other cake books and tutorials on line, RTR fondant may also be referred to as 'sugar paste' and 'plastic icing' or called 'wedding cake icing' by non-decorators.

   Some professional instructions will advise you to dust the work surface with cornflour before rolling out fondant. This is because cornflour is a non-stick agent, which prevents the fondant from sticking to the bench or mat. If I only have a small amount of fondant to roll out and I'm confident that I will only need to roll it once or twice, then I will use cornflour.

However, for really large amounts of fondant (say cakes larger than 8 inches) I use **Icing mixture** (see page 42 for more details)—a mix of cornflour and pure icing sugar. This is because rolling out a larger amount of fondant (or if you are new to rolling out fondant) takes a lot longer meaning there is more bench/mat and fondant contact time—the fondant is worked more which requires more dust to the work surface to avoid the fondant sticking. More dusting equals more drying for the fondant, and cornflour is the most drying agent of all.

Fondant can only take so much dry powder before it starts to dry out itself and when it becomes too dry it is no longer malleable and you can get rips or tears, or 'elephant skin'-like wrinkles.

I have found that when I work with a mix of cornflour and pure icing sugar, I get all the benefits of the cornflour, but because the bulk of the dry dust is pure icing sugar, which is the main ingredient in fondant, it won't dry out as quickly.

   Effectively, you are asking the fondant to take up more of its own main ingredient and therefore it will take more dust before it dries out.

is smoothed over the edge—this will avoid the weight of the fondant hanging down the sides pulling at the top and ripping it. Once it is secure over the top edges, work down the side. Do not just smooth straight down the sides—it may look nice in the first two places but it will start to fold over and wrinkle as you move around the cake.

8 Smooth down the sides a bit at a time—smooth down a little and then using clean, dry dusted fingers, move the edges of the fondant outward away from the cake, slightly pulling them outwards, this gives a smooth surface and avoids folds. Work around the cake

consistently. You are lifting the fondant away gently as you would gently lift the edges of a skirt. If you need to wash, dry and re-dust your hands at this point do so. Work all the way around the cake and smooth down the sides.

9 Cut away the excess fondant with a large kitchen knife or fondant knife in and down at a 45-degree angle. Wash and dry your hands and re-dust them.

10 To smooth the fondant, run your dusted hands over the cake so that it has a light layer of icing mixture. Using your hands and the fondant smother, smooth the top of the cake first and work your way around the sides in long, even strokes with a very small amount of pressure. If you have folds or minor tears, use some double-sifted pure icing sugar compacted into the space and use the heat of the palm of your hand rubbed in a circular motion to warm the fondant, this melts it slightly and when it is warm and tacky it sucks up dry powder, as it absorbs the icing sugar it repairs the damage to leave a smooth, clear surface.

Note: this will not work in all cases and should be avoided if ganache is coming through. Do not try this with icing mixture as the cornflour will prohibit the binding and make the blemish worse.

Want pointy/sharp edges?

Sharp edges on fondant-covered cakes are really in fashion right now. There are two ways to finish this look with fondant but both work infinitely better if you have sharp edges on your ganache for the fondant to take the shape of in the first place. Once the fondant is on the cake and smoothed out you can either use two fondant smoothers or a specific tool called a sharp top edger. If you use the specific tool, follow the instructions that come with the brand of tool that you buy.

If you use the two smoothers method, hold one smoother against the side of the cake, run the other smoother across the top of the cake with your other hand from the centre towards the edges. Using a small amount of pressure, push the fondant edge up against the smoother on the side of the cake and repeat this around the edge of the cake. You are effectively just squeezing the edges into a point.

To get nice sharp edges on the sides of your square cake, you can use the same method described above, guiding and pushing or you can smooth from the centre of each side to the point. This will create a peak of excess fondant at the sharp edge that will need to be removed by a knife or squeezing your smoother ends together and then smoothed down with your finger.

How to cover a cake board

It is preferable to cover your cake board with a light layer of piping gel, applying it with a wide brush. In the absence of piping gel you can dampen the cake board with a very small amount of sugar glue or water. Set this aside and roll out your fondant on a lightly dusted non-stick mat. Follow the same principles for rolling out fondant for a cake. Make sure the length and width of the rolled fondant matches the size of your cake board. When you have rolled it out evenly, pick it up and lay it over the cake board. Smooth the fondant with your hand first and then a fondant smoother if you have one. To trim the excess from the sides you can either cut it away with a fondant/kitchen knife—by holding the board in one hand and gliding the knife along the edge of the board in a downwards motion—or by using the fondant smoother to smooth down the edge of the board to create a slope of fondant that tapers off at the edge of the board. The excess will fall away as you work your way around the board.

Gum paste

Gum paste is ideal for making figurines and decorative detail. It may be called sugar paste, modelling paste, moulding paste or flower paste. It feels and behaves similar to fondant but is slightly dryer and stiffer to work with. Due to its difference in formula it will hold its shape better when modelled into a figurine and will dry rock hard. It is edible however after it has dried it might be a bit hard on the teeth! The ratio of ingredients in gum paste varies according to the purpose for which it is manufactured, for example fine flower modelling or bulky figure modelling. For the purpose of this book we will use standard gum paste or we will add CMC (*carboxymethyl cellulose*) powder to fondant.

Making fondant into gum paste

In simplified terms, the key recipe difference between fondant and gum paste is that fondant contains glycerine. Glycerine allows fondant to form a 'crust' or 'skin' on its surface that sets hard enough to the touch on the surface, but underneath the skin, the fondant remains very soft. The removal of glycerine from the formula creates a product that is stiffer to work with and that will dry completely hard given enough time and air. The powder I use to add to my fondant to turn it into gum paste is CMC powder starting at a ratio of 1 teaspoon to 250g (8¾ oz) of fondant. You can add more than this to get it to set quicker however you must work quicker to avoid it drying out and cracking. Like fondant, this is a feel-as-you-go situation that is definitely affected by the weather.

Whether it is fondant or gum paste, make sure it is always covered in an airtight seal, with cling film or if you're working with it and need regular access, plastic bags—both products will dry out very quickly in the air and will require 'work' by kneading to add the warmth of your hands if they have been left too long.

Color me up! A note on food colors

For baking and decorating I use gel food coloring. The color from this product is intense so you don't need much of it. Even though gel food color is a water-based color, it is in a concentrated gel form and the small quantity that you need to add to the cake batter, buttercream, fondant or gum paste to get a dramatic color effect will not affect the texture or consistency.

The only exception to this rule, of course, is royal icing. You can add a very small amount, for example, 2 small drops of gel food coloring to royal icing, however if you want to color royal icing a deeper color you will need to weigh the color when you weigh the liquid content.

If you already have a stock of 'liquid food coloring' which is the stuff that pours like colored water, save these for cake batter and buttercream but make sure you make weight allowances for it in the recipe—remember this is colored water and water affects the ingredient ratios of your batter or icing. Never use liquid food color in fondant or gum paste as water breaks down the sugar bonds and reduces the overall elasticity of the fondant and gum paste.

CMC GUM POWDER

CMC powder has many trade or brand names, so be sure to look for *carboxymethyl cellulose (CMC)* as the whole ingredient list. CMC can be referred to as gum but be careful not to confuse it with gums used for bulking or glazing. CMC powder is an ingredient used in medicinal tablet production. The addition of this to fondant can turn it into gum paste. To put it simply, the CMC powder works on the glycerine and counteracts it so that the fondant can dry hard like gum paste. Gum paste made from fondant and CMC will work perfectly well. It will be softer and take a little longer to dry than purpose made gum paste, however, it's unlikely that you'll register the difference unless you are making very fine decorations.

COLORING FONDANT AND GUM PASTE

If I am coloring a large amount of fondant, I divide the product into fist-sized balls and after coloring one ball at a time, combine all of the balls together. This gives me greater control over the final color and makes the physical toll of coloring a lot easier.

With a fist-sized amount of fondant or less, knead it with your hands until it 'warms up', making it more pliable. Roll it into a ball and make a well in the centre. Add one to two drops of gel food color at a time, close over the well and carefully knead the ball, folding over the fondant to contain any food color that has not yet been kneaded in. Repeat this until the color starts to become a visible part of the fondant.

Then take the ball between your palms and roll it into a sausage shape , folding it back on itself and repeating this action until the color is mixed through. The rolling action takes a lot less muscle work than kneading. Using these techniques you will get the color to a streaky effect. Finish mixing the color through evenly by kneading on the bench. If you require a darker color than the one you have mixed, add a few extra drops to the fondant at the streaky phase and repeat the process until you have the desired color. If the fondant feels very soft, do not add icing (confectioners') sugar yet. Instead, wrap it in cling film (plastic wrap) and allow it to sit for half an hour to cool down. After you have let it settle, check to see if it is still very soft and unworkable. If so, add some pure icing sugar to it to make it more workable.

Black and red

I always purchase red and black fondant ready colored, as it is near impossible to color fondant black. This is an industry wide issue for black and bright red so you are likely to find smaller quantities of black and red sold at your local cake decorating supply store or on line.

Skin color

No matter what skin tone I am trying to achieve I always start with a warmed ivory base color and work with a ball of gum paste about half the size of my fist—it is easier to handle and I know my ratios in this size, so all of the following information relates to this amount of gum paste.

Base color

Once you have an ivory base, either purchased or colored up, add ½ –1 small drop of soft/pale pink to your gum paste and knead in thoroughly. This will not change the color of the gum paste but it will bring a warmth to the tone of it. This makes the skin seem alive and flush as opposed to flat and cold. Do not use a smaller amount of a deep or bright pink; the darkness of the pigment will not give you the same effect. This base color may seem redundant, until you put the below colors into plain white gum paste, then you really see a difference in the end result—trust me, I've spent a lot of time on this, it's worth it.

Caucasian or European

For a very pale Caucasian the base color will be enough. If they are tan or European, add ½ drop of warm brown.

Asian

Starting with the base color, first add another drop of ivory. Then add ½ drop of warm brown and ¼ drop of gold and knead through thoroughly. If this is too dark, add some more plain white gum paste. For a very pale skinned Asian look use ½ drop warm brown and omit the gold.

Indian

Starting with the base color, add two drops of warm brown and one drop of chocolate brown. Assess the color and add more chocolate brown, half a drop at a time, if required.

Arabian and Mediterranean

Starting with the base color, add two drops of warm brown and assess the color. Add an extra 1 drop to 1½ drops of warm brown for Arabian and after that a ½ drop of chocolate brown if required. If the Mediterranean skin tone needs to be more sun-kissed first add another ½–1 drop of pale pink for warmth and if this is not quite enough add ½ drop of gold.

African

Starting with the base color, add 1 drop of warm brown for every 2 drops of chocolate brown. Start with 1 and 2 two drops respectfully and then add more as required until you achieve the accurate skin tone. If you have put 3 drops of warm brown and 6 drops of chocolate in and it still not dark enough, continue to add chocolate brown only 1 drop at a time.

If you require a tone closer to ebony, you can add ½ drop of black food color or a small ball of black fondant to the gum paste but only after you have already colored it to a dark brown, any earlier and the complexion will have a grey tinge you cannot get rid of.

Latino/Hispanic

Starting with the base color, add ½ drop of warm brown and ¼ drop of gold. Add ¼ drop of warm brown at a time as required until you reach the desired skin tone. If the tone you are seeking is darker you can add ¼–½ drop of chocolate brown.

Go for gold: Painting with edible metallics

I use both pre-made edible metallic paint and also (gold) metallic dust that I mix with cake decorators rose spirit. Rose spirit is a liquid with a very high percentage alcohol content so it will evaporate quickly so keep the lid on at all times! I mix up the metallic dust and rose spirit in an egg cup because it has high sides and a deep well, when I am not using the paint I place a clean wet cloth over the cup to reduce the evaporation of the rose spirit and spare my materials. The rose spirit is used to make a paste—as the alcohol evaporates off it leaves the color stuck to the fondant/gum paste. To apply it, dip your paint brush into the well of color, remove it and push it against the side of the cup letting the excess rose spirit run back into the well and paint as normal. Adding a small amount of color at a time is better than risking drips or runs. As it dries the color may be more transparent than it looked going on—simply go back over it when it has dried with more color. Allow the paint to dry before using or adding additional color over the top.

Coloring chocolate/ganache

For the purposes of this content of this book, the only chocolate you may need to color is white chocolate and white chocolate ganache.

White chocolate is made up of fat compounds, which are the components that are dyed with edible color. It is best to use oil-based food coloring and if you can, chocolate specific, oil-based food coloring to color chocolate. This is because fat will evenly mix with fat a lot easier than fat will mix with a water-based gel food color and as there is no emulsifying (mixing on high) steps there is no opportunity for emulsification like we have for buttercream and cake batters.

If the cake you are making is a one off and you already have gel food coloring and you are using compound chocolate, you can *try* to use gel food coloring. I have experimented and used this for the Duck Pond Cupcakes and it was effective. However, I had low expectations of the outcome. First you must not try to dye the chocolate too dark, instead use less of a darker color dye—I used royal blue to get medium water blue. Also, the end effect was a light blue with royal blue flecks in it. There is every chance the color will split, in which case you need to discard it and start again. So don't try this unless you have ingredients to spare.

To color white chocolate with oil-based chocolate food coloring or gel food coloring the process is the same; put the chocolate pieces in a heatproof bowl and set it over a pot of water that has boiled but is no longer on the heat. Add the food color before the chocolate starts to melt and gently move the chocolate around the bowl until it melts then use it immediately. Never let it get hot or continue to heat after this point otherwise it will dry out and become granular. If this happens, it has overheated— discard it and start again.

To color white chocolate ganache with oil-based chocolate food coloring or gel food coloring, add the color to the cream just before you add the chocolate and stir it through together. Cream contains both fat and water so it will take gel food coloring better than chocolate alone.

Sugar glue

You can buy sugar glue in nail polish bottle-like containers—complete with brush inside, fairly cheaply and super-convenient. But if you want to make your own there are two ways. You can add CMC powder to water and allow it time to first clump and then disperse, try 1.5 teaspoons in 250ml (8½ fl oz) and add more water if required and use this as sugar glue.

Or you can use the traditional recipe of 50% white sugar crystals (that you put in your tea) 50% boiling water. Pour the boiling water over the sugar and stir until dissolved. Allow the mixture to come to room temperature and then place it in the fridge. Once it has dropped to fridge temperature remove it and bring it back to room temperature, and it is ready to use. Keep any leftover sugar glue in a container to use next time. This does not need to be refrigerated again; the refrigeration step is only to bring the mixture to a glue-like consistency which it will maintain at room temperature.

To fill a piping bag

Trim off the end of the piping bag and insert the coupler (if you are using a small tip) or large piping nozzle of your choice. Secure the bag with a piping bag clip or clothes peg just above the tip, to avoid leaking. Place your hand halfway down the outside of the piping bag and fold the top half of the bag down over your hand to make it easier to get the filling closer to the nozzle. The bag should stay in your hand, no pressure required. Hold the bag over the bowl of batter/icing and using a spoon or spatula, scoop the batter/icing into the bag. To avoid air bubbles it is best to wipe the content of the spoon or spatula against the side of the bag and fill inwards.

PIPING BAGS

There are many different piping bag options on the market. If you are going to do a lot of decorating, try them all out and see which one you like working with the most and then invest in a set of different sizes. If you are going to make a cake once a year perhaps invest in a small pack of disposable bags. I have a set of reusable piping bags that I use for cake decorating and pastry work, they feel like material on the outside and have a plastic-feel coating on the inside, which makes them easy to wash.

If you have reusable piping bags, wash them in hot soapy water, making sure to turn them inside out as well to get a good clean and hang them over the door handle of your oven to dry—the oven heat will help ensure the bags are dry thoroughly, essential before you put them away to avoid mould. Alternatively clip them to clothes hangers and dry in the sun.

When I am piping cake batter I use disposable bags—I find cake batter harder to clean away and I also usually need a lot of bags of the same size, so it is simply easier.

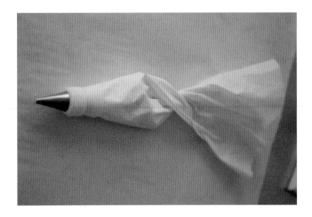

For icing, only part-fill the bag. Though refilling a piping bag is one of my least favourite jobs, when it comes to icing having less in the piping bag and adding more icing later helps keep your icing at the optimal consistency. The heat of your hand, when applied directly to icing through a thin piping bag is sufficient to melt the icing contained within. The only time I load up my piping bag is if I am piping with cake batter or soft ganache.

Pied-piping: A few piping tips

No matter what piping nozzle or technique is used, once you start to pipe you need to apply consistent pressure with your hand on the piping bag, don't change otherwise your design will look different in size and sometimes shape.

When you want the flow of icing to stop abruptly, you stop applying pressure and move your piping away. To leave a tail behind, move the bag in a downward, flicking motion. To cut it off clean make a very small, sharp circular motion as you pull the bag directly away without applying any pressure. If you would like to continue the shape into a tapered point, ease the pressure off the bag as you slowly pull the piping bag away.

If I am going to be doing a lot of piping, I have a new, damp, cloth balled up on hand ready to wipe clean the end of my piping nozzle as needed. You will get to know your piping nozzle and icing and how often you need a quick wipe clean, for small, detailed royal icing piping I wipe the nozzle frequently.

If you have been piping for a while and suddenly the consistency of the icing alters or starts to look different, especially the color and texture, the bag's contents may have melted under the warmth of your hand. Don't waste time, empty the contents of the piping bag into the bowl of icing and refill the piping bag with fresh icing, squeezing out the excess of the older stuff in the bowl get a nice even flow going before applying it to the cake or cupcakes again.

Silicon moulds, shape and letter cutters

I love silicon moulds, they are quick, easy and super-effective. You simply push your gum paste (or fondant) into them; they take the shape of the mould and simply pop back out again … perfectly formed. This is such a time saver. When using silicon moulds remember that gum paste holds it form better and is less likely to pull out of shape when you remove it from the mould and handle it. It will also dry quicker so you need to work fast in securing it to the place you want your shape.

Whether you use fondant or gum paste, they are both still temperamental to the weather and can be a bit sticky. For ease of reference I will refer to only gum paste from here.

To avoid getting your gum paste stuck in the mould: before your first use and after each use, wash and clean them in warm soapy water and allow to dry thoroughly.

If your silicon mould is a shallow one with no small, fiddly bits and the weather is not humid, a light dusting of cornflour (cornstarch) should be sufficient to allow your gum paste to be removed easily.

For deep moulds, or ones with small, fine details that are slightly closed off, compact the silicon mould with cornflour and then tap it out. This gives it a heavy coat and makes it easier to remove the gum paste. If this doesn't work, spray the silicon mould with vegetable oil release spray, but make sure it's clear oil, not yellow, otherwise it will affect the color of the gum paste shape. This option will leave the figure with an oily sheen. In this case wait for the figure to dry and gently brush the surface with cornflour—this attracts moisture away from the surface—use a clean dry brush to remove excess cornflour residue.

Sometimes a mould you have used dozens of times with no problem starts to be difficult to use. First clean it in warm soapy water to make sure no oily residue has been left, if that doesn't work, the problem could be caused by the weather. Incredibly damp weather affects how gum paste performs. Incredibly hot, humid weather changes how the gum paste will work in the mould and you may need to use the spray oil method. If problem persists, you can place the mould into the freezer for 3 minutes, which will harden the paste, making it easier to clean out of the mould.

When it comes to letter and shape cutters that are ejector cutters or cut-and-push/tap cutters I use the same procedure as I do for silicon moulds. This is because there is more contact surface between the cutter and the gum paste and more small areas for the gum paste to get stuck.

Standard shape cutters need very little preparation, I simply use them as is when cutting gum paste shapes. When I am using them to cut out shapes from slices of cake however, I always give them a light spray with vegetable oil—I find this helps them to glide through the cake slice better and assists the removal of the shape from the cutter with less risk of damage.

A note on flat-top cupcakes

Having an even, flat top on your cupcake makes it a lot easier to decorate. To avoid my cupcake doming, and to get the most even, flat top I can, I beat my cake batter for an extra 30 seconds on high and place it into the cupcake cases immediately. I then allow the batter to sit in the cases for 15 minutes on the bench *before* putting them into the oven. I find that the extra air I have beat into the batter leaves and the batter settles into the cupcake cases and when put into the oven will rise evenly.

If you do this, have all of your cupcakes all point in the one direction, so that they are pointing to the hottest part of your oven. Then place a small oven-safe dish of cold water in that corner and the extra heat will be taken up trying to heat your cold water and the oven should come back to an even heat—just be careful when opening the door in case there is steam.

Recipes

· ·

Whether you use a recipe provided here or one of your own favourites, it is important to consider the icing you will be using to decorate the cake before you decide on the cake recipe. Fondant looks great but it has trade-offs. Because fondant is heavy the cake you put it over must be dense enough to take the weight of the fondant without being crushed by it. A light sponge for example has a lot of air in it—the weight of the fondant would push down the sponge and the cake would start to bow at the sides giving a bulging or pregnant look. The structural integrity of the cake would also be compromised and would not cut very nicely. A light royal icing or buttercream however can coat a lighter cake such as a sponge with no impact.

Don't despair, this does not mean you are limited to fruitcake or plain chocolate mud cake. Madeira cake and some carrot cake recipes can be dense enough and white chocolate mud cake, like a vanilla sponge, will take on whatever flavor you can dream up … so get inventive.

A NOTE ON EGGS

It is important to weigh your cracked eggs. Recipes work on the science of ingredient ratios and the role of eggs is to both combine the ingredients and hold them together as well as provide structural support to hold up the flour. Six small eggs are different to six large eggs and what constitutes a small or large egg in one region of the world may be vastly different to another. That said, there is a little wiggle room. When you are weighing your cracked eggs if you are a little over or under the recipe will cope, although it is always better to be a little over rather than under.

BANANA CAKE

Bake in a preheat oven set at 190°C/375°F for 40 minutes.

Makes 1 medium loaf tin (approximately L:21cm/W:11cm/D:7cm)

225 g/8 oz butter, at room temperature
225 g/8 oz caster (superfine) sugar
3 eggs

390 g/13¾ oz ripe bananas, mashed
100 g/3½ oz self-raising (self-rising) flour
125 g/4½ oz cornflour (corn starch)

1 Start with your butter at room temperature and mix it to combine with the caster sugar, once combined, scrape down your mixing bowl and mix them together on high for 2–4 minutes to create a creamy mix, you will know when it is ready because the butter will change color and become slightly lighter. Add the eggs and mix on medium. Scrape down the bowl and add the mashed banana.

2 Mix on low until combined.

3 Sift in the flour and cornflour and mix on medium for 2 minutes.

CARROT CAKE*

Bake at 180°C/350°F for 60 minutes

Makes 1 23cm/9 inch round cake

220 ml/ 7.7oz vegetable oil
5 eggs
200 ml/7 oz water
230 g/ 8 ¹⁄₁₀ oz grated carrot
435 g/15 ⅓ oz sugar
245 g/8½ oz self-raising (self-rising) flour

230 g/8 ¹⁄₁₀ oz wholemeal (whole-wheat) flour
10 g /⅓ oz baking powder
25g / ⁹⁄₁₀ oz skim milk powder
1 teaspoon salt
1 teaspoon mixed spice

1 Add your liquid ingredients to your mixing bowl and place your dry ingredients on top.

2 Mix until combined and then beat on high for 5 minutes.

*Recipe courtesy of The Northern Sydney Institute, part of TAFE NSW

SPICED PUMPKIN CAKE

Bake at 150°C/300°F for 40-60 minutes

Makes 1 small ball tin

220 g/7 ¾ oz butter, at room temperature
220 g/7 ¾ oz caster (superfine) sugar
2 large or 3 small eggs
175 g/6 oz mashed cooked pumpkin
140 g/5 oz plain (all-purpose) flour

140 g/5 oz self-raising (self-rising) flour
1 teaspoon cinnamon
½ teaspoon nutmeg
¼ teaspoon ginger

1 Start with your butter at room temperature and mix it to combine with the caster sugar. Once combined, scrape down your mixing bowl and mix them together on high for 2–4 minutes to create a creamy mix—you will know when it is ready because the butter will change color and become slightly lighter. Add your eggs and mix on medium until clear.

2 Scrape down your bowl and add your mashed pumpkin. Mix on low until combined.

3 Sift in your flour and spices and mix on medium for 2 minutes or until clear.

CHOCOLATE MUD CAKE

Bake at 130°C/265°F for 2 hours 40 mins (check at 1 hour 40 mins)

250 g/9 oz butter, at room temperature
250 g/9 oz compound chocolate
470 g/16 ½ oz caster (superfine) sugar
120 ml/4 ¼ fl oz milk (add an extra 2 tablespoons, if needed)
60 g/2 oz unsweetened cocoa powder

150 g /5 oz self-raising (self-rising) flour
150 g /5 oz plain (all-purpose) flour
100 ml/3 ½ fl oz oil (rice bran, grape seed or olive oil)
4 eggs

1 Melt the butter in a saucepan set over low heat. Add the chocolate and sugar and stir constantly until the chocolate has also melted. Add the milk and keep stirring over a low heat until the ingredients combine.

2 Set aside and allow the mixture to cool, I find transferring it to a mixing bowl works best to remove it from the heat of the base of the saucepan that can still keep cooking it.

3 When the chocolate mix has returned to room temperature, place it into your mixing bowl and sift the cocoa powder and flour placing it on top of the liquid and mix on low until just combined.

4 Add the oil and eggs to the mix combine on low speed and mix on high for 3–4 minutes.

5 Transfer the batter to a greased and lined cake tin and set aside for 10 minutes before baking. This rest time allows the batter to settle after being mixed on high and helps the cake to rise evenly. If you are making one of the cakes with frozen shapes inside, allow the batter to sit in the mixing bowl for 10 minutes before adding it to the tin with the shapes and baking immediately.

Psst! Butter will melt down better if you start with it at room temperature.

Note: I use a combination of olive, rice bran and grapeseed oil in my cakes. I find the combination is lighter and creates a more subtle taste. Use whatever cooking oil suits you best, or you have to hand.

WHITE CHOCOLATE MUD CAKE

Bake at 130°C/265°F for 2 hours 30 mins (check at 1 hour 10 mins)

Fills a 9 inch round or 8 inch square cake tin

270 g/9 ½ oz butter, at room temperature
300 g/10 ½ oz white chocolate
470 g/16 ½ oz caster (superfine) sugar
250 ml /9 fl oz milk

300 g/10 ½ oz plain (all-purpose) flour
260 g/9 ¼ oz self-raising (self-rising) flour
4 eggs
Edible food color and flavoring, as desired

1 Melt the butter in a saucepan over low heat. Add the chocolate, caster sugar and milk and stir constantly until the chocolate has also melted and the ingredients combined. Transfer to a separate bowl and leave to cool.

2 When the chocolate mix has returned to room temperature, place it into your mixing bowl and sift flour placing it on top of the liquid and mix on low until just combined. Add the eggs one at a time to the mix on low speed until clear. Mix on high for 2 minutes.

Remember: if you are coloring your batter you want to be adding your food coloring before you mix the ingredients on high to ensure the color is emulsified into the batter.

3 Transfer the batter to a greased and lined cake tin and set aside for 10 minutes before baking. This is rest time allows the batter to settle after being mixed on high and helps the cake to rise evenly. If you are making one of the cakes with frozen shapes inside, allow the batter to sit in the mixing bowl for 10 minutes before adding it to the tin with the shapes and baking immediately.

Note: this recipe makes a very dense cake, ideal for carving, stacking and remaining structurally sound despite having the centre removed. I only use this recipe for my surprise inside cakes.

You will notice that all of the cake balls and cakes that we cut shapes out of and bake again are mud cakes. We use a mud cake batter due to its density, which makes it more structurally sound, allowing for the double handling of cutting it out, freezing it, placing it and re-baking it. Mud cakes also withstand the re-bake a lot better than a sponge, both in terms of moisture (due to the high fat content) and in the retaining its form so it doesn't liquefy and disappear.

LIGHT FRUIT CAKE

Bake at 180°C/350°F for 40-60 minutes

Makes 1 medium loaf tin (approximately L:21cm/W:11cm/D:7cm)

Cake

4 eggs
275 g/9¾ oz caster (superfine) sugar
250 g/9 oz plain (all-purpose) flour, plus
  1 tablespoon extra
125 g/4½ oz self-raising (self-rising) flour
20 g/¾ oz cornflour (corn starch)

230 g/8¹⁄₁₀ oz butter
2 teaspoons salt
20 ml/¾ fl oz milk
130 ml/4½ fl oz water
Dried fruit, to taste

Fruit Soak

Dark rum 200 ml
White rum 200 ml
Tequila 50 ml
Sugar syrup 100 ml (flavor with ginger at Christmas)

Water 200ml
A sprinkle of cinnamon sugar stirred through the
  liquid before pouring over the fruit.

If you don't like to use alcohol you can soak the fruit in plain water or a flavored sugar syrup overnight in the fridge.

If you don't mind cooking with some alcohol, I use the following ratios of ingredients (adjust the volume to make enough liquid to adequately cover the fruit as the fruit will absorb the liquid):

1 Soak the dried fruit in a bowl overnight.

2 Strain and rinse the fruit before spreading it out onto plates lined with kitchen towel to dry.

3 Bring all the ingredients to room temperature.

4 Mix the egg and sugar together on high until the egg becomes light and fluffy.

5 Add the flours gradually on medium speed; do not worry if the egg loses volume.

6 Add the room temperature butter and the salt and mix on low until just combined.

7 Add the milk and water and beat on medium for 2 minutes.

8 Toss the fruit in plain (all-purpose) flour until it is lightly coated* and then add it to the cake batter and mix on low until evenly combined.

*This will prevent the fruit from falling to the bottom of the batter when the cake is put into the hot oven. Thanks to the teachers at The Northern Sydney Institute, part of TAFE NSW for that most helpful tip!

OPTION ALERT! If you mix all of the ingredients together at the same time the result will be a denser fruit cake. It won't rise as far but will be quicker to make. The baking time stays the same.

SPONGE CAKE*

Bake at 180°C/350°F for 15-20 minutes

392.5g/13⁹⁄₁₀ oz caster (superfine) sugar
227.50g/8 oz cake margarine**
5 eggs
400g/14¹⁄₁₀ oz soft or high ratio flour**

7.5g/0.3oz baking powder
15g/0.5 oz skim milk powder
147.5g/5.2 oz water
Vanilla essence to taste

A traditional, or 'conventional' sponge is very light and rises a great deal. For the cakes that feature in this book, traditional sponge cake may be too light and rise too much. The recipe below is perfect for whenever sponge cake is required.

1 Mix the cream cake margarine with the sugar until light and white. Gradually add the egg and essence (in several additions) to the fat, emulsifying well between each addition.

2 Add the flour, milk powder and baking powder and blend until smooth and free of lumps—do not over mix. Stream in the water on low speed and mix until smooth and free of lumps.

Recipe courtesy of The Northern Sydney Institute, part of TAFE NSW

** Where the recipe refers to cake fat or margarine, I use unsalted butter. If you want to use cake margarine you can, this is usually used commercially to give a more shelf stable product. Similarly, hi-ratio flour has been milled finer and treated and is used in commercial mixes. I replace this with 250g / 8.8 oz self-raising flour 150g / 5⅓ oz plain flour sifted together.

BUTTERCREAM

500 g/1 lb 2 oz unsalted butter, at room
    temperature

1 kg/2¼ lb icing (confectioners') sugar
¼ cup of melted white chocolate (optional)

1 Put the butter in the mixing bowl and beat on high until the butter just starts to turn white (change to a lighter color).

2 Add the icing sugar a little at a time. Scrape down the sides regularly.

3 If you are using buttercream on a hot day and are worried about the low melting point of butter or if you simply want it to taste a little more like a dense mousse, simply add ¼ cup of melted white chocolate after all of the icing sugar has been added, and make sure it is mixed in thoroughly.

If you add this you will need to apply/pipe the buttercream right away before the chocolate starts to cool or else it may become too stiff to work with. Once applied, put the cake/cupcakes in the fridge. Once the chocolate and butter combination has come down to refrigeration temperature, it can be brought back out to room temperature and will not be affected by the hot weather so easily, thanks to the higher melting point of the chocolate. Plus, it's super yummy.

Troubleshoot: If your butter is too cold or you have added too much icing sugar the standard buttercream will be dry and unspreadable. If this happens, add 30 ml/1 fl oz of milk and mix through. Alternatively, lightly heat the butter and icing sugar to soften the butter and place it back on the beaters. Note, you must now keep your cake/cupcakes refrigerated otherwise the milk can spoil.

Note: If you are going to attempt to use buttercream underneath a layer of fondant, mix the butter and icing sugar together until combined—do not cream the butter.

ROYAL ICING

500 g/1 lb 2 oz icing (confectioners' sugar)   Lemon juice
1 egg white

1 Double sift the icing sugar into the mixing bowl.

2 Add the egg whites and mix on low–medium until peaks form.

Recipe courtesy of The Northern Sydney Institute, part of TAFE NSW

Notes:

- Only a drizzle of lemon juice is required: I usually squeeze ¼ of a lemon over my hand and the small amount of juice that runs off is enough—the presence of acid helps the egg white develop.

- To conduct the peak consistency test: stop the mixer, using the back of a teaspoon push the teaspoon up against the royal icing and pull it away—a trail of royal icing should follow the spoon in a peak.

- If you want a sweet icing to act as soft glue or give you a melted icing look (like the circus cupcakes), stop mixing when the formed peaks bend over themselves. If you want royal icing that is a load-bearing glue and that will hold its shape (like the Halloween cupcakes), keep mixing until the peaks stay peaked and do not fall.

- To color royal icing, add the edible food color just as the egg white and icing sugar are forming soft peaks; the final mixing on high that stiffens the peaks will also evenly distribute the color throughout the mixture. Note: any more than 2–3 drop of color may adversely affect the mixture; the water content may interfere with the egg whites forming stiff peaks. Choose the shade carefully, this is not a time to buy a lighter shade and simply add more to the recipe to get a darker tone.

- Use egg white powder to substitute the raw egg white if the recipient of the cake/party attendees may have dietary restrictions. This is particularly important for pregnant women.

ITALIAN BUTTERCREAM*

400 g/14 oz caster (superfine) sugar
100 ml/3½ fl oz water
Juice from ½ lemon

1 egg white
500 g/1 lb 2 oz butter
125 g/4½ oz creaming fat**

1 Place the caster sugar, water and lemon juice in a saucepan and bring to the boil. Using a candy thermometer cook to 115–118°C/239–244.4°F. Cool before adding to egg whites.

2 Whip egg whites (use your whisk attachment on your mixer) until light and fluffy and slowly add the boiled syrup. Once combined, set aside and allow to cool completely (do not refrigerate). Once cool, add the butter and creaming fat to the mixture and whisk on high speed to smooth out and aerate the fats.

3 Add cocoa powder to make this a chocolate buttercream. I adore this recipe, it tastes so fabulous it is worth the extra effort to upgrade from standard buttercream.

Recipe courtesy of The Northern Sydney Institute, part of TAFE NSW

**Creaming fat is a shelf stable commercially used product, if you don't have easy access to it simply substitute it for more unsalted butter.*

CREAM CHEESE ICING*

225 g/7⁹⁄₁₀ oz cream cheese
112.5 g/4 oz cake fat

312.5 g/11 oz pure icing (confectioners') sugar

1 Cream together the cream cheese and cake fat. Sift the pure icing sugar into the mixing bowl and combine well.

*Recipe courtesy of The Northern Sydney Institute, part of TAFE NSW

This is so simple, reduce or increase the recipe as required. I like to add the juice of ¼ of a lemon for a bit of a tart taste to the cream cheese. Note: For cake fat, you can use butter, margarine or a myriad of different commercial products designed for shelf stability for these sorts of icing. I like to use plain, unsalted butter.

Helpful Hint: Start with butter at room temperature to make the creaming process easier.

MASCARPONE CREAM

150 g/5½ oz mascarpone
150 g/5½ oz thickened cream

100 g/3½ oz icing (confectioners') sugar

1 Combine the ingredients in a mixing bowl and whisk thoroughly.

Note: most recipes call for a 1:1 ratio of Mascarpone to cream. Rarely do these two items come in the exact same size from the supermarket—you can adjust the ratio slightly to use up your ingredients and not have any waste. Just note if the ratio of cream is higher you may need to add a little more icing sugar as the dry ingredient to offset how wet the cream is; use your best judgement to control the consistency of the icing.

GANACHE

1.2 kg/2 lb 10 oz dark (bittersweet) chocolate
600 ml/1 pint cream
(2:1 ratio)
OR
1.8kg /3lb 15½ oz milk chocolate
600 ml/1 pint cream
(3:1 ratio)

OR
1.8 kg/4 lb white chocolate
450 g/1 lb cream
(4:1 ratio)

1 Break the chocolate into small pieces (or buy chocolate buttons and place into a large mixing bowl).

2 Place the cream into a saucepan with a heavy base and bring it to the boil stirring regularly. Pour immediately onto the chocolate and keep stirring until the chocolate has melted and it is thoroughly combined with the cream. Set it aside and allow to cool a little. When it is close to room temperature beat it with your mixer until it becomes lighter in texture and is combined well. Bring down to room temperature and store. I like to leave mine covered in the refrigerator overnight to set before using. If you are not using it under fondant, you can use it to decorate immediately. If you are making it well in advance (or a larger batch than you need) you can freeze it.

For under-fondant ganache, use couverture or compound. If you have worked with chocolate before and are comfortable with tempering chocolate then I suggest that you use couverture chocolate in your ganache to coat your cakes. It has a rich, taste and smooth texture, a luxury that will be reflected in the price. If this is your first foray into working with chocolate and making ganache, use compound chocolate—it is easier to use and less temperamental with heat.

When ganache is used as the only icing for the cake or the 'outer covering' for a cake, it needs to look pretty and taste good, but this covering type can be softer. For outer-covering ganache you can experiment with blocks of your favourite eating chocolate and not worry if it never really 'sets'.

ICING MIXTURE

9 parts icing (confectioners') sugar
1 part cornflour (corn starch)

1 Sift these two ingredients together in the above ratio, making as much as you need to roll out fondant and other decorative elements.

Note: You can buy cornflour dispensers, or secure a handful of cornflour in a cleaning cloth with mesh holes, muslin wrap or cheesecloth. These make the best dispensers of a fine cornflour dust.

Daisy Hill and the Cow Face Cupcakes

DIFFICULTY: ✏️✏️✏️✏️✏️

TIME TO MAKE: ⏳⏳⏳⏳⏳

This cake is so cute and versatile, perfect for kids discovering farmyard animals or for anyone who loves cows—and it is so easy to make. If you don't have a hemisphere tin, substitute an oven-safe soup or mixing bowl for it, as long as it has the domed shape.

Because cows are associated with milk and cream, I have used creamy white chocolate and a dairy milk chocolate in the mud cake recipe, replacing the suggested compound chocolate in the basic recipe. I have done this for the creamier, chocolaty taste. You can replace cooking chocolate for your favourite chocolate for any of the recipes but you must remember that chocolate on the shelf is designed to be eaten right away, not for cooking and baking at high temperatures, so you may need to adjust the temperature of your oven down slightly. Also understand that because this chocolate behaves differently at high temperatures the batter will not hold its shape as well, you can see from mine here it gives a nice milky swirl, not defined 'cow spot' shaped blobs.

OPTION ALERT! If you want to have a more definition between the white and chocolate brown spots in the cake to make it more cow spotted, simply use the cooking chocolate recommended in the recipe section, chill the batter and follow the steps below.

PSST! I used a heart-shaped cake board because it resembles the shape of the spots I have put on Daisy the Cow and it allows me room to play around with my gum paste, making a muddy path and stepping stones leading up to the gate. If you're feeling adventurous and have the time, you can add ducks and rabbits and even a small pig to the board for interest.

YOU WILL NEED

Large hemisphere cake tin—20 cm/8 inch round and 10 cm/4 inch deep (or use an oven-safe soup bowl)

Grass tip/nozzle, for piping (I use the Wilton 233 grass tip)

2 piping bags, for the batter

Piping bag and coupler, for the icing

Gum paste and fondant

Butter & icing sugar (see page 38 for buttercream recipe)

Gel food color: leaf or forest green, brown and pink

2 batches of mud cake batter (I used white chocolate mud cake from page 35 for one cake, and then replaced the white chocolate with the same quantity of milk chocolate for the second batch)

Modelling tools: ball tool, Dresden tool, wheel cutter

Cutters: heart shape, small blossom circle

Sugar glue

Embroidery scissors

Black edible pen

Cupcake cases

Cupcake tray

Cake board

Icing sugar and cornflour mix

MAKING THE CAKE

1 Preheat the oven to 120–130°C/250–266°F for mud cake, or 180°C/350°F if you are making sponge cake. Grease and flour the hemisphere tin or spray with cake release/vegetable oil spray. If you are using packet mix cakes, follow the instructions on the packet for temperature but be flexible with your cooking time, this tin is a different shape and may take a little longer than a standard round tin.

2 Stabilise the hemisphere tin on a baking tray and egg ring, or preferably in a small round cake tin with water in the base (but ensure the water doesn't touch the dome of the hemisphere tin).

3 Fill two piping bags with the two cake batters. Seal the end of the piping bag with a clip or elastic band. Have two tall jugs (or bowls) to hand so that you can rest the larger end of the piping bags in them when you need to swap bags.

4 Cut the ends off the piping bags (small end up so you don't lose any batter!) and start piping large oval/kidney shaped beads of white batter into the hemisphere tin. When you have piped one layer of white spots, pipe the chocolate batter over the top to just cover the spots. Using the white batter, pipe another layer of large oval/kidney shaped beads of batter on top the of

 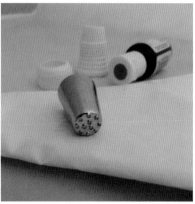 

the chocolate layer and then cover it with a thin layer of the chocolate batter. Repeat this until you have filled the tin to the required level.

5 Bake for 60–75 minutes for the mud cake, or 30–40 minutes for a sponge cake, or until a skewer, when inserted into the middle of the cake, comes out clean. Be sure to test your cake 10 minutes before the timer is due to go off to get an idea of where it is up to and reassess the baking time from there.

HOT TIP! When I make a sponge cake, I beat the batter on high for an extra 30 seconds to add extra air to it, and then after I have placed it into my cake tin I let it sit for 15–20 minutes before putting it into the oven. The extra air leaves the batter, the batter settles and I get a flat, even rise to my cake and cupcakes. If you have used sponge cake batter for the Daisy cake I recommend you follow this advice to get a flat base to the hemisphere shape.

PREPARING THE CAKE

If your cake has risen to a dome in the oven, don't despair! Let the cake cool and then refrigerate it. Once it is cold, return the cake to the hemisphere tin so it is secure, stabilising it on top of a round tin so it doesn't rock about and using the top of the hemisphere tin as a guide, simply take a bread knife and level the cake.

Once you have a flat cake base, cover the part of the cake board that the cake will be sitting on with your buttercream. Place the cake, flat side down, into the buttercream. This will secure the cake to the board and help keep the base fresh (I do this even if I am not levelling the cake).

OPTION ALERT! Want to add an extra surprise to this baked cake? Why not add the milk bottle lollies to the centre, so when the cake is cut the milk bottles come tumbling out! After baking the hemisphere, follow the instructions for cutting, filling and sealing the cake back together in the Gender Reveal Belly Cake on page 311. You can make the space as large or small as you like, but remember will reduce the number or size of the cake slices you have available to serve.

DECORATING THE CAKE

Put the grass tip (nozzle) into the piping bag and part fill the bag with buttercream. Pipe grass all over the cake. I start by piping from the tip of the dome down the side of the cake, creating four equal portions. Then I fill in these portions one at a time working in a line from top to bottom to ensure that the grass looks even.

There are three tricks to using the 233 grass tip: pressure, angle and using a small amount of buttercream in the piping bag.

Unlike most other tips, the 233 grass tip is held vertically above the area to be piped, and not at an angle. The gap between tip and cake should be the height you wish the grass to be, and it should be consistent across the cake. When you pipe, apply pressure until the buttercream is close to the tip, closing the gap between the tip and the cake, stop applying pressure to the bag and then move the tip away from the cake, still a vertical movement. This will give the effect of short mown grass. If you want longer grass in some areas, simply ease the pressure off the piping bag as you pull the tip away from the cake. The length of time you keep applying pressure will determine the length of the long grass.

Refilling a piping bag is one of my pet peeves, however, this type of icing requires it—butter has a low melting point and because your hand holds the piping bag for an extended period of time, the butter will start to melt. You will notice this because the buttercream stops performing, meaning that it won't form the grass shape as well or sit up like short mown grass. When this happens, empty the contents of the bag back into the bowl of buttercream. Replace it with solid buttercream and squeeze the bag over the bowl until all the melted buttercream has passed through the tip and only firmer buttercream starts to flow out in a more grass-like consistency. If this doesn't work, then you may have to remove the tip from the coupler and wash it under hot water, dry, reattach and keep going.

MAKING DAISY THE COW

1 Take two balls of white gum paste. Make one slightly smaller than the other; the smaller one will be the head and the larger one the body so it is important to get the proportions correct.

2 On a non-stick surface, shape the smaller ball of gum paste into a teardrop shape by rolling the outside edge of your little finger back and forth across the one-third point of the ball, if the base does not automatically become teardrop shaped, finish moulding the shape with your fingers. Shape the body into a teardrop in the same way and position with the point facing up.

3 Place the teardrop-shaped head on its side so the small and large ends are both in contact with your work surface. Using your thumb and forefinger squeeze the top of the fatter end of the shape to make it flat-ish. It will look like a small a flat rise and will be where the eyes are situated. Ensure the top of the flat rise is still rounded to give a head shape and has space to add ears and horns.

4 With the body and head next to each other, using your fingers, mould the end of the nose, checking the length against the body to keep it in proportion.

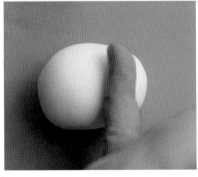

5 Color a small portion of white gum paste with pink food color. Thinly roll out the gum paste. Using a circle cutter cut out a circle that will fit over the end of the nose.

6 Brush a thin layer of sugar glue over the end of the nose and stick the pink circle in place. Smooth over the edges from top to bottom so any creases disappear under the nose. Trim any excess with a small fondant knife or embroidery scissors.

7 Using your ball tool, make two indentations in the end of the nose for nostrils.

8 For the legs, take two smaller balls of gum paste and roll each into sausage shapes. On a non stick surface using two fingers from each hand, roll the sausage shape into a more defined, neat sausage shape that is thicker on one end—this will be the hoof. Once you have two identical sausage shapes with one end larger than the other and of equal lengths, you can shape the hoofs. Taking one shape at a time hold the sausage vertically with the larger end facing down, gently drop the fat end onto the non stick surface several times and the end will start to blunt and become flat and round. Repeat for the other sausage and ensure they are the same length afterwards, trimming if necessary.

9 Paint the bottom edge of the cow's body with sugar glue. To attach the legs to the cow, place the fat end of the hoof at the front of the figure and wrap the limb around the back of the cow, securing the end to the centre of the back of the cow (if it is too long simply trim away with scissors). Repeat this for the other limbs. Always start with the bottom legs first as the top legs will sit on top of the bottom legs for support until the figure dries.

10 Color a small portion of gum paste brown. Roll it out thinly and using a heart-shaped cutter, cut out 1 heart for the tummy spot. Brush sugar glue to the back of the heart and stick in place.

11 Using the same brown gum paste, rolled out thinly, cut out small, simple blossoms. Using a wheel tool (or kitchen knife) cut each blossom in half. Using the sugar glue again, stick the half blossoms to the cow to give her spots.

12 Roll 4 small balls of brown gum paste; apply sugar glue to the end of the legs and using your finger press the balls of brown gum paste onto the end of the legs to create hooves.

Smooth the edges with your finger as required (wash and dry your hands and dust your fingers with cornflour to stop it sticking if necessary). Once the hooves look neat, use the Dresden tool to indent the top of the hoof to create a cleft.

13 Add the head to the body by first inserting a stick of raw spaghetti into the body. Eventually the spaghetti will soften due to the moisture content of the gum paste, however, it will provide stability while the glue dries, and it is edible! Using embroidery scissors, cut the spaghetti to the right length to fit into two-thirds of the head. Apply sugar glue to the top of the body where the head will rest, then carefully place the head onto the spaghetti stick so it is resting on the body.

14 Take a small ball of the brown gum paste and cut it in half. Roll each half into a ball and ensure they are equal size. On a non-stick surface, (dust it and your fingers with cornflour) using your forefinger, press directly down onto each brown ball to make a flat disc. Pushing them flat before sticking in place ensures they are the same size. Brush sugar glue on the back of the disc and stick to the face of the cow to make the base of the eye. The closer and larger they are the more cartoonish and cute they look.

15 Repeat to make the eyeballs using white gum paste balls, making them slightly smaller. Stick the white discs directly in the centre of the brown discs.

16 Repeat the steps to make the black pupil of the eye, this time placing them toward the bottom of the white discs.

17 Take very small, equal-sized balls of white gum paste, brush a small spot of sugar glue onto the top right corner of each black disc of the eye. Using your finger, place the white ball directly onto the glue spot on the black disc and flatten it onto the eye with your finger while attaching it.

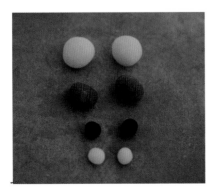

18 To make the ears, using your fingers, roll a small amount of white gum paste into two equal, tic-tac shape cylinders. Using the small end of the Dresden tool on a non-stick surface, push down into three-quarters of the shape to make an indent. Using your fingers pinch the last quarter to make the tip of the ear a little more pointed.

19 To make the inner ear, using a small amount of pink gum paste, make a smaller version of the cylinder, as above. Apply sugar glue to the indented part of the white ear and using the small end of the Dresden tool, depress the pink gum paste into the indent. Apply a small amount of sugar glue to the cow's head, and then attach the ears. You may need to use the Dresden tool at the back of the ear to secure it in place if necessary. Do not worry if this looks unsightly, you can cover it with cow hair.

20 To make the hair, shape a medium ball of brown gum paste into an elongated oval. On a non-stick surface, flatten this shape with the palm of your hand or lightly with a rolling pin. Trim the edges to fit the piece neatly onto the head and down the neck/back. Use embroidery scissors to cut into the shape at a 45-degree angle, to create peaks of hair. Once you are happy with its texture, apply sugar glue to the back of the shape and stick in place. You may need to cut a few extra pieces or lift some tufts after handling it.

21 For the horns, roll a small piece of white gum paste into a very small sausage. Using scissors cut this shape in half. Using your fingers, roll these two equal parts into shape, one end pointy the other end flatter. Apply a small amount of sugar glue to the flat end and secure in place using the Dresden tool to flatten the base of the horn to the hair. Lastly, bend the horns to make a crescent pointing inward to the face.

22 Last, but not least, we make Daisy a happy cow! To create the smile, using a circle cutter at a 45-degree angle, insert it into the base of the nose area to make an indent. Using the small end of the ball tool, tidy the edge of the smile by pushing directly inward at each end of the indent to create dimples.

MAKING THE FENCE AND FLOWERS

1 Roll out white gum paste on a non-stick surface dusted liberally with cornflour. Using a ruler, measure the height and width of the fence, keeping it in proportion to the size of the finished cake. Use a sharp edged ruler or a ruler and a fondant/kitchen knife to cut out the fence palings.

2 Align the fence palings equal distances apart, ensuring they can easily move across the non-stick surface, add additional cornflour at this point if required. Remember the fence is going to dry on the spot so you don't want it to stick.

3 Secure the last fence paling as a rail, diagonally across the fence palings using a liberal amount of sugar glue. This is the support beam so ensure it is stuck to all of the fence palings. Using the small end of the ball tool, make indents at each end of the rail to look like nail divots. Place two small balls of brown gum paste into the divots, securing with sugar glue. Leave this to dry before we decorate it any further. Drying time will vary, depending on the weather, where you live and how dry/damp your house is. In the Australian summer this takes 24 hours to be rock hard.

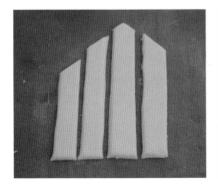  

4 Write on the fence. You can use cut out letters but as this is a small space and I wanted a hand-painted country fence look I have used a black edible pen. Be sure to measure twice and write once, thinking letter height and spacing before commencing.

5 Decorating Daisy! Cutting out the flowers is the easy part. Color up a small amount of gum paste whatever color you would like your flowers to be, I have chosen a coral color (on the red color spectrum) to contrast with my green grass. Roll out your colored gum paste and cut out as many flowers as you would like to hide in the grass of the finished cake and one for the fence. Cut out each flower, rubbing the cutter back and forth on the board/mat to ensure the flower is cleanly cut. Transfer the gum paste onto another non-stick surface. Use the small end of the ball tool in the centre of the flower to push it out of the cutter. This will indent the centre of the flower and make the petals curl inwards slightly giving a lively 3D effect. For the flower centres, color a small amount of gum paste in a contrasting color (I used egg yellow) and make little balls, attaching them with sugar glue. Use sugar glue to attach the flowers to the fence at the start and end of Daisy's name … and voila, a lovingly created country fence for Daisy!

Making the Cow Cupcakes

1 Preheat the oven to 120°C/250°F for mud cake, or 180°C/350°F for sponge cake batter. Line the cupcake tray with paper cases.

2 Fill two piping bags with the two cake batters (brown and white), the batter that will be the heart of the cupcake should be half the amount of the other batter (as you will use a lot less of it). Clip off the end of the piping bag with a clip, peg or even elastic band. Have two jugs to hand that you can rest the larger end of the piping bags into (tip facing upwards) when you need to swap bags.

3 Pipe the larger amount of batter into the cupcake cases and fill to two-thirds full. Take the other piping bag and insert it into the centre of one paper case of cupcake batter. Apply pressure to the piping bag as you pull it out of the cupcake case—this will create a different color heart in the cupcake. You may need to wipe over the end of the piping bag in between each cupcake insert. Fill the cupcake cases to 1 finger width lower than the top of the paper case, this allows for rise.

Note: for this part I use a large round piping tip to give me better control.

4 Bake for 25–35 minutes for the mud cake, or 17–20 minutes for a sponge cake, or until a skewer, when inserted into the centre, comes out clean.

DECORATING THE CUPCAKES

1 Apply a thin layer of ganache or buttercream on top of the cupcake; this keeps it moist on top and gives the fondant something to adhere to. Be inventive with colors and flavors here if you wish.

2 Roll out the brown fondant about 4mm/²⁄₁₀ thick, as you smooth it out, this will reduce down to approximately 3mm/¹⁄₁₀ in thickness.

Use a circle cutter that is big enough to fit over your entire cupcake. This allows for depth as well as diameter. If you don't have big circle cutters you can use an egg ring. Cut out your brown topper and lay it over the top of you cupcake. Use clean dry hands to smooth out the topper. You may also use an acetate square if you have it, this will give a nice shiny smooth finish. Smooth down the sides so they cover and tuck under the edges of the cupcake. Do this for all of the cupcakes.

3 Roll out your pink fondant very thin (we are using it for color not cover) and using the same circle cutter, cut out pink circles. Cut these pink circles in half and apply half to the bottom of the cupcake, rounded side up to create a nose. Smooth down the pink to disappear under the lip of the cupcake, use a fondant knife or embroidery scissors if you need to, to neaten it.

Using the techniques explained for the daisy cow figurine:

4 Make two eyes for each cupcake as for Daisy the Cow.

5 Make and attach two ears to each cupcake as for Daisy the Cow.

6 Make and attach two horns for each cupcake as for Daisy the Cow.

7 Make, cut and attach blossoms as cow spots for each cupcake. Because the cupcakes have brown cow faces, I have made my cow spots white. This is reverse of Daisy Cow's colorings and creates a more diverse color palate for interest when they are all plated up together on the party table. (Never lose sight of the big picture! Always imagine your finished product in the space it will be displayed, not just in context of your smaller decorating space).

8 To make a smile, take your circle cutter and insert it in and upwards at a 45 degree angle in lower the ⅓ of the cupcake face. Make dimples by inserting the large ball tool at each end of the cut made to represent the smile. You can do this by applying pressure directly down, or also at a 45-degree angle, or applying pressure inwards and upwards to help shape cheeks. The indentation for nostrils is achieved the same way using the larger end of the ball tool.

If you have time and want to get creative, you can add different colored flowers or hats to each of the cupcakes, personalising them as Daisy's friends.

Circus Tent and Cupcakes

DIFFICULTY: ✎✎✎✎✎

TIME TO MAKE: ⧗⧗⧗⧗⧗

A circus-themed cake is super-popular and never goes out of style. Kids love it and it is so easy to make it the focus of a circus-themed party—so bright and fun. The great thing about this cake is that it is easy to personalise too— just add the recipient's name in the circus banner and boom! Instant hit! I have made only the circus tent here. If you are having a large party, you can make a square cake (approximately 7.5 cm/3 inches larger than the round cake in order to increase the quantity of cake you have). Use a contrasting color such as blue with opposite shaped detail, striped tent and star spangled box or vice versa is a great option.

TROUBLESHOOT

My gum paste roof ripped as I draped it over the shape. This can happen for several reasons:
- If the roof point is too narrow or sharp for the weight/amount of gum paste that needs to hang from it, it will keep ripping no matter what you do.
- Most commonly paste rips because the gum paste has been rolled out too thick. Try again and roll it out a bit thinner.
- The gum paste may be too wet/not dry enough. Knead through some more pure icing (confectioners') sugar and if that doesn't work add another ½ teaspoon of CMC powder to the gum paste. Sometimes it can be a combination of all of these things but it is important to address each one at a time.

YOU WILL NEED

Round cake tin. The size will depend on how many people you need to feed with it. I have used an 18 cm/7 inch round and 7.5 cm/3 inch deep cake tin and made 2 cakes.

2 batches mud cake batters for 2 round mud cakes

1 batch mud cake batter, for the cake balls (see page 34)

Cake ball trays

Gel food color: blue, green, red, orange, yellow

Red fondant

Black fondant

White fondant

Gel food coloring: blue, yellow and orange (or buy pre-colored fondant)

CMC powder to turn fondant into gum paste

Star cutter

Blossom cutter

Fondant or kitchen knife

Rolling pin

Non-stick mat

Icing mix, for dusting

750 g/1 lb 10 oz chocolate ganache

22 gauge wires

Sugar glue

Chocolate and/or lollies, to fill roof

Cupcake cases

Cupcake tray

2 cake boards, the same size as your cakes

Cake board, for display

1 drinking cup/glass or non-stick shape, to use as a mould for the circus tent roof

Letter cutters

Plaque cutter or paper template (download from the internet and adjust the size to suit your cake design)

Piping bag

1M piping tip/nozzle or piping tip/nozzle of your choice for the cupcake design

MAKING THE CAKE BALLS

1 Mix up one batch of white mud cake batter and divide it equally into 4 bowls, using kitchen scales to ensure that the batches are even. Color the batter with your choice of bright gel food colors.

White chocolate mud cake is a creamy yellow color, so a light, bright blue color coloring will turn teal green when mixed into the batter. I prefer to use royal blue; it has a weighty base and will turn the batter darker blue. If you want a light blue cake, color the batter white first. This is best done with beaters on the cake mixer, and it will be easier if you lighten the entire batch of batter before you divide it between the bowls. It just means your other colors will be lighter too.

Flavor ALERT! Because the cake balls are so different in color I wanted to give them a distinct taste too. Mud cake has such a strong chocolate taste, and in keeping with the fun party food theme

I flavored my cake ball batter with marshmallow flavor. Another popular option is the Cotton Candy—a flavor that is synonymous with the circus and fairs, but I saved this one for my cupcakes!

2 Preheat the oven to 150°C/300°F. Grease both sides of the cake ball tray with cake release agent/vegetable oil.

3 Spoon the batter into the base tray. I make one color at a time to avoid dropping one color into another.

4 Cook for 17–20 minutes (cooking times may vary, depending on your oven and the cake batter recipe you use). As a general rule the cake batter should come out of the top of the cake ball tray a little or at least be visible and when you put a skewer in it, the skewer should come out clean. I always sacrifice one cake ball from the centre of the tray to cut open and check—this also means you get to eat it!

5 Once you have cooked all of the batter and allowed the cake balls to cool to room temperature, they need to be frozen—follow the instructions on page 13.

MAKING THE CAKES

1 Preheat the oven to 120–130°C/250–265°F for the mud cake. Grease and line the cake tin. You can use a vegetable oil or grease and flour option however for cakes that are going to have other cakes re-baked inside them, I line the tin with baking paper coming up at least 2.5 cm/ 1 inch higher than the tin sides in case of additional rise.

2 Make the chocolate cake batter. Place approximately one-fifth of the batter into the tin, use this as a base to secure the cake balls in place. Space the still-frozen cake balls no less than 1.5–2 cm/3–4 inches apart. Resist the temptation to push all of the cake balls down to the base, do this with only one-third of the balls. They will rise, but you don't want them all on one level.

3 Once the cake balls are in place, disperse the rest of the batter into the cake tin between them. I do this with a piping bag because it gives me greater control over the batter being

The number of cake balls you will use in the cake will depend on the size of your tin and how many layers of cake you need to bake for the size of your design. Be sure to place different colors next to each other and an even amount of each color.

carefully and evenly placed between the balls. If you don't want to get a piping bag out, you can do this, more slowly, with a spoon.

4 Once the cake batter is in the tin, smooth over the top with a spatula or knife (slightly dampen it to avoid the batter sticking to it) and put into the oven right away. Bake for the time specified for the size tin you have, until cooked through, and when a skewer, inserted at three different points across the cake, comes out clean.

5 Make a second cake in the same way. Allow both cakes to cool completely, wrap in cling film and refrigerate.

HOW LONG TO BAKE CAKE BALLS

The cake balls do take up space and there is less raw cake batter to be cooked, but the cake batter is being heated by the oven and at the same time cooled by the frozen cake balls, this competition of temperatures slows baking time down and the balance must be just right to ensure the cake is cooked and your cake balls are not liquefied.

BUT I CAN'T WAIT! Can't wait to see if it turned out? Worried it won't have turned out and you don't want to find out on the big day when you cut it? Yes you can cheat! Make sure the cake is refrigerator-cold, and that you have the ganache and boards ready to go, cut one neat clean wedge out of the cake and check it. Put the wedge back into the cake. Apply ganache to the board that the cake will be set on. Set the cake on the board and apply ganache over the cut area on the top and sides of the cake. Return it to the refrigerator to harden. Wait until the ganache is rock hard before moving on to the next step. Cutting weakens the integral structure of the stacked cake, so be careful. It is important to remember where the cut is and aim to cut a slice of cake over the same place, you can always put markers over the cuts, such as carefully placed stars on the tent, and so on.

DECORATING THE TENT BASE

1 Follow the instructions in the How-To section to stack and stick your cakes together with ganache.

2 Measure the height and circumference of the cake. Roll out and cut a rectangle of black fondant slightly taller than the cake. At the point you wish to be the front of the cake, secure the black fondant to the side and top of the cake as well. This should stick directly to the ganache.

3 Knead half a teaspoon of CMC powder into the red fondant you will be using to cover the cake. This will make the fondant a bit stiffer—so the tent flaps can maintain their shape without drying too hard.

Roll out the red fondant long enough to fit the circumference of the cake and slightly wider than the height of the cake. I recommend rolling this piece of fondant 0.5 cm/¼ thick.

4 Pick up the fondant, draping it over your forearms, and gently wrap it around the cake starting

WHAT TO DO IF FONDANT RIPS

If your fondant is too thick and has ripped, don't despair. If the rip is close to the top it will be covered by the roof—use your fingers and the heat of your hands to repair the rip and mould it back together, smoothing and thinning as you go. A few rips lower down can be covered by stars or carefully spaced stripes. If it is too hard to salvage don't worry if you need to remove the red fondant and start again—this happens to me too sometimes.

with the centre of the red fondant sheet at the back of the cake, wrapping it around the cake like a towel. Be sure the straight edge lines up with the base. The excess will peak over the top of the cake and is to be folded onto the top of the cake to help secure it. At the front, join the red fondant at the top and then gently part it away from the black rectangle, manipulating the folds to look like draped curtains pulled aside—this may take some fiddling. The extra thickness will make this heavy, if it is too thick it could rip at the top, if it is too thin or dry, it may crack and dry out and look ragged on the edges—it is a fine balance. If you do get cracked edges you can (very carefully!) trim the edges of the tent flaps with embroidery scissors and then pinch the fresh edges so they appear to come together.

5 OK so you have covered the base of your tent—that was the hardest step—it's all fun from here. For the stripes on the tent, roll out the white fondant and using a fondant or kitchen knife cut it into equal-sized strips. Apply sugar glue to the back of the strips and carefully place them on the cake. Start at the base to ensure the stripe ends flush with the skirt of the red tent—any excess at the top can be trimmed away after it has been secured down. Do not be tempted to place the stripes too far into the centre of the cake; this space is reserved for another surprise.

6 Once the stripes are on you can add your stars. Roll out the yellow fondant and cut out multiple small yellow stars. Apply sugar glue to the back of them and with clean, dry, cornflour-dusted fingers, and apply the stars one at a time to the opening of the tent.

7 Apply a thick layer of ganache to the top of the cake. This will secure the red fondant and white stripes to the top of the cake.

MAKING AND APPLYING THE TENT ROOF

It is a good idea to make this several days in advance.

1 Find a shape that you are happy with to be the point of the roof and hold up your gum paste to the right height. The height of the roof must be in proportion to the height of the base cakes. For my 18 cm/7 inch round cakes, a short drinking glass with a rounded base is perfect. Secure your shape to a non-stick surface with scrap fondant. If you are worried it is not a non stick surface, you can spray with vegetable oil for this step.

2 Knead 1½ teaspoons of CMC powder into each 250 g/ 9 oz of red fondant. This will turn the fondant into a very stiff gum paste and will help expedite the drying and structural integrity of the roof.

3 Roll out the red gum paste to 2.5 mm/¹⁄₁₀ inch onto a non-stick, cornflour-dusted surface. Once you are happy with the size, shape and thickness of the gum paste, gently pick it up and drape it over the secured shape. Gently manipulate the edges to fold and fall where you want it to. Decide what will be the front of the tent roof and ensure that there is a space flat enough to fit the plaque you are going to use. Use your template to test this.

4 Leave the shape to dry rock hard (this could take several days). This is a relatively flimsy structure, if you have time and spare materials, make two 'just in case'.

NOTE: Gum paste, like fondant, will at some point get beyond repair—too much cornflour, CMC, icing sugar, kneading, glue—it can only take so much. If this happens, don't be afraid to discard it and start again.

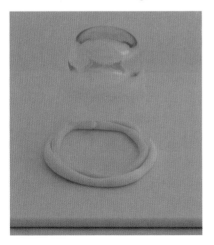 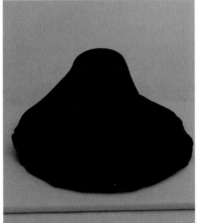 

5 Once the roof is dry, add more ganache to the outside rim of the top of the base cake ready to be the glue that will stick the roof down. Carefully lift the roof from its shaping structure. Then, either:

(a) Turn it upside down and very carefully fill the roof space with chocolate and lollies, place thick paper over the hole, turn the roof back up the right way, holding the paper in place with your hand, place the roof on the base cake and gently pull the paper out from between the roof and the base cake. Note: this gives maximum fullness of lollies but carries with it the most risk of the roof cracking and the ganache smudging on the base cake. If you don't want to risk it:

(b) Simply build a pyramid of chocolate/lollies on top of the base cake that you slot the roof over.

Either way, when your roof is on it is best to leave the ganache to set. When the roof is ready, simply add stripes to it the same way you did the base cake.

MAKING AND APPLYING THE FLAG, SIGN AND BUNTING

It is a good idea to make these at the same time as you make the roof so that they can be drying at the same time and you can assemble it all at once.

1 If you don't have a plaque-shaped cutter or need a specific size of plaque, download and print out a paper template from the Internet. Roll out the yellow gum paste 2.5 mm/$\frac{1}{10}$ inch thick and using a knife or cutter, cut out the shape. Use a cranked handle spatula to move the plaque to a non-stick surface such as baking paper, to dry. If you have rough edges, use the edge of your finger and the heat of your hands to smooth the edges, otherwise a wheel tool works well.

2 Roll out the white gum paste and cut out the desired lettering. Using sugar glue, add the lettering to the plaque and allow it to dry.

3 One the plaque is dry you can add it to the flat part of the roof using sugar glue. If you have misjudged the shape or size of the roof and plaque and only part of the plaque rests on the roof, use royal icing to secure it.

4 For the flag, roll out the yellow gum paste 5 mm/$\frac{1}{5}$ inch thick and, using a fondant or kitchen knife, cut out a triangle. Tidy the edges as you did for the plaque.

5 Dip the end of a 22-gauge wire into sugar glue, wipe off the excess and insert the wire all the way through the triangle so it sticks out of the top slightly. Wait for it to dry.

6 Cut out a yellow gum paste star to lie over the top of the roof. Insert a plain wire into the centre of this star and thread carefully through the top of the roof.

7 Remove the wire, roll a ball of blue gum paste and insert the flag wire, trimmed to size, through it and into the star and cake below. Use this fresh blue gum paste to secure the wire, mould it with your fingers to grip the wire and provide extra support.

8 Take a smaller ball of blue gum paste and, with sugar glue, affix it to the small piece of wire sticking out of the top of the flag.

9 Bunting is not a necessary addition but if your roof edges are uneven, some bunting will covers it and add a bit of pizzazz. Use a contrasting color. I rolled out blue gum paste very thin to 15mm/0.06 inches thick and cut out blossom shapes. I then cut the blossoms in half with a wheel tool and set aside to dry. If you want a more rounded shape, cut them and add them directly to the roof with sugar glue and your finger, this will allow them to the take the shape of the roof. I let mine dry so they look more squared off and stiff, this helps to correct the shape of my roof a little more. If sugar glue doesn't work to stick the dry ones, apply royal icing to the back of the bunting and attach it to the roof that way.

Making and Decorating the Cupcakes

1 Preheat the oven to 120–130°C/250–265°F for mud cake. Line a cupcake tray with paper cases.

2 Make the chocolate mud cake batter. Divide approximately one-tenth of the batter between the cupcake cases. This is only to stop the ball form rolling around away from the centre of the case.

Add one cake ball to each cupcake case—pushing them firmly to the base of the liner. They will rise and we don't want them to rise too much.

Once the cake balls are in place, pipe the rest of the batter into the cupcake case around the cake ball. The batter will not cover the cake ball. Once the batter is in, smooth some of the batter over the top of the frozen cake ball with a spatula or knife (slightly dampen it to avoid batter sticking to it). This creates a join between the batter and the top of the ball and will

hopefully guide the direction of the rising batter, helping to keep the frozen ball down.

3 Put into the oven right away. Bake in oven for 25–35 minutes or until skewer comes out clean. Depending on your oven, the type of chocolate used and the size of your cupcake cases your cooking time may vary. Be sure to check the centre and outsides of your cupcakes to determine if it is cooked.

4 Once the cupcakes are cooked and have cooled completely you can pipe royal icing (or buttercream if you wish) in a spiral motion using a 1M tip/nozzle or similar. For these cupcakes I wanted a soft ice cream look rather than a stiff swirl so when I beat my royal icing I stopped when it formed a peak that slowly folded over. If you want icing that swirls up and stays up, beat your royal icing until peaks form that stay upright.

5 Add brightly colored stars. You can purchase these or make them in advance with gum paste and your star cutter.

Flavor ALERT!! Cotton candy is synonymous with the circus and fairs so I couldn't miss an opportunity to flavor my royal icing with a cotton candy flavor. You can flavor royal icing but remember, flavor is a liquid and should be weighed up with the liquid in your recipe.

DOUBLE UP OPTION

If you have left over ganache and wanted to put in a double dose of chocolate taste,
apply ganache to the top of your cupcake and let it harden a little before adding the royal icing.
No waste and extra taste.

Dad's Freighter

DIFFICULTY: 🥄🥄🥄🥄🥄
TIME TO MAKE: ⏳⏳⏳⏳⏳

My dad has been driving trucks for almost as long as I can remember, it is his passion and he is really good at it, holding all sorts of licenses for all types of trucks and he can tell you all about them ... for hours.

Also, his favorite color and chocolate flavor is orange so this birthday cake design for him was a no brainer! Of course the surprise inside for him was all of his favorite sweets— Clinkers, chocolate orange and mint chocolate balls and of course, mint slice biscuits for wheels.

Not limited to grown-ups, big trucks are always a favorite for many little boys at some point. This design is generic with colors and flavors easily interchangeable, for example, if your little one is obsessed with the garbage truck, simply modify this design by either having an open top with the hole full of lollies exposed or keep the lollies inside as a surprise.

YOU WILL NEED

Loaf tin (pan), 10 x 24 x 7 cm (5½ x 9½ x 2¾ in.)

Small square tin, 10 cm/4 inch (if you don't have a small square tin, use a larger one, cut smaller squares after baking and stack them to create the size, shape and height required)

2 batches white chocolate mud cake batter (see page 35)

½ batch mud cake batter, for small square cake (see page 34)

Gel food color to color the cake batter and fondant

Fondant (white or pre-colored)

Letter cutters

Gum paste (Or CMC powder to turn fondant into gum paste)

Sugar glue

Fondant or kitchen knife

Rolling pin

Non-stick mat

Icing mix, for dusting

750 g/1 lb 10 oz ganache

Chocolate and/or lollies, to fill trailer and cab

Cake board, for display

Gold and silver edible metallic paint

Modelling tool: ball tool

Ruler

MAKING THE TRAILER CAKES

1 Preheat the oven to 120–130°C/250–265°F for the mud cake. Grease and flour or line the cake tin.

2 For the trailer, mix up one batch of white mud cake and color and flavor it.

If you have two identical loaf tins (pans) make and bake both batches at the same time.

3 Once the cakes have cooled completely, wrap and refrigerate them. Once they have reached refrigeration temperature, stack them so that the tops are sandwiched together in the centre of the cake; this gives a sharp, clean edge at the base and top. Using a bread knife (or sharp kitchen knife), trim the sides of the cakes using the top and lower edges of the cake as a guide. A bread knife is sharp and if moved slowly and gently in a sawing motion it will carve the cake easily and neatly for you. Remember that the ganache and fondant that are to be applied and will help shape the cake too, so don't be overzealous with your trimming!

4 Once you are happy with the shape of your two loaf cakes, separate them so that the 'tops' that were sandwiched together are facing upwards. You now need to decide how many chocolates/lollies you want to put into the trailer. For this cake I have put chocolates in the bottom half of the trailer leaving the top half as pure cake since there were a large number of guests to feed. If you want to put more chocolate/lollies in there, simply repeat the same steps for the top loaf.

FLAVOR ALERT

White chocolate is the vanilla base of the mud cake world so add any flavors you like—
see the Recipes and How To section for more ideas!

Remember more lollies = less cake.

5 To make room for the chocolates/lollies, you need to cut out a portion of the cake from the centre of the loaf. First find the centre of the cake, I use a skewer to (mark this point) and measure outward a rectangle shape. Always make the cavity the same shape as the cake. As a rule, I never make the hole any longer or wider than two-thirds of the size of the cake—both of these factors affect the structural integrity of the cake. Remember, you are removing the heart of the cake and asking it to take the weight of a second layer, chocolate ganache and fondant. The more cake you remove, the more structural support there isn't.

To make the hole, use a small kitchen knife (paring knife) held vertically, to cut the sides of the

TROUBLESHOOT

If you place the cakes on top of each other and they don't sit flush, you have too many chocolates/
lollies in the centre. The best thing to do is remove the top cake, remove lollies and try again.
If you don't want to do this you can back fill the gap with ganache at this point but there is fairly
high chance this will become visible through the fondant. If you have a detailed truck design
that will hide it, power ahead. If you are going for a flat-side design like mine here, sorry—
lift that top cake and start removing.

shape into the cake. You always hold the knife vertically to ensure you are reaching the same depth all the way around.

Once you have cut out the shape, remove your centre skewer and using a small, flat-ish teaspoon, scoop out the cake inside the cut rectangle. Do this gently and slowly to avoid cake cracks or ripping. If your cake cracks slightly, don't despair; go very easy in that area and patch repair it with ganache.

6 Fill the cavity with the treats. Using a cranked handle spatula, apply ganache liberally around the chocolate/lolly centre to the edge of the cake. This will be the glue that binds the cake layers together. Place the top cake over the lower cake.

HOT TIP! If you are putting sweet treats in the top cake, to avoid the treats from falling out of the cake when you flip it over, place a sheet of paper over the cavity , then placing your hand on top of the paper and cavity, gently place the top cake on top of the bottom cake, removing

your hand as you do so. Gently pull the paper out from between the cakes. This will drag some ganache so keep this in mind when choosing the treats.

7 Following the techniques outlined on page 17, ganache the trailer cakes.

CHEAT: At this point I cheat a little with my ganache, taking a portion and heating it in the microwave until it is a soup-like consistency. With my cakes on a set up board, I pour the soupy ganache over the top a bit at a time and work quickly to smooth it down the sides of the cake. This will not look good. While it adds an extra step to the ganache process, I find that for carved cakes it makes the perfect glue and crumb coat all in one. Refrigerate the cake until the ganache turns hard. Take the cake out of the refrigerator, cut away the hard chocolate on your set up board and let it come to room temperature before adding your 'proper' layer of ganache in step 7.

DECORATING THE TRAILER CAKES

1 Color the fondant following the instructions on page 24. Because navy, like black is so hard to color I have purchased navy fondant and recommend you do the same. If you can't buy navy fondant, buy royal blue and add the navy color—you will use less dye this way.

My trailer cake was not too large so I was able to roll my fondant out in one piece and cover the cake, smoothing down the sides and edges (see the instructions for covering a square cake with fondant in the How To section on page 20).

If your cake is quite large, you can attach the fondant in segments to your cake. Measure the length and height of each side of the cake, roll out your fondant and trim the fondant to shape. Carefully, using two flat hands, lift the fondant and gently attach it to the side of the cake, securing it with a smoothing motion with warm, flat palms. If there is excess fondant sticking up above the cake top, trim with embroidery scissors, for excess at the base use your fondant/ kitchen knife as per normal. Do this for all five sides and pinch the joins together to make sure the fondant is sealed and in a nice straight line.

NOTE: Cut and attach the top of the shape first, not only does it act as a guide so that all other attachments will sit flush with it, it also makes the joins at the top a lot less visible, the top part disappears and when the seams are visible they are straight and look like joins of the metal trailer.

2 Navy is a tricky color and I wasn't 100 per cent happy with my sharp edges so I added a nice

contrasting white border to the sides of my truck. Not only does this give me a sharp line, it draws focus to the signage and creates overall impact. To create a border, roll out some white fondant very thin and leave for 2–3 minutes to become a little dry and stiff. Using a ruler, measure the length and width you need each border to be and cut to size. They should be pliable but stiffer than usual. Dust the cornflour from the back of the border and brush with sugar glue. Gently, using your fingers and a soft touch, apply the border to the cake.

Following the same techniques as the white border cut out and apply the lettering for the signage for the trailer.

OPTION ALERT! If the recipient of the cake has a specific company logo, favorite beer or a cartoon you can theme the truck by adding an edible image to the sides of the trailer, cutting it to the exact shape and hiding the joins with your borders. If you are going to go this far, you can also add a small picture of their head to the edible print out and place this in the truck window!

TIP

White onto a dark color has room for error, if you miss or have to reposition, you may see tiny patches where the glue has been (which you can reduce with cornflour) but the overall color has not been affected. Putting a dark border onto a white or very pale surface requires precision and accuracy—a slip, miss or reposition will cause a colored smear across your pale surface that is a lot harder to fix. So once you have decided on a color combination to go with, make it easier on yourself and use the darker of the two to cover the cake and the lighter for the detail.

MAKING THE TRUCK CAB CAKE

1 Preheat the oven to 120–130°C/250–265°F for mud cake. Grease and line a 10 cm/4 inch square cake tin.

2 Mix up the required amount of mud cake batter for your tin. I used a 4-inch square tin, lined with baking paper and filled to the top, causing it to ride up the baking paper and become 4 inches tall. For this I only needed half of one mud cake recipe and I still had a little left over (If this ever happens, simply add these to some cupcake cases, bake, freeze and use as lunch box snacks at a later date). If you are making a larger square cake you intend to cut down you may need to make up one whole mix to fill your tin.

OPTION ALERT! You don't have to use chocolate mud cake. If the recipient of the cake has other favorite flavors, simply follow the flavoring directions from any one of the cake recipes in the recipe section and make it your own.

3 Once the cake has reached refrigeration temperature, remove from the refrigerator and using a bread knife start to carve it. Measure the depth and cut the cake in half (this is called torting).

4 Stack the cakes so that the cut edges are sandwiched together in the centre to give a sharp, clean edge at the base and the top. I always make the base of the cake the top of the cab—this is a quick, easy way to ensure a flat top and sharp, clean edges at the top.

5 Separate the cakes again so that the surfaces that were sandwiched face upward.

Cut and scoop out the centre of the cake and fill the cab with sweet treats, following the instructions above. Use different treats in different sections of the truck if you like.

6 Once you have constructed the truck cab, follow the ganache and fondant covering instructions set out for the trailer above, this is the same technique applied to a square on a smaller scale. You might think smaller is easier but it is not. The most common mistake made at this point is rolling your fondant out too thin—I still do this too, so don't worry!

REMEMBER: Allowing the ganache time to set (overnight or at least 4 hours, see the techniques section) gives you a firmer base to work with when applying your fondant. That means you can be a bit firmer smoothing out the fondant and getting super-sharp edges on your square and rectangle shapes.

DECORATING THE TRUCK CAB CAKE

1 Adding CMC powder to my left over fondant pieces to turn them into gum paste, I then model the shapes required to detail the cab.

2 For the side windows, thinly roll out the gum paste and cut 2 to size and shape (hold it up in front of the door to get an idea of its proportion). Using edible silver paint, paint the windows. Leave until touch dry but still malleable (we need it to take the shape of the truck and sit flush without cracking), apply sugar glue to the back and stick in place. Make the windscreen in the same way, cut to size and apply.

3 Make the truck grill using the same technique but this time roll the paste out a little thicker, cut it to size, then use the edge of a ruler to make indents into the paste at equal distances apart. Paint the grill silver.

4 For the headlights, roll two equal-sized balls of gum paste. Press the top of the ball squashing it between your finger and the work surface, creating two flat sides with bulging round edges. Gently pick up the headlight and using a knife or ruler, make indents into the bulging sides at equal distances apart. This will give the headlights texture and also flatten the bulge slightly. Choose the flatter side to attach to the cab. The other side is the light. With light side up, use your ball tool to make indents— headlights are concave. Set aside until mostly dry, then paint the outside silver and the inside gold with edible metallic paint. Stick in place using sugar glue or, if they are too thick/heavy, use royal icing to attach them.

5 For door handles, model sausage shapes using gum paste. Cut these to the size, pinching each end to make them smooth, paint and stick on with sugar glue.

6 The exhaust pipes take a bit more work and a modelling tool! Make a sausage in the same way you did for the handles and hold in your fingers leaving 0.6 cm /¼ inch free. Using your small ball tool in tiny circular motions create a hollow in the end of the exhaust—this will create a small indented hole but also expand the edges of the exhaust so it looks like they get bigger in a flute shape at the top. Unlike the rest of the decorations these need to dry completely before you put them on to ensure they hold their shape. If the cake is for an adult you can add a wire to the centre of the exhaust to ensure structural integrity and speed up the decorating process however it is very important that everyone at the party is aware the decorations are not edible.

FEELING CREATIVE? You can make a wind resister for the top of the cab and other metal bits and pieces to make your truck more realistic—just make sure you use gum paste and allow plenty of drying time. If they are an odd shape or need to stand up, use royal icing to glue them together … your imagination (and time) is the limit!

HOT TIP ON WHEELS! For this cake I went old school kids-cake style with the wheels made from my Dad's favorite biscuits and secured them in place with the left over chocolate ganache. If you want to make the truck more realistic you have several options. There are silicon moulds you can buy to make wheels really quickly with gum paste. If you are not going to have a need for this mould again—you can make it by hand. Simply follow the same instructions for the headlights on a larger scale. Instead of using a knife or ruler to indent the sides, you need tyre tread, which is easily achieved with a toy or model car—the softer the gum paste the easier it will take the indented pattern. Try making this with black gum paste and paint the indented part with silver lines in a circle to make hot wheels … simple!

Carrot Cake

DIFFICULTY: / / / / /
TIME TO MAKE: ⧗ ⧗ ⧗ ⧗ ⧗

I adore this cake. It's so sweet and is suitable all year round. It's just so easy to make for the huge wow factor it brings—and let's face it—we all feel like we are being a bit more healthy when we have carrot cake, right?

To achieve this surprise inside, we need to bake an orange colored mud cake in a loaf tin, cut out carrot shapes from it, freeze them and then re-bake them inside the carrot cake, in the same (or larger) loaf tin.

For the orange-colored cake I have used white chocolate mud cake which I have colored orange and flavored with an oil-based cheesecake flavor to give it some oomph. We are used to carrot cakes coming with a cream cheese frosting, so instead of creamy, cheese flavor on top, we are putting it in the centre.

YOU WILL NEED

Loaf tin (pan) (10 x 24 x 7 cm/5½ x 9½ x 2¾ in.)
1 batch carrot cake batter, see page 33
1 batch white mud cake batter, see page 35
Kitchen knife
Buttercream (see recipe on page 38)
Grass tip, for piping. I used Wilton 233 grass tip
Piping bag and coupler, for icing
Gum paste
Sugar glue

22-gauge wires (or 18 or 20 if you already have them)
Gel food coloring: green, brown and orange
Display board
Cheesecake food flavoring
Cake board
Icing mixture, for dusting

TO MAKE THE CARROTS

1 Preheat the oven to 120–130°C/250–265°F. Grease your loaf tin with vegetable oil or cake tin release spray or grease and flour it.

2 To make the carrots, make one batch of white chocolate mud cake batter, color it orange and add an oil-based cheesecake flavor. Pour the batter into the loaf tin and bake until cooked through and set aside to cool.

3 Once the loaf has cooled completely, wrap the cold cake with cling film and put it in the refrigerator. Once at refrigerator temperature, bring it out, and using a bread knife, cut the loaf into 2–2.5 cm/ 1 inch thick slices.

4 Find the mid-point of the base of the slice. Using a kitchen knife, cut from this point on an angle outward to the corner of the slice, stopping short of the crust. This should create a V shape. Trim the crusty top off of the slice. This is your first carrot; use this as a cutting guide on the rest of the slices so that your carrots are fairly uniform in size.

HOT TIP! You won't use all of the carrots you cut out so select the best ones and put the others aside. There will also be a lot of unused orange cake. Trim the crust from this spare cake, then crumb the cake. Tip into a freezer proof container and keep for cake pops or your next pound cake! YUM!

5 Wrap each carrot individually in cling film and put them in the freezer.

Remember: we need the carrots to be frozen so they don't over bake, dry out or liquefy when we re-bake them in the carrot cake.

TO MAKE THE CAKE

1 Preheat the oven to 180°C/350°F. Grease your loaf tin with vegetable oil or cake tin release spray or grease and flour it.

2 Make one batch of the carrot cake recipe on page 33, or your own favourite carrot cake recipe or packet mix.

Place about one-fifth of the batter into the loaf tin and use this as base to secure the frozen carrots. Space the cake carrots upright and about 2 cm/¾ apart in the batter. Push them all the way to the base of the tin.

3 Pour the rest of the batter into a large piping bag and pipe the batter between the carrots. Make sure there are no air pockets. When piping, I work in a loop, around the edges and zigzag through the carrots and repeat. You may need to keep propping your carrots up—the more batter you put in, the more they will stay in place. Carrots do not organically grow in dead straight lines; there is some variation on their angles so your end look will be fine.

You may have carrot slices slightly sticking out of the top of the batter. I chose to keep these and after baking I trimmed the crusty bit off of top. This gave me a distinctive row of carrots from the top view but runs the risk of drying out the top of the carrot slices. If you prefer a more buried carrot look—use a small cranked handle spatula to smooth the carrot cake batter over the top of the orange carrots note: a wet spatula will glide over the batter without any batter sticking to it. Be sure to mark where each carrot is so that you can accurately place the leaves later. Use can skewers or cocktail sticks for this, however my oven burns them to a crisp so I simply mark the batter with a cross at each point.

4 Bake immediately for 40 minutes or as per the time required for the recipe you have used. When it comes time to check if your cake you will know it is cooked through when a skewer inserted at three different points across the cake, comes out clean. Set aside to cool, then turn out of the cake tin onto a wire rack. Once it has cooled to room temperature, it is time to decorate!

TO DECORATE THE CAKE WITH BUTTERCREAM GRASS

1 To secure the cake to the cake board, spread some buttercream on the board in the place where the cake will sit and place the cake on the buttercream.

2 Once the cake is secured you can start to pipe the grass. I have piped grass across the top of the cake only, leaving gaps so that the orange carrots can be seen peeking through and then continued the grass over the board to cover it—this makes the carrot cake itself appear as a mound of dirt, in a line, with grass growing wild in ditches at each side and between the carrots.

USING THE GRASS TIP

See the Daisy Cow recipe for tips on how to best use the 233 grass tip.

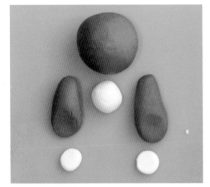

TO MAKE A SNEAKY BUNNY

1 To make the body, make a ball of brown gum paste. Roll on a non-stick surface with the palm on your hand to make an oval.

2 For the tail, make a small round ball of white gum paste. Use it as it is or roll it over a clean dishcloth to give a furry texture. Attach the white cottontail to the centre of the brown oval body shape with a small amount of sugar glue—too much and it will slide off. If the tail won't stick, use a small piece of raw spaghetti, like a wire, inserted into the body, trimmed to length and place the white tail onto it to hold it in place.

3 For the feet, make two equally sized balls of brown gum paste, about two-thirds of the size of the body. Apply sugar glue to the flat base of the feet and roll each between your palms to make an elongated oval. Using your palm or fingers, press it lightly onto a non-stick surface to make it flat on both sides. Using your knife or Dresden tool make indents in one end to give the impression of toes.

4 Place the body against the side of the carrot cake, using the buttercream grass to secure it. Apply a small amount of sugar glue to the each side of the body and stick the feet in place. It should now look like the back end of a rabbit.

TO MAKE THE LEAVES

1 Add tylose to your fondant to turn it into gum paste. Color up your gum paste green. See page 24 in the techniques section for advice on how best to do this.

2 Roll out your green gum paste on to a cornflour-dusted surface and using a long leaf cutter, cut out your leaves. I always make two more than I actually need to make sure I'm covered for any breakages. If you do not have a long leaf cutter and are not likely to use one again, draw or print out a picture of one to the right scale, cut it out of paper and use that as a template, carefully cutting around it with a small sharp kitchen knife

HOT TIP! If you knife starts to 'drag' the fondant causing puckered edges you are either not gliding it smoothly or it is dirty. Clean the blade and keep going.

Note: You want your fondant thick enough to be able to insert a 22-gauge wire through the centre but not so thick that it won't dry or takes too long to dry. My leaves were roughly 2-2.5 mm/ ⅒ inch thick. If you don't like a blunt edge look, simply pinch the edges of the leaf with your fingers to make them thinner, or work them over in a circular motion with your ball tool.

3 While your gum paste is still soft, use your Dresden tool or fondant scriber to gently indent a main vein down the centre of the leaf, stopping short of the tip. The best way to do this is one fluid movement from just below the top to the bottom of the leaf. If that does not work for you, use small short strokes to avoid puckering.

Using the same motion, indent branches that come off of the main vein. You can stop at this point or continue to add sub branches off the main branches and so on, depending on how detailed you want to get. The important thing is to work quickly before the gum paste starts to dry out otherwise it will wrinkle. Cover each leaf you have not yet worked on with a piece of plastic (wrap, bag, sleeve—whatever is to hand).

4 Lastly, using no thinner than 22-gauge wire, cut the wire to length and dip one end into sugar glue. Remove the excess glue from the end of the wire with your fingers and carefully insert the wire into the centre of the leaf , guiding it in to about ¾ of the length of the leaf. Leave flat to dry.

Betty's Butterflies

DIFFICULTY: ✎ ✎ ✎ ✎ ✎

TIME TO MAKE: ⧗ ⧗ ⧗ ⧗ ⧗

How sweet is this cake? I designed this for my Nan who just loves butterflies and everything purple. This is actually a small cake; just 18 cm/7 inches square, which is perfect for a small family gathering or just a couple of friends over for tea.

Small, unassuming and a big wow factor when you cut it! Bring out the best china and tablecloth or team it up with dainty butterfly napkins and paper plates.

HOT TIP!

While this looks like a nice, clean icing job, you never want to do this directly on your display board or cake plate. Even seasoned professionals get ganache everywhere and even the slightest smear of it makes the plate/board look messy and dirty. It is always best to ganache, let it set and then transfer your cake to its display area.

YOU WILL NEED

Loaf tin (pan) (10 x 24 x 7 cm/
  5 ½ x 9½ x 2 ¾ inch)
18 cm/7 inch square cake tin
1 batch chocolate mud cake batter (see page 34)
1 batch white chocolate mud cake batter (see
  page 35)
Kitchen knife
Butterfly cookie cutter
Butterfly silicon mould or shape cutter (smaller
  than the cookie cutter)
Chocolate ganache

Crank-handled spatula, to smooth the ganache
  over the cake
Gum paste
Sugar glue
22-gauge wires
White, florist tape (also known as parafilm)
Gel food coloring: regal purple
Display/cake board
Optional food flavoring for the purple butterfly
  cake. I have used oil-based marshmallow flavor
Set up board (or baking paper on your bench)
Icing mix, for dusting

TO MAKE THE BUTTERFLY CAKE

1 Preheat the oven to 120–130°C/250–265°F. Grease and flour or line the loaf tin.

2 Make one batch of white chocolate mud cake; color and flavor it. I have colored this one Regal Purple and flavored with an oil-based marshmallow flavor to give it some oomph. Remember, purple is the most unstable color on the spectrum and will fade when heat is applied, you will be baking these butterflies twice so make the batter a little darker than you intend the butterflies to be at the end.

3 Tip the batter into the tin and bake the cake until cooked through. Leave to set for a few minutes before turning out onto a wire rack to cool. Wrap the loaf in cling film and refrigerate the cake. Once at refrigerator temperature, bring it out and, using a bread knife, cut the loaf into 2–2.5 cm/¾–1 inch thick slices. The slices need to be as cold as possible without being frozen to get the best cut out. Refrigerate again, if necessary.

4 Lightly spray the butterfly cookie cutter with vegetable oil, this helps the cuter glide through the cake slice easier with less crumb and breakages.

Position the butterfly cutter over a slice and cut out the shape. Remove excess cake from around the edges of the cutter and gently push out the butterfly a little at a time, working your way around the shape evenly so it does not crack. Repeat this for every slice. You will make a lot more butterflies than you need but with odd shapes like this there are bound to be casualties, you may very well need your spares so cut them out!

TIP! Put aside all your spare butterflies and scrap purple colored cake that was cut away from the crust edge. You can crumb these left over pieces with your fingers into a bowl and make cake pops or pound cake with it at a later date—useful and yummy. Remember frozen cake crumbs will keep well in the freezer. See page 16 for how to do this.

5 Wrap the butterflies individually in cling film and freeze them. The butterflies need to be frozen so they don't over bake, dry out or liquefy when they are baked again.

Making the Square Cake

1 Preheat oven to 120–130°C/250–265°F. Grease and flour or line the square tin.

2 Make one batch of chocolate mud cake, following the recipe on page 34. If you use an 18 cm/7 inch square tin you will have batter left over. Use to make cupcakes or reduce the recipe by approximately one-quarter. Or you can make your own favourite recipe or packet mix.

3 Place approximately one-fifth of the batter into the loaf tin, use this as base to secure the butterflies. Because we are baking in a square tin, I put my butterflies in upside down, so that when the cake is cooled and I am decorating it—the top and top sides of my cake is perfectly flat, with clean sharp edges. This is a great time saving cheat. Whichever way you decide to put in your butterflies, place them no less than 2cm/¾ inch apart. When you put the butterflies into the batter, push them down but try not to connect them all the way to the base of the tin, we want them to ideally be hovering in the centre of the cake.

Once all of the butterflies are in place, disperse the rest of the batter into the cake tin between them. Again, I highly recommend using a piping bag for this—you really want to make sure there are no pockets of air where you have missed pushing batter between the butterflies

and make sure the batter is even. When piping I work in a loop, around the edges and zigzag through the butterflies and repeat. You may need to keep propping your butterflies up—don't worry, the more batter you put in the more they will stay in place.

4 Once the batter is in the tin, use your crank handled spatula (slightly wet to avoid batter sticking to it) to smooth the batter over the top, so no butterflies are sticking out of the batter. Use a kitchen knife or skewer markers if your oven will allow it, to mark where the butterflies are.

5 Put into the oven right away. Bake for 45–60 minutes or as per the time required for the recipe you used. When it comes time to check your batter, be sure to check the cake with a skewer at three different points across the cake, to ensure you are accurately checking the cake batter not the butterfly parts! Once the cake is cooked and cooled completely, it is ready to decorate!

ICING THE CAKE WITH CHOCOLATE GANACHE

I wanted to give this cake an old fashioned 'just out of my home kitchen' look so I didn't use a base board, two board or lid method to ganache it, I free handed it. Is that a gasp I hear? Don't worry—remember the top part of my cake was the base of the cake in the tin so I have cheated a little and now have a nice shaped cake to work with.

1 Trim the excess cake, cutting away any doming to make a flat base. Using a set up board, or baking paper on your bench, and with the cake right side (original base) up, apply ganache with a cranked handle spatula making fluid back and forth motions. Wipe clean your spatula regularly if you find it is pulling ganache off rather than putting it on. Dipping the spatula in hot water and drying it lightly will assist the smooth application of ganache. If you struggle with this step, make your ganache that little bit runnier (not soup consistency though!), this can help get it nice and smooth. Let the ganache set before transferring the cake to the display board or cake plate.

TO MAKE A KALEIDOSCOPE OF BUTTERFLIES

1 First things first, make your structure. Take a 22-gauge wire (this will be your central line), then take a second 22-gauge wire and cut it into three different lengths. Wrap the ends around the central wire in a spiral motion. Once secured, bend the wires outwards at angles, always with the ends facing upward—this will give you an all around 3D structure—the butterflies are attached to the end points.

2 Once you are happy with your structure, use your parafilm (florist's tape) to cover the wire from underneath the lowest attachment all the way to the base of the central line—this will cover any exposed ends of the wire before it is inserted into an edible food product.

3 To make the butterflies, follow the advice on page 23 on how to use gum paste in silicon moulds. Be sure you use gum paste here otherwise the butterflies will not dry.

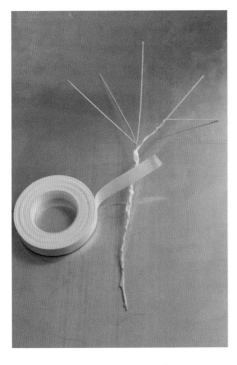
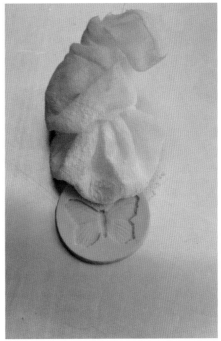

When you attach each butterfly to the wire, coat the end of the wire in sugar glue and remove any excess with your fingers. Holding the butterfly between your clean, dry, flat fingers, guide the base of the butterfly onto the end of the wire, inserting the wire into the centre of the butterfly as far as you can manage it without damage (aim for ⅔ of the way in). When the butterfly is on the wire it will still be very soft and floppy and at risk of ripping and falling off of the wire. To avoid this, place scrunched up aluminium foil underneath each butterfly to provide support for it as it dries. This is also an excellent opportunity to shape the wings at different angles, to give the effect of butterflies in flight.

Repeat this for all of the wires and butterflies and allow them time to dry hard—at least 48 hours. Make more than you need in case of breakages. Make some additional butterflies and dry them without wires, these can sit flat on the cake itself to carry the theme through.

Mother's Mug and Cupcakes

DIFFICULTY: ✎ ✎ ✎ ✎ ✎

TIME TO MAKE: ⧗ ⧗ ⧗ ⧗ ⧗

This is a perfect cake for a mother who loves her coffee. Mother's Day or birthday, this cake shows the love with a big WOW factor!

My mother loves chocolate and strawberries so for this design I have made the cakes using a moist chocolate mud cake recipe with strawberry flavored white chocolate mud cake balls. You can change up the flavor combination quite easily to whatever your mother likes best. I have also tried pink raspberry white chocolate mud cakes with caramel mud cake balls, and for the real coffee lover—a coffee cake with butterscotch cake balls. Your flavor combinations are endless; just make sure you pair flavors that complement each other. Don't be tempted to be heavy handed with your flavors— remember less is more. And lastly, choose colors that represent the flavors and contrast with each other, there is nothing worse than going to all this effort and not being able to really see the cake balls you have hidden inside.

YOU WILL NEED

Round cake tin (pan) (size is dependent on size of your design and how many you need to feed; I used a 20 cm/8 inch round, 7.5 cm/3 inch deep cake tin and made three cakes)

3 batches of chocolate mud cake batter (page 34)

1 batch white mud cake batter, for the cake balls (page 35)

Cake ball trays

Gel food color, deep pink for the cake balls, pink and brown for the fondant (or you can buy chocolate fondant that is super yummy and a nice dark shade of brown)

White fondant

CMC powder, to turn fondant into gum paste

Circle cutter

Fondant or kitchen knife

Fondant smoother or acetate square

Rolling pin

Non-stick mat

Icing mix, for dusting

1–1.5kg/2 lb 3oz–3lb 5oz chocolate ganache

Sugar glue

Royal icing

Cupcake cases

Cupcake tray

2 cake boards, the same size as your cakes

Cake board, for display

Letter cutters

Plaque cutter or paper template (you can download these from the internet easily and adjust the size to suit your cake design)

Piping bag

1M piping tip/nozzle or piping tip/nozzle of your choice, for the cupcake design

20 or 22 gauge wires (if the handle is too heavy)

MAKING THE CAKE BALLS

1 Mix up one batch of white mud cake batter. Add your choice of flavor and color early to make sure it is emulsified through the batter. If you want to color your cake with a pale tone, whiten the batter with white food coloring first. Ensure the color is emulsified through the entire batter to avoid color shrinkage when baking.

2 Preheat the oven to 150°C/300°F. Grease both sides of the cake ball tray. Spoon the batter into the base tray.

3 Bake for 17–20 minutes. As a general rule the cake batter should come out of the top of the cake ball tray a little or at least be visible and when you put a skewer in it, the skewer should come out clean. I always sacrifice one cake ball from the centre of the tray to cut open and check—this also means you get to eat it!

4 Once you have cooked all of the batter and the cake balls have cooled, you need to freeze them. I use freezer wrap or 'go-between' between each cake ball to ensure they don't stick together and to avoid icicles forming on them. The balls need to be frozen when we bake them again, so they don't dissolve and disappear into the mud cake batter, so don't skip this step!

MAKING THE CAKES

1 Preheat the oven to 120–130°C/250–265°F. Grease and line the cake tin, with the baking paper coming up at least 2.5 cm/1 inch higher than the tin in case of additional rise.

2 Make the chocolate mud cake batter. Place approximately one-fifth of the batter into the cake tin; use this as a base to secure the frozen cake balls. Space the frozen cake balls no less than 1.5–2 cm/ ½–¾ inch apart. Push one-third of the balls to the base of the tin, resist all temptation to push all of the balls to the bottom—they will rise during the baking process and you don't want them all on the one level.

3 Once the cake balls are in place, disperse the rest of the batter into the cake tin between them. I do this with a piping bag because it gives me greater control over the batter being carefully and evenly placed between the balls. If you don't want to get a piping bag out, you can do this, more slowly, with a dessertspoon.

4 Once the batter is in the tin, smooth over the top of the batter and cake balls with a spatula or knife (dampened slightly to avoid batter sticking to it) and bake immediately. Bake for the appropriate time for the tin size remembering that your oven and cake batter recipe may vary the cooking times. To check your batter, insert a skewer at three different points across the cake (to ensure you are accurately checking the cake batter and not the cake balls). If the skewer comes out clean, the cake is ready.

5 Repeat for the second and third cakes. Allow the cakes to cool completely, wrap in cling film (plastic wrap) and refrigerate until cold.

MAKE A MUG OUT OF ME: DECORATING THE CAKE

1 Follow the instructions on page 16 to stack and stick the cakes together using ganache. Leave to set.

2 When the ganache on your cake is set and you are ready to cover it with fondant, put your cake on your covered display board.

Measure the height and circumference of your cake.

Roll out your pink fondant as long as the circumference of the cake and slightly wider than the height of the cake. I would recommend rolling this fondant 0.5cm/¼ inch, which is quite thick.

3 Measure the height and circumference of the cake. Roll out the pink fondant as long as the circumference of the cake and slightly wider than the height of the cake—this excess will become the lip of the mug. I would recommend rolling the fondant to 0.5 cm/⅕ inch. Cut each long side with your fondant knife so that they are straight.

OPTION ALERT! If you are proficient at using fondant and are comfortable working with stiffer fondant, add some CMC powder (about 1½ teaspoons per 1 kg/2¼ lb). This will help the top lip of the mug stay erect and hold its shape until the fondant sets. I did not use this option in the cake photographed here; you can see the lip edges of my mug are not even. I have an 'old mug I made Mother at school' look to my design, which works; I made the shape and it went where it wanted to go!

4 Pick up the fondant, draping it over your two forearms and gently wrap it around the cake starting with the centre of the pink fondant sheet at the side of the cake, wrapping it around the cake like a towel. Be sure the straight edge lines up with the base. The excess will peek over the top of the cake and will be moulded into the lip of the mug later. At the side, join the pink fondant together to make a seam, trimming away any excess to create a straight seam. Use sugar glue to secure the seam at the top otherwise the weight of it will pull the rest apart, then quickly place an acetate square or fondant smoother over the seam. Work in a circular motion, so that the heat of your hands melts the fondant and the seam should all but disappear.

Troubleshoot: If you have underestimated the fondant length and your seam doesn't meet up, work quickly smoothing the fondant with the palms of your hands around the cake—stretching the elasticity of it to reach further around until the two seams meet. Be careful though, the fondant may rip in one spot if you smooth from the same point too much so try and smooth from up and down the cake. Additionally the action of smoothing the fondant edges forward to meet each other may pick up some ganache and cause chocolate smudges on your fondant— leave it and cover with spots later.

5 Before the air starts to dry the fondant too much, start to work the lip of the mug between thumb and forefingers in a pill rolling movement, this will smooth and round the lip as well as stretch it a little so that you can roll it outward lightly to give an old coffee mug look. This is a job that takes a bit of work to get done neatly but once it is done stop touching it—it is tempting to keep going and going and going until you realise your mug lip is now a fluted glass. If this happens, cut it away with embroidery scissors and start again with the thinner fondant that is left.

6 Lastly, apply more ganache to the top of the cake; you want it thick so you don't risk drips. I used the back of a teaspoon to smooth this out and made circular motions with it so it looked like ripples in hot water.

OPTION ALERT! You don't have to use a pink and brown combination; I have used this color scheme because it is the inverse color scheme of the surprise cake inside. If your mother has a favourite mug, you can personalise the cake by making a replica of that.

Making and applying the handle

Note It is best to do this several days in advance to allow ample drying time. As with other fragile structures, if you have time and resources make two, just in case.

1 First design how you would like your handle to look. I used a scroll design for my handle. It gives me a large contact surface with the side of the cake and it also matched my 'old-style, much-loved mug' look.

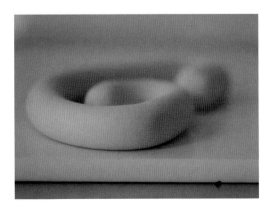

2 Next step is to decide how big the handle needs to be so that it is proportionate to the size of your cake. I have a piece of string or ruler to hand that is the same length that the handle needs to be so I can refer to it.

3 Add CMC powder to the fondant to make it gum paste. Roll the paste into a long sausage shape (I would recommend you make this thick so it is not fragile but not so thick that it is too heavy and doesn't dry).

Tidy up the ends of the sausage and roll the fondant into the required size. Once this shape is achieved, I put my handle up against something long and flat, so that the edges of the handle that will be in contact with my mug have a flat-ish edge. Allow this to dry hard.

4 Once the handle is dry and the cake has been covered you can attach the handle to the cake. Attach this to the side of the mug over the top of the seam—this covers your mechanics and takes focus away from the seam. Apply royal icing to the flat, contact points on the handle and hold it against the cake for a minute or two to glue it on.

Troubleshoot: If the handle is heavy you have two options:

i) you can bunch up aluminium foil under the handle to hold it up in place until the royal icing dries or;

ii) if you think the handle will be too heavy to be held by royal icing only, you can insert 20 or 22 gauge wires into each flat contact point of the handle (even space 3 or 5 prongs) before it dries and use royal icing around the wires to secure the handle in place when it is dry.

However, if you use wires you must note exactly how many you use and ensure that all of the wires have been removed and accounted for before cutting up the cake to serve it.

Making and applying the sign and circles

1 To make the sign, use a plaque-shaped cutter or download and print out a paper template from the Internet.

2 Add CMC powder to the chocolate fondant to make it gum paste, this will help it to hold its shape when you pick it up to attach it to the cake. Roll out the chocolate gum paste to 0.25cm/⅒₅ inch thick and using a fondant or kitchen knife or your cutter, cut out the shape. If the gum paste is very soft, use a cranked handle spatula to move the sign to a non-stick surface such as baking paper to dry just a little.

3 If there are ragged edges, use the edge of your finger and the heat of your hands to smooth them over, otherwise use a wheel tool.

4 When the sign is stiff enough to hold its shape (but not so dry that it cracks) apply sugar glue to the back of it, and using clean, dry fingers dusted with cornflour, apply it to the front of the mug.

5 Roll out the white gum paste and cut out the lettering. Using sugar glue, add the lettering to the sign.

6 I like to add the circles last. Using a circle cutter, thinly roll out the chocolate gum paste; the circles need to sit flush on the cake, not look 3D. Cut out several circles at a time and using sugar glue on the back of them, add the circles to the cake, first covering any rips, tears or wrinkles on your fondant (if there are any) and then place other circles accordingly so the design looks visually balanced.

OPTION ALERT! This doesn't have to be a 'Mother' cake. If you have a friend or relative who loves coffee and would appreciate this cake, make the plaque on the mug larger, using your letter cutters you can cut out a phrase—either a replica of the phrase on their favourite mug or simple 'Coffee Addict', 'Coffee makes life better', 'Keep Calm and Drink Coffee'. Likewise, if the recipient is a tea drinker, use white chocolate ganache and color it appropriately, green for green tea, light brown for English breakfast, and so on.

Making and decorating the cupcakes

1 Preheat the oven to 120–130°C/250–265°F. Line the cupcake tray with paper cases.

2 Make, color and flavor the chocolate mud cake batter. Divide approximately one-tenth of the batter between the cupcake cases. Use this as base to secure a frozen cake ball, and stop it from rolling away from the centre of the case.

3 Add one cake ball to each cupcake case, pushing it firmly to the base of the liner so that it doesn't rise too much. Once all the balls are in place pipe the rest of the batter into the cupcake case around the cake ball. The batter will not cover the cake ball, once the batter is in, smooth some of it over the top of the frozen cake ball with a spatula or knife (slightly dampen it to avoid batter sticking to it). This creates a join between the batter and the top of the ball and will hopefully guide the direction of the rising batter, helping to keep the frozen ball down.

4 Bake the cupcakes immediately for 25–35 minutes, or until a skewer comes out clean. Leave to cool on a wire rack.

NOTE: Depending on your oven, the type of chocolate used and the size of your cupcake cases your cooking time may vary. Be sure to check the centre and outsides of your cupcakes to determine if it is cooked.

5 Once the cupcakes have cooled completely, you can pipe royal icing or buttercream in a spiral motion using a 1M tip or similar. For these cupcakes, I wanted an upright swirl that would hold its shape in the heat so I used royal icing and beat it until it formed a peak that did not fold over—this makes it stiffer to pipe with but gives a great look. If I was to make this same cake in winter, I would use buttercream for a softer finish and eating texture.

OPTION ALERT! You don't have to create a swirl with icing. You can use a more sedate finish and simply ganache the cupcake tops, if you want to do this but still bring through the feminine pink theme, add small, basic pink roses to the top of each cupcake.

Bunny's Silhouette

DIFFICULTY: ✎ ✎ ✎ ✎ ✎

TIME TO MAKE: ⧗ ⧗ ⧗ ⧗ ⧗

I designed this cake in a whimsical, romantic mood around the time of Easter and my wedding anniversary, inspired by one of my favourite books from my childhood and Rob Ryan's artwork, which I just adore.

He creates the most beautiful, romantic silhouettes out of hand cut paper and since discovering him I have been looking for projects I can incorporate silhouettes into. I am not sure who first designed a silhouette cake but it's such a great idea, beautiful simplicity sometimes says so much more, and the variations are limitless. Like Betty's Butterflies, this cake is so sweet and so effective on a small scale.

Don't feel you need to fill up the entire sides of the cake, the wide expanse of negative space between the painting and the top creates more drama, drawing focus to your design.

OPTION ALERT!

Try painting with a dark color on to a lighter background for a very different look, with the same dramatic effect.

YOU WILL NEED

Loaf tin (pan),10 x 24 x 7 cm (5.4 x 9.5 x 2.85 inch)

18 cm/7 inch square cake tin (pan)

1 batch chocolate mud cake batter (see page 34)

1 batch white chocolate mud cake batter (see page 35)

Batter whitener—optional

Kitchen knife

Bunny cookie cutter (or 2 if you want different bunnies like in this design)

Flower cookie cutter

Chocolate ganache (white or dark)

Chocolate fondant

Crank-handled spatula, to smooth the ganache over the cake

Gum paste

Sugar glue

22-gauge wires (if you have 20g or 18g wires form other cake/craft activities these will work just fine)

Display/cake board

Food flavoring of your choice for the bunny cake (I have used marshmallow)

Set up board, or use baking paper on your bench

Icing mix, for dusting

Rolling pin

Non-stick mat

Baking paper

Pencil

Sticky tape or pearl-headed pins

Modelling tools: Dresden tool

Paint brush

Egg cup

Rose spirit or white gel

White gel food color or edible dust/chalk

MAKING THE CAKE BUNNIES

1 Preheat the oven to 120–130°C/250–265°F. Grease and flour, or line the loaf tin.

2 Make up a batch of white chocolate mud cake. I added some white food coloring to lighten it. Bake until cooked through, then leave to set for a few minutes before turning the cake out onto a wire rack to cool.

OPTION ALERT! You can flavor the bunnies with food flavoring to provide additional taste and contrast, consider marshmallow, caramel, cheesecake, or whatever your favourite combination with chocolate is.

3 Wrap the cold cake in cling film (plastic wrap) and put it in the refrigerator. When at refrigerator temperature bring it out, and using a bread knife, cut the loaf into 2–2.5 cm/¾–1 inch thick slices. If your cake starts to return to room temperature refrigerate it again; the slices need to be as cold as possible without being frozen to get the best bunny shaped cut out.

4 Take the bunny cutter and spray it lightly with vegetable oil. Position the cutter over the slice (at whatever angle you need to) and cut out the shape. Remove the excess cake from around

the edges of the cutter and then gently use your fingers to push the bunny out of the cutter, a little at a time, working your way around the shape evenly so it does not crack.

5 Make as many bunnies as you can—the ears are fragile so there are bound to be casualties. Also with this cake, in a square tin you may be able to fit two rows of bunnies depending on the size of your cutter and tins.

6 Wrap each bunny individually and place in the freezer. The bunnies need to be frozen so that they don't over-bake, dry out or liquefy when re-baked in the chocolate mud cake.

MAKING THE CAKE

1 Preheat the oven to 120–130°C/250–265°F. Grease the square tin and dust the tray with flour, or line with baking paper.

2 Make one batch of chocolate mud cake. If you make an 18 cm/7 inch square cake you will have batter left over. Either make these into cupcakes to freeze or reduce the recipe by approximately one-quarter.

3 Place approximately one-fifth of the batter into the loaf tin and use this as base to secure the bunnies. Because we are baking in a square tin, I put my bunnies in upside down, so that when the cake is cooled and I am decorating I, the top and sides of my cake are perfectly flat, with clean sharp edges. Space the bunnies no less than 2 cm/¾ inches apart. Push the bunnies down but try not to connect them all the way to the base of the tin, ideally they will hover in the centre of the cake.

4 Once all of the bunnies are in place, disperse the rest of the batter into the cake tin between them. Again, I highly recommend using a piping bag for this as you really want to make sure there are no pockets of air where you have missed pushing batter between the bunnies and make sure the batter is even. When piping I work in a loop, around the edges and zigzag through the bunnies and repeat. You may need to keep propping your bunnies up—don't worry, the more batter you put in the more they will stay in place.

Put into the oven right away. Bake for 45–60 minutes or as per the time required for the recipe you used. When it comes time to check your batter, be sure to check the cake with skewer at three different points across the cake, to ensure you are accurately checking the cake batter not the bunny parts!

5 To avoid bunny feet or ears sticking out of the batter, use a cranked handle spatula (slightly wet to avoid batter sticking to it) to smooth the batter over the top. Use a kitchen knife or skewer markers if you oven will allow it, to mark where the bunnies are.

6 Bake immediately for 45–60 minutes, or following the instructions for the recipe you used. Insert a skewer at three different points across the cake, to ensure you are accurately checking the cake batter not the bunny parts. If the skewer comes out clean, the cake is ready.

Once the cake is cooked and cooled completely—it is ready to decorate!

TO COVER AND PAINT THE CAKE

1 Follow the steps in the How-To section to ganache your square cake.

2 Roll out the chocolate fondant large enough to cover the entire cake, and smooth down the edges, following the instructions for covering a square cake with fondant on page 21. Once neatly covered, transfer the cake to a display board.

3 Find a design you like online and print it out to scale or, take several different designs, tracing the parts of each that you like to create your own scene on baking paper. For those of you who are gifted with the talent for drawing, freehand a design of your own (and blog how to do it for the rest of us!). Whatever path you take, you need to end up with a size-appropriate scene traced onto baking paper. The key here is a straight line at the bottom. It's a good idea to start with a straight line and trace your images on and above this line, never below it, using it as a guide to keep your design straight.

Note: I am not gifted with the skill to draw and paint well, embracing this I have deliberately designed my cake to look like painting on an old vintage china pattern—this works best putting light paint on a darker surface. If you choose to put say black onto white you need to be a lot neater with clean lines as it will show so much more.

HOT TIP! The more you put in your design, the more you need to trace and paint. Go easy for your first one. Also remember, what looks like very little on a large sheet of white baking paper will look very different on the small side of a dark cake—don't be tempted to add too much or it may look cluttered. Likewise, space out your images— when you add paint to them the paint will be going on and slightly over the edges making each image larger—you want to make sure you leave enough space for each to avoid crowding.

4 Repeat on all four sides of the cake. You can do four different designs and tell a story on each side or you can repeat two designs or the same one all the way around.

5 Working on one side at a time, attach the baking paper to the cake at the base and mid point. If the fondant is set and hard to the touch use a small amount of sticky tape to hold it in place. I prefer to secure the baking paper in place with pearl head pins (pearl head so you can see them and don't accidently leave one behind).

6 Once in place, use a Dresden tool to trace around each shape. Use the flat side not the point of the Dresden tool and apply pressure evenly. Work from one side to the next so that you don't miss images but also so that you can take a sneaky peak to see how effective your pressure is.

TIP: This step and the painting is infinitely easier in a bright, sunlit space.

7 Once the tracing is complete, mix white edible color dust/chalk with rose spirit. I use an eggcup for this because it is convenient and it is a small well. The rose spirit used to make a paste and make dust liquid is alcohol, so it evaporates off leaving the color stuck to the cake.

If you cannot use alcohol, paint white gel food coloring directly onto the cake, this is a bit gluggy and you need to be more careful, allowing more drying time. When I am not using the paint I place a clean wet cloth over it to reduce the evaporation of the rose spirit and spare my materials.

8 Using your paintbrush in careful, small strokes start to fill in the outlined shapes. Again, move from one side to the other, whichever direction suits your left or right-handedness. If you have a rose spirit mix, dip your paint brush into the well of color, remove it and push it against the side of the cup letting the excess rose spirit run back into the well. Adding small amounts of color at a time is better than risking drips or runs. As it dries the color may be more transparent than it looked going on. You can either leave this chalky-white effect or go back over it when it has dried with more color.

9 Allow the paint to dry and then add your topper.

OPTION ALERT! Either trace all four sides then paint all four sides, or trace and paint one side at a time.

MAKING A BUNNY SILHOUETTE AND FLOWER FOR THE TOP

It is a good idea to make these toppers first so they have time to dry. You could use a bunny and flower cutter or a shape you have drawn or found online, cutting out a paper template and using a knife to cut out the design.

1 Roll out the white gum paste 0.25 cm/⅒₅ inch and using a fondant or kitchen knife, or your cutter, cut out the shape. Use a cranked handle spatula to move the shape to a non-stick surface such as baking paper, to dry. If there are ragged edges, use the edge of your finger and the heat of your hands to smooth them over, otherwise a wheel tool works well. Repeat for your second shape.

2 Once all shapes have been cut out and moved to clean, dusted, non-stick surfaces to dry, cut the wires to length, and using a small amount of sugar glue on the ends to be inserted, insert the wires two-thirds of the way into your shape. Leave them in place to dry while the shape is drying.

3 Once the shapes are dry, lift them, dust off any excess cornflour and place the shapes atop the cake by inserting the wires. It is important that you know exactly how may wires have gone into the cake and remove the topper before cutting it up to serve.

Pink Ombre

DIFFICULTY: ✎✎✎✎✎
TIME TO MAKE: ⧖⧖⧖⧖⧖

This cake is so soft and feminine. Ombre; simply meaning a graduation in color tone, is a testament that less can be more. I get a lot of orders for simple ombre cakes for first birthdays and christenings. Traditionally the three (or more) layers of cake are evenly colored. For this cake, I am using a white chocolate mud cake base that I have flavored with a raspberry food flavoring oil to give a hint of berry in the cake. Mud cake is a dense cake and the overall look of this design is soft and light, so with this in mind I flavored my royal icing with a small amount of cotton candy food flavoring, this flavor is not intense or very obvious to the tongue—it gives more of a 'fairy floss' sensation of lightness in the mouth. Raspberry and cotton candy complement each other on the flavor palate and the light sensation of cotton candy balances the denseness of the mud cake.

OPTION ALERT!

This cake also looks great as a square stack! Square tins hold more batter than their rounds of the same size, so this is a great option if you need to feed a lot of people.

YOU WILL NEED

Round cake tin (pan) (size of your choice depending on size of your design and how may you need to feed; I used a 23 cm/9 inch round, 7.5 cm/3 inch deep cake tin and baked three cakes)

3 batches white chocolate mud cake batter

Gel food color (I used deep pink and rose)

White chocolate ganache

Royal icing

2 cake boards, the same size as your cakes

Cake board, for display

Sugar roses

Lace and ribbon

Flavoring (optional)

Large cranked handle spatula

STOP! See Ombre cakes and Coloring batter on page 11 of the techniques section before proceeding.

MAKING THE CAKES

1 Preheat the oven to 120–130°C/250–265°F. Grease and flour, line the cake tin. I like to line the tin with the baking paper coming up at least 2.5 cm/1 inch higher than the tin in case of additional rise.

2 Make the cake batter and color it as required. Bake the cake for the specified time for the size tin you have, or until cooked through. Check the cake is cooked by inserting a skewer into the centre of the cake, when it comes out clean the cake is ready.

3 Allow the cakes to cool completely, wrap in cling film (plastic wrap) and refrigerate to chill. Make 3 cakes in all.

STACKING THE CAKES

1 Cut off the cake crust. Cutting a dark or domed top off of a cake is fine but you need to make sure each cake is of equal height after you have finished the trimming, otherwise it can look uneven.

TROUBLESHOOT: What if I got a bit over enthusiastic with the trimming of one of my cakes and now its half the height of the others? If this happened, don't panic, own it and make it look like you did it on purpose. If you have very set ombre shades keep them in order, if your shade order/placements can be flexible I like to put super-thin layers either at the top or second from the bottom, this helps the eye travel either up or down the cake when you view it. A different size in the centre of the cake will draw focus to itself and the eye will stop there. Remember: it's just a cake!

Be careful trimming the sides. This can be tricky on circular cakes because you are working on a curve with a straight-edged knife. If one cake has more crust than the others you still need to trim all cakes and trim each as required, then with the smallest cake on top cut down the others, one at a time, so that they are all the same size when stacked. It is better to take a longer amount of time removing small amounts of cake with a sharp bread knife than too much really quickly.

2 Spread ganache between each layer, stacking the cakes. Add a thin layer of ganache to the outside of the cakes as well using the pumpkin-soup consistency for a shell coat described on page 17 of the techniques section. This will provide a crumb coat so that the royal icing will stick to the cake and not remove the crumbs from the raw edges as well as providing much needed structural support. Put the cake in the fridge and allow the ganache to set.

OPTION ALERT! The taller your cake stack, the less stable it is and the greater the chance of the weight of each cake bearing down on the one beneath causing the sides to bow or if you are travelling with it, topple and fall. You may wish to place dowels through the layers.

The simplicity of this cake and its decorations means that I can make it close to the day of delivery and the three dense layers will be fine because I am using both ganache and royal icing, which lend structure, support and glue like properties to the cake. So for this example I have not needed to put any support dowels in my cake.

3 Cover the display board and using a small amount of ganache in the centre of the board, place the ganache-coated cake onto the board—the ganache on the board will set and help secure the cake in place.

ROYAL ICING AND DECORATING

For this cake, I have created a double sweet treat with the icing, putting a cotton candy flavored royal icing outer layer over the white chocolate ganache that is holding the cakes together. Apply only a thin coat of ganache and thin coat of royal icing though. Thinner layers allow them to complement each other and not compete.

ICING

1 If the ganache was set in the refrigerator, make the sure it has come back to room temperature and finished its 'sweat'. Blot any chocolate sweat with a paper towel—moisture will discolor a royal icing finish.

2 Make and color the royal icing (see page 39).

3 When applying the royal icing, I use a large cranked handle spatula and work from the base up. If you don't have a spatula, a butter knife will do, it will just take longer.

I have achieved a rustic-rendering look in the royal icing with long vertical lines, which are visible in the finish. To replicate this, apply the royal icing to the cake and once it is on and even, take a clean, dry spatula and run it from the base to the top all the way around—the flat edge against a circular cake creates the visible ridges.

Alternatively you can create hundreds of little peaks instead, if you like, by using a small cranked-handled spatula (or flat side of the bread knife) flush against the cake and making a flicking motion with your wrist.

Want it to be smooth? Use a long cranked handle spatula, flush against the cake and move it around the cake in a circular motion. If your royal icing still looks a little rough, try this action with a warm (not hot) spatula.

DECORATING

For this cake I have taken the quickest, easiest option—the roses are made entirely of gum paste and were purchased colored and finished. You can make these quite easily and it is a rewarding thing to see your work come to life but as I do not intend to include sugar flower step-by-step instructions in this book, I have used store bought ones! If you are interested in making these you'll find many great free tutorials on YouTube, but do not leave it to the last minute. Sugar flowers take time because you need to let layers of petals dry before adding more. Lastly, if you do this, follow my advice of making more than you need 'just in case'.

Big flowers come on paper-wrapped wires, which are safe to use as an anchor to insert into the cake. When working with royal icing you need to insert these wires shortly after icing application because once royal icing is dry, it is hard and almost impenetrable without causing cracks.

The lace at the base is real, purchased from a local haberdashery store with a thin pink ribbon

threaded through the holes in the lace, tied in a pretty bow at the back of the cake for a small feminine little detail. Again, you can make edible lace and it looks fabulous! I personally love it however because I do not intend to include step-by-step instructions for edible lace in this book, I have used real lace—which is actually a lot cheaper!

Blue Ombre Christening Cake

DIFFICULTY: / / / / /

TIME TO MAKE: ⏳⏳⏳⏳⏳

This design is so elegant and formal for a christening. The majestic wallpaper-style print below an expanse of white fondant that encourages the eye to travel up to the freestanding gold ornate cross, really makes an impact … more so when you cut into it to find a blue ombre layering with a gold cross inside. I have chosen to do this cake in blue as the standard ombre design included in this book is pink—you can see how easily these colors can be interchanged.

YOU WILL NEED

Round cake tin (pan) (size of your choice depending on size of your design and how may you need to feed; I used an 18 cm/7 inch round, 7.5 cm/3 inch deep cake tin and baked three to get 3 cakes

3 batches white chocolate mud cake batter (page 34)

1 white cake to crumb (sponge or mud) (page 35)

Gel food color to color the cake, royal blue, sky blue, egg yellow and gold

Flavoring (optional)

White chocolate ganache

White fondant

2 cake boards the same size as your cakes

Cake board, for display

Gum paste

20 or 22-gauge wires

Cross cutter or silicon mould

Edible gold paint, or edible gold dust and rose spirit

Edible blue metallic paint, or blue dust and rose spirit

2 A4 size edible 'wallpaper' images

Circle cutters (pastry size)

Large mixing bowl

Cranked-handled spatula, small (or butter knife)

Sugar glue

MAKING THE CAKES

Make 4 cakes in total: 3 blue mud cakes and one gold sponge.

1 Preheat the oven to 120–130°C/250–265°F.

2 Grease and flour or line the cake tin.

3 Make, color and flavor the cake batters one at a time, see advice on batter coloring and ombre cakes on page 11, and bake until cooked through.

4 Allow the mud cakes to cool completely, wrap in cling film (plastic wrap) and refrigerate to until cold.

5 Make the gold cake, coloring and flavoring as required.

For this cake I used a 50/50 combination of egg yellow and gold food colors. Gold on its own is very muted, egg yellow is a golden yellow and adds vibrancy and depth to the gold. Bake the sponge until the skewer in the centre of the cake comes out clean. Invert onto a wire rack and leave to cool but do not refrigerate.

6 Once the gold cake has cooled completely, cut away all of the crust (which means anything that is brown) so you are left only with the golden part of the cake—this will be very crumbly.

Holding the gold cake over a large mixing bowl start to break it into pieces with your hands. As the pieces fall away, pick them up and rub between your palms to make a fine crumb.

7 Once you have a fine crumb, add a quarter of a cup of melted white chocolate ganache. First stir this through with a spoon, this will help start the mixing process and also cool it a little. Once this is achieved use your hands to crumb the cake again but this time you are rubbing through the chocolate ganache. Depending on the size of your gold cake you may need half a cup of ganache. I used half a cup of ganache for an 8 inch tin sponge cake.

MAKING THE SURPRISE CAKE CROSS

1 Trim the crust from the three cakes and make sure the top of each is level.

2 Once your cakes are the right size and shape, stack them in the right order and find the centre of the top cake using a ruler. Insert a long blade bread knife directly down through the centre of the top cake and the two cakes below. This is how I get my 1 central point. You can also do this by inserting one central dowel. Remove the knife and separate the three cakes.

Using a circular cutter, cut out the centre of the bottom and middle layer cakes. For the third cake, which is your top layer, cut only three-quarters of the way into the cake and scoop out the cake left behind—this will make the top section of the cross shorter than the bottom.

3 To make the arms of the cross, take the middle layer/centre cake, and using a larger circle

cutter align it so that the small hole is in the dead centre, cut out a larger circle. This will make the arms of your cross.

4 Starting with your base cake (first layer), fill the hole of the base cake with golden cake crumb mix. With a cranked handle spatula or knife, apply a layer of ganache around the hole on the cake top to create a 'glue' to which the next layer will stick.

5 Place the middle layer on top of the base layer refrigerate the cake stack for 20 minutes. This will set the ganache enough so that the top cake will not to move too easily as you add cake crumb. If you are time poor you can skip this step but be very careful your cake does not move, you don't want errant gold crumbs.

6 Fill the hole of the middle layer with golden cake crumb mix as before. Really push this down to ensure it connects with the layer below. Apply a layer of ganache as before to the cake top around the hole containing the cake crumb.

7 For the cake that will be the top layer, compact the gold crumb into the hole and apply a layer of ganache to the cake all around the hole. Turn upside down and stick to the middle layer using your straight cake sides as a guide. Do this quickly before gravity has time to make the gold cake crumb fall out. You should not get any falling crumbs if you used enough ganache in your gold crumb mix.

ICING AND DECORATING THE CAKE

1 Now you have the cakes stacked, follow the normal instructions to ganache the outside in preparation for the application of fondant. See page 17 in the techniques section.

2 Cover the cake with white fondant, following the instructions on page 20.

3 Cover the display board, if you like, and transfer the covered cake to the board.

4 Remove your edible image from its backing sheet and attach with a small amount of sugar glue or as per the instructions for the edible image you have purchased.

NOTE: you may need two A4 sized edible images for your cake, my cake required 1¾ images which required me to cut down the second one, lining it up with the pattern on the first. Remember the old age adage of 'measure twice, cut once!' Line everything up and measure it before taking it off the backing paper to avoid rips and tears. When you do apply the image to the cake, choose the front of your cake and put the centre of the first image on the front of the cake, lining the image up with the base of the cake—smoothing upwards and then outwards to stick it down.

Repeat this for the second image if it is required.

TROUBLESHOOT: I aligned the paper with the bottom of the cake for both first and second image but when I applied the image, one is higher than the other. If this happens don't panic! First try and see if you can gently remove the taller image by peeling it back. If you can't, don't force it. If you can remove it, lay it flat, trim the height by the exact amount needed and reapply it. If you haven't been able to remove it you have two options: you can remove it entirely and start again with a new image or you can 'botch it' and by this I mean peeling back one corner of the image that is too tall and with small, long nosed sharp embroidery scissors trim it on an angle. This will mean it meets the lower image and angles gently upwards to its normal line—do this both sides. If it is a busy pattern you may get away with this as busy patterns play tricks on the eye and you don't so much see a straight line as perceive intense pattern and blank space. It's not ideal, but if you're at home, it's close to midnight and the christening is tomorrow, it will do; remember its only cake and only you will look that close and be that critical of it.

MAKING THE FREESTANDING CROSS

First let me say, if you are never going to use the tools for this topper again, you can buy toppers, really pretty and color specific ones like this fairly cheaply online—you just need to be organised ahead of time to allow for shipping. Wherever feasible, buy a spare 'just in case'. Supporting local cake ladies like myself is also great—they will make them for you fairly cheaply too.

You can make a cross several ways and they all involve gum paste and wires! You can use a cutter or a silicon mould to get the cross shape. For this cake I used my favourite cross mould.

1 If you are using a cutter then roll out the gum paste as thick as you want it to look and move on to step 4.

2 If you are using a silicon mould, make sure it is clean and dry. Dust the mould with cornflour and tap out the excess. Ensure you fingers are also clean, dry and lightly dusted. Place a ball of gum paste into the centre of the silicon mould and using your fingers, pressing downward and out towards to the edges, smooth the gum paste into the silicon mould so that it reaches all of the edges. The back of the gum paste figure, facing you should be flat. If your mould is detailed with a lot of small pieces resist all temptation to run your rolling pin over the back of the mould otherwise it may get stuck.

3 Remove the shape from the mould by bending your mould back gently—the shape should start to come away at the edges first and drop out of the mould. If not, gently coax it with your fingers without pulling out of shape. Place the shape onto a dry, cornflour-dusted surface, flat side down, ornate side up.

4 Apply sugar glue to your wire and remove the excess with your fingers. Then gently insert the wire at the base of the cross and insert it three-quarters of the way into the shape or as far as you can go without it emerging from the other side. Leave to dry and make several more if you have the time and materials.

TIP: If your gum paste gets stuck in the mould, place it in the freezer for 30 seconds—3 minutes maximum. This shrinks your gum paste and will allow the shape to come out easier. Remember you have frozen it so you need to let it sit, flat side down and dry before using it. I don't recommend this if you can avoid it!

5 Once the cross is hard to the touch you can paint it. Start on the back, so that if the back is blemished it doesn't matter as much; it also gives you a feel for the paint. I use both pre-made edible metallic gold paint and gold dust that I have mixed with rose spirit. Adding small amounts of color at a time is better than risking drips or runs. As it dries the color may turn translucent, simply go back over it with more gold color when it has dried. Leave to dry. Using a fine-tipped paintbrush and edible blue metallic paint, paint the blue embellishments (optional). Leave to dry, then insert your cross into the centre of your cake by feeding the wire into the cake until the cross is sitting atop the cake.

TROUBLESHOOT: HELP! I have gone through all of the steps but my cross won't sit facing forwards—the wire keeps spinning around.

WHY? This means that you have inserted the wire into the cake crumb and it isn't gripping the wire. To fix this, add a small amount of white royal icing to the top of the cake below the cross to hold it in place. Being white it will blend into the white fondant and not be too noticeable.

Do not paint the royal icing gold as the alcohol will reduce the cohesive bonds in the icing and it will not hold your cross in place.

Alternately, you can use a small round ball of white fondant to sit atop the cake, around the wire and under the cross, like a stand. You don't need much and you can paint this gold so it looks like a stand or leave it white to disappear into the blank part of the cake. FIXED!

Name Cakes

Name cakes are all the rage at the moment and what a great idea it is—you have a nicely decorated birthday cake in the recipients' favourite flavor and when you cut it there is the personalised surprise. All that extra effort really gives it a WOW factor and it is not that hard to do … just a bit fiddly and takes some preparation time.

YOU WILL NEED

Large, wide loaf tin (pan) (10 x 24 x 7 cm/5½ x 9½ x 2¾ inch) or deep square tin

Square tin, 18 cm/7 inch

1 batch chocolate mud cake batter, for the Ben Cake, or 1 batch sponge cake batter, for the Ava cake*. (see page 34)

1 batch white chocolate mud cake batter to cut out letters for the name (1 cake per name)

Large letter cutters

Gel food coloring of your choice. I have used deep pink, leaf green and royal blue

Fondant to cover the display board, I have used red, and white colored soft pink

100s and 1000s (Ava Cake)

Gum paste (Ben Cake)

Sugar glue (Ben Cake)

Edible image (Ben Cake)

20 or 22-gauge wires

Kitchen knife

Butter and icing (confectioners') sugar, for the buttercream

Food flavoring of your choice for the letters inside (optional)

Set up board, or baking paper on your bench

*You can re-bake the letters in either mud cake or a standard sponge cake as the icing and decorations for these designs are not heavy.

MAKING THE LETTER CAKE

1 Preheat the oven to 120–130°C/250–265°F. Grease and flour or line the loaf tin.

2 Make up one batch of white chocolate mud cake and color it deep pink for the girl's cake.

Divide the cake batter for the letters for the cake into two bowls. For the boy's cake I colored half of it royal blue and the other half leaf green. Add both, bit by bit to the loaf tin directly from the mixing bowls with a spoon, no piping bags required. Once the two colors are in the tin, swirl a butter knife around in the cake batter, to give a swirly under-the-sea effect.

Bake until cooked through. Leave to cool, wrap in cling film (plastic wrap) and refrigerate.

3 Remove the pink/blue mud cake from the refrigerator and using a bread knife, cut the loaf into 2–2.5cm/¾–1 inch thick slices. If the cake has started to come to room temperature as you are cutting it, return it to the refrigerator as you need the cake to be as cold as possible without being frozen to get the best cut out.

4 Give your letter cutters a light spray with vegetable oil to help guide them through the cake

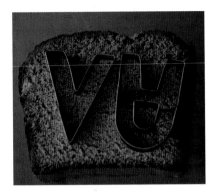  

easier with less cracks and breakages. Position the letter cutters over the slice at whatever angle you need to and cut out your shape. Once you have cut the letter shape it will still be in the cutter, remove excess cake from around the edges and gently use your finger to push it out a little at a time working your way around the shape evenly so it does not crack. You need to make enough letters to fill the cake tin and have some left over to account for potential breakages.

TIP: Choose large letter cutters. Not only do the larger letters make more of an impact, they are more likely to hold their own consistency when re-baked. Smaller letters with their smaller density are more prone to being heated to the point of dissolution in your finished cake upon re-bake.

5 Wrap each letter individually and put them in the freezer. We need them to be frozen so they don't over bake, dry out or liquefy when we re-bake them in the final cake.

MAKING THE NAME CAKE

1 Preheat the oven to 120–130°C/250–265°F for chocolate mud cake, or 180°C/350°F for sponge cake batter. Grease and flour or line the square tin.

PSST! It is likely that you will have batter left over. Either make these into spare cupcakes to freeze for lunch boxes or crumb the cupcakes into a bowl and freeze for cake pop mixture at a

2 Spread approximately one-fifth of the batter in the base of the tin, and use this as base to secure the letters. I put my letters in upside down, so that the base becomes the cake top with perfectly flat, clean sharp edges. I start by standing my letters in front of an upside down tin and as I turn the tin upright I turn the letters with it so I know exactly what order and way around they need to be placed. Place the letters no less than 2cm/¾ inches apart and push them all

the way down to connect them to the base of the tin, this will help keep them in place and not 'wander' in the batter as it is cooked.

3 Part-fill a piping (pastry) bag and pipe between the letters ensuring that there are no pockets of air. Make sure the batter is even. When piping, I start with any holes in the letters and then work in a loop, around the edges and zigzag through the letters and repeat.

You may need to keep propping your letters up—don't worry, the more batter you put in the more they will stay in place.

Once the batter is in the tin, use your cranked handle spatula (slightly wet to avoid batter sticking to it) to smooth the batter over the top, so you can't see any part of the letters sticking out of the batter. Use a kitchen knife (or skewer markers if your oven will allow it), to mark where the letters start and end—whatever sequence makes sense to you so you can be sure to get the cake the right way around when decorating and cutting it.

4 Bake immediately for 45–60 minutes, or as per the time required for the recipe you used. Test to ensure the cake is baked through by inserting skewer at three different points across the cake. If the skewer comes out clean, the cake is baked.

5 Invert the cake onto a cooling rack and mark it immediately with flour or a marker of your choice so you know which side is the front of the cake. Leave to cool.

DECORATING THE AVA CAKE

I wanted to give this cake a fun, party vibe and what decoration says kids' party better than 100s and 1000s?

1 Place the cake on a cake board the same size as the cake.

2 Apply a layer of buttercream to the cake and edge of the board, so now the board has become the false base of the cake. I kept my buttercream cream colored because it blends in with the 100s and 1000s; you can color it if you wish.

3 Decant 100s and 1000s into a shallow bowl or clean baking dish that is a little wider than the cake itself. Now you have two options to apply the 100s & 1000s: the professional way and the heavy-handed cheats way. I'm including both and will let you guess which one I use.

Place your hand under the cake board and hold the cake low over the dish then use your free hand (make a cup shape with it) to scoop up 100s and 1000s and apply them to the cake using a very small amount of pressure so that they stick. Repeat until the cake is completely covered and no buttercream is really visible.

Alternately use the cheat's method but note it carries its own risk to the cake, don't say you weren't warned! Ensure your dish is wide enough and adequately full of 100s & 1000s. Apply buttercream to the cake sides only, leaving the top of the cake free from icing. With one hand under the base of the cake and the other on the top of the cake I very gently hold the cake on its side and dip each side into the 100s and 1000s, the soft buttercream and light pressure from the dip should create an instant covering. Repeat for all four sides and then place your cake right side up and apply buttercream to the top of the cake and then gently turn the cake upside down into the dish of 100s and 1000s and while it is inverted in the dish finish applying 100s and 1000s to the sides. The trick here is removing the cake without it falling off the board or damaging the shape of the sides. To do this I use a large cranked handle spatula or egg flipper and my hand on the base board and invert the cake back up the right way. Be warned though, 100s and 1000s will go everywhere. It is quick and easy, has risk and requires definite vacuuming.

Alternatively for the top you can simply use the cupped hand method for less risk and less mess.

NOTE: Through all of this you need to keep a marker on the 'front side of the cake'.

4 Secure the cake to the display board with buttercream making sure the front is facing forward. To make sure I don't get confused later I put the back of the cake almost flush with the back of the display board so there is a wider space in front of the cake—this allows a nice falling spot for the front of the cake when you cut it away to reveal the name.

DECORATING THE BEN CAKE

Nautical themes have made a comeback in fashion for kids' cakes recently and I wanted to incorporate this idea into the Ben Cake. Blue and red provide a fresh, crisp look to almost any design, and are bright and happy. Note: if you are going to make the 3D boat you need to prepare this in advance to allow it time to dry and turn hard.

1 Place the cake on a cake board the same size as the cake itself.

2 Make and color one batch of buttercream blue. Apply the buttercream to the cake, including the board edges, so that the board becomes the false base of the cake.

3 Once the cake is evenly covered, go back over the buttercream with a small, clean cranked handle spatula (or use a butter knife), and in small areas at a time, I use a back and forth motion over the buttercream and flick my wrist at the end point to create a peak. I do this all over the cake to give the effect of waves.

4 Refrigerate the cake so that the buttercream sets hard and retains its shape.

OPTION ALERT! If you want to go one step further, when the buttercream is hard, add white royal icing to the tips of the waves to make the water look choppy.

5 Add the boat topper. I have made mine out of gum paste, an edible image and cake decorating wires. You can use your child's favourite toy or buy a new one and make that part of the present—this is a particularly good option if your child is at an age where they will want to play with the 'toy' on top of the cake. Gum paste toppers that contain wires can never be given to children.

MAKING THE BOAT

I had a simple image of a boat in red, white and blue printed on edible paper. You can have this printed at your local cake decorating supply store or order it online. Be sure to have several printed on the one sheet in case you rip it when cutting it.

1 Remove the edible boat image from its backing and cut around it. Cut this shape out using a sharp craft knife or embroidery scissors—whichever works best for you.

2 Stick the image to some rolled out gum paste using sugar glue.

3 Using a kitchen knife, cut around the shape of the edible image, and discard the excess gum paste.

4 Applying sugar glue to the ends of the 20-gauge wires (or skewers) and remove the excess with your fingers. Insert the wire two-thirds of the way into the gum paste at two different spots for stability. Leave to dry on a cornflour dusted surface until rock hard.

Insert wires into the cake to complete the decoration. Note: it is very important to check that the wires/skewers come out of the cake before serving it for consumption!

Number Cakes

Age cakes, like name cakes, are all the rage right now. These cakes are most often made into loaf shapes and are perfect for small parties, family birthday gatherings and lunch box treats.

OPTION ALERT! You can re-bake the numbers in either mud cake or a standard sponge cake as the icing and decorations for these designs are not heavy.

YOU WILL NEED

Loaf tin (pan) (10 x 24 x 7 cm/5½ x 9½ x 2¾ inch)

1 batch white chocolate mud cake batter colored royal blue for the number 7 and

1 batch chocolate mud cake batter for the number 7 cake (see page 34)

1 batch chocolate mud cake batter for the number 5, and

1 x butter sponge cake batter colored pink for the 5 cake (see page 37)

Large number cutters

Gel food coloring: deep pink, teal, turquoise, sky blue, royal blue and cornflower blue

Fondant, to cover the display board, I used chocolate brown and blue

Fondant, to make the blue balls (#7 cake)

Chocolate ganache

Sugar flowers, pink roses (#5 cake)

Optional: food flavoring, for the numbers

Set up board, or baking paper on your bench

MAKING THE NUMBER CAKE

1 Preheat the oven to 120–130°C/250–265°F. Grease the loaf tin and dust it with flour, or line the tin with baking paper.

2 Make one batch of white chocolate mud cake for the digit and color and flavor it as desired. Bake immediately and test with a skewer to check that the cake is cooked through. Invert on to a wire rack to cool.

3 Wrap the cold cake in cling film (plastic wrap) and put it in the refrigerator until cold. Remove the cake from the refrigerator, and using a bread knife, cut the loaf into 2–2.5cm/¾–1 inch thick slices. If the cake has started to come to room temperature, put it back in the refrigerator, you need these slices as cold as possible without being frozen to get the best cut out.

4 Spray the number cutter lightly with vegetable oil. Position the cutters over the cake and cut out the shape. Remove the excess cake from around the edges and gently use your finger to push out the cake a little at a time, working your way around the shape evenly so it does not crack. Make enough numbers to line the cake tin and have some left over in case of breakages.

5 Wrap each number individually in cling film (plastic wrap) and put them in the freezer. They need to be frozen so they don't over bake, dry out or liquefy when we re-bake them in the final cake.

Making the cake

1 Reuse your same loaf tin or choose one that is slightly wider. Grease it and dust it with flour. Preheat the oven to 120–130°C/250–265°F if you are making mud cake or 180°C/350°F for sponge cake batter. Make one batch of cake batter.

2 Place approximately one-fifth of the batter into the tin, and use this as base to secure the numbers. Put the numbers in upside down, so that the edge at the base of the tin becomes the cake top and it is perfectly flat, with clean sharp edges.

NOTE: If you put numbers in upside down check that they read correctly when turned right way up. I start by standing a number in front of an upside down loaf tin and as I turn the tin upright I turn the number with it so I know exactly what order and way around they need to be placed.

Place the numbers no less than 2 cm/¾ inches apart and push them all the way down to the base of the tin, this will help keep them in place.

3 Once all of the numbers are in place, part fill a piping (pastry) bag with the rest of the batter and fill the cake tin. I start with any holes in the numbers (#4, 6, 8 and 9) and then work in a loop, around the edges and zigzag through the numbers and repeat to ensure there are no air pockets in the batter. You may need to keep propping your numbers up—don't worry, the more batter you put in the more they will stay in place.

4 You don't want to see any part of the numbers sticking out of the batter, so use a cranked handle spatula (slightly wet to avoid batter sticking to it) to smooth the batter over the top. Use a kitchen knife or skewers, to mark where the numbers start and end so you can be sure the cake is the right way around when decorating and cutting it.

5 Bake immediately. When it comes time to check your batter, be sure to check the cake with a skewer at three different points across the cake, to ensure you are accurately checking the cake batter not the number parts!

6 Once the cake is cooked invert it onto a cooling rack and be sure to mark the front of the cake. Leave to cool.

PSST! You will have a small amount of left over batter. Either make these into cupcakes to freeze for lunch box treats or crumb into a bowl and freeze to use in cake pop moisture at a later date.

DECORATING THE NUMBER 5 CAKE

I wanted to give this cake a feminine, formal-ish feel but still keep it suitable for a little girl. Pale pink and dark brown is so rich in color contrast and effective in its simplicity, I didn't want to overdo it, so I kept the decorations simple with sugar roses, using one on the top as a marker.

1 Place the cake on a cake board the same size as the cake.

2 Ganache your cake, including the board, so now the board has become the false bottom of your cake. See How To section for details. Remember this design has a polished finished but not a flawless shape, so your ganaching doesn't have to take a long time. Once applied allow the ganache to set in the fridge, bring it back out and let it come back to room temperature.

3 Remove your cake from your set up board and carefully place it into your display board, in this cake I have covered a cake board with pale pink fondant. I have colored the icing pale pink by using the tiniest amount of the deep pink that I used to dye the batter. It is important with so many darker colors going in the cake to keep the board a lighter shade of pink—it lightens the overall design and the eye is naturally drawn to the darker colors first, creating focus.

4 Secure the sugar flowers to the cake and board by inserting the paper-covered wires into the cake and using the ganache to help adhere them into place.

Note: For this cake I have taken the easy option and purchased sugars flowers. You can make these quite easily and it is a rewarding thing to see your work come to life but as I do not intend to include sugar flower step-by-step instructions on this book, I have used store bought ones! If you are interested in making these you'll find many great free tutorials on YouTube, but do not leave it to the last minute. Sugar flowers take time because you need to let layers of petals dry before adding more.

OPTION ALERT! Instead of sugar flowers you can use fresh ones. If you do, be sure they are food safe. If you purchase these from a florist, explain what they are for so that they can wrap the ends to make them food safe for you. If you are doing it yourself, search YouTube for a guide on how to wire the flowers and wrap the ends in floral tape (parafilm). You can also get cake-picks from your local cake decorating supply store/online, which allows you to sit the flowers upright with no petals touching the cake.

DECORATING THE NUMBER 7 CAKE

A loaf-shaped cake in plain chocolate was a bit too boring for a birthday, I wanted to give this cake some boyish interest but keep the decorations simple. Making a blue ball base around the cake looked great and decorative arches naturally followed, providing me with the perfect markers for where to cut the cake.

OPTION ALERT! Like the base but not the arches? You can proceed with just balls around the base OR use smaller balls arranged on top of the cake to make the number 7. If you do this, end your 7 at the point you want to cut the cake for the best surprise reveal.

1 Place the cake on a cake board that is the same size as the cake.

2 Apply a layer of ganache to the cake, including the board, now the board has become the false bottom of your cake. See how to sections for details. Remember this design has a polished finished but not a flawless shape, so your ganaching doesn't have to take a long time. Once you have covered the cake with ganache, use the flat side of your spatula or butter knife and smooth it lengthways down the cake top and sides—this will make long lines in the ganache and give it texture.

3 Cover your display board and place your cake in the centre.

4 For the balls, divide the white fondant into batches according to the number of colors you would like to use. I used teal, turquoise, sky blue, royal blue and cornflower blue. You can just use royal blue and color the fondant three different levels of intensity, or add a small amount of yellow to the sky blue shade to get a turquoise color.

5 Make balls from the colored fondant by rolling a small amount between your palms and in a circular motion. Add the balls around the base of the cake first. Place the remaining balls in the middle to form arches, or arrange on the cake top in the figure of a 7. Make the balls to whatever size suits the proportion of your cake. Remember the larger they are the less you need to make.

Individual Rainbow Mud Pies

DIFFICULTY: / / / / /

TIME TO MAKE: ⏳⏳⏳⏳⏳

A cool twist on a classic design, this is a deconstructed rainbow cake the size of a standard cake slice. Made into individual cakes, it is small, distinctive, and everyone gets their own one! The layers of this cake are best baked in a brownie tray. The great thing about this design is because it is small and put together with buttercream; you can use any white cake recipe you like. I used my favourite butter sponge cake recipe because I just adore how light and fluffy it is.

YOU WILL NEED

Brownie tray
1 batch white cake batter of your choice (mud, sponge, Madeira or your own favourite recipe– see page 35)
1 batch royal icing (see page 39)
3–6 gel food colors of your choice
Chocolate buttercream

(also nice with Italian meringue buttercream)
Sugar rainbows
Royal icing, white
1 candle
Small cranked handle spatula
Paring knife or small, sharp kitchen knife
Square cutter (optional)

MAKING THE CAKE LAYERS

1 Make up one batch of cake batter and decant equal measures of it into different bowls—the number of bowls depends on the number of colors you are going to include. A rainbow mud pie in a brownie tray makes a perfect cube with three layers (trimmed) so I would advise choosing a number of colors divisible by 3. For this design I have made 6 colors: leaf green, royal blue, orange, red, regal purple, and electric pink. Add the color to each bowl, and using a teaspoon or a whisk, thoroughly mix the color through the whole batter.

Remember: For red batter, dye it orange first then add red coloring.

2 Preheat the oven to 120–130°C/250–265°F for mud cake, or 180°C/350°F for sponge cake batter. If you are using packet mix cakes, follow the instructions on the packet for temperature but be flexible with your cooking time, as this a brownie tray not a cake tin so the time will vary significantly; my sponge took only 17 minutes to bake.

3 Grease the brownie tray well with vegetable oil/cake tin release spray or grease and flour it. Add batter to each well and bake immediately.

4 Bake for 17–25 minutes, depending on your cake recipe. When the tops of the cakes spring back when gently touched, test them with a skewer—if this comes out clean, they are ready.

5 While the cakes are cooking, get a head-start on making the chocolate buttercream.

HOT TIP! When I make a sponge cake, I beat the batter on high for an extra 30 seconds to add extra air to it, then after I have placed it into my cake tin I let it sit for 15–20 minutes before putting it into the oven. The extra air leaves the batter, the batter settles and I get a flatter top to my brownie shaped cake with less to trim away!

TRIMMING THE CAKE LAYERS

1 If a crust has formed, trim the sides off of each layer using a paring knife or small sharp kitchen knife. Remember if you do this for one you must do it for all of them and be careful to trim the same amount from each.

CHEATERS NOTE: If you are like me and don't have an eye to cut straight but you own a set of square cutters, get them out and use one of the larger square cutters to evenly trim the sides of all layers.

2 If you cake has domed (which it likely will as it cooks so quickly at high heat), using the same paring knife cut the domed top off of the layer. I find sitting in a chair in front of my kitchen bench so I am eye level with the layer helps me achieve a nice flat, even cut.

TO ICE AND DECORATE THE CAKE

1 Once you have trimmed each layer, decide which 3 colors will be put together. For me, I have put all of my lighter gelato colors together and all of my super bright colors together to give two very different effects when the cakes are cut or bitten into.

2 Stack each of these and using your small cranked handle spatula to apply the chocolate buttercream between each layer—stack them on top of one another. If this starts to become difficult because of cake crumbs, clean and dry your spatula between layers using warm water so that the blade of the spatula is warm—the cleanliness reduces sticking and the warmth helps the butter to spread more easily.

3 Once you have done this for all of your individual cakes, put them in the refrigerator for 5–10 minutes. You want the buttercream in between each layer to set before you put on the outer layer—the nature of soft butter is that it will attract more of itself and you will find more comes off of your cake onto your spatula rather than applying it, let alone smoothly.

4 Remove the cakes from the refrigerator and apply the room temperature buttercream to your cold cakes. To get a smooth finish, apply long, smooth strokes with the flat blade of the spatula around the cake once the buttercream has been applied. To create a rough, peaked texture use small back and forth motions with the flat edge of the spatula. Twist the spatula at the end of the stroke by flicking your wrist to cause a peak. I like to use smooth for one set of colors and rough peaks for the alternative set of colors so I know which is which.

5 Now you have individual mud pies they just need a little party dressing. Make up a batch of royal icing. Fit a 1M piping tip or #9 thermo nozzle to a piping bag, then part fill the bag with royal icing. Pipe two white rounded bulbs of royal icing at each end of the mud pie to look like clouds. Quickly insert the sugar rainbows into the clouds and down into the buttercream of the

cake for a little bit for support—you may need to hold it for a few seconds while the royal icing starts to crust over in the air. Repeat this for all of the cakes and voila, your individual mud pies are done … quick as that!

VARIATION: Leave them without dressing, or opt for stars or hearts or, for an adult, some edible gold sprinkles.

PARTY IDEA

These individual cakes are great in a little take-home cupcake box as a party favour when the main birthday cake of the party was a large rainbow cake OR serve these up instead of cupcakes to accompany a smaller rainbow cake for the birthday boy/girl, to round out the party food.

Om Chakra Cake

DIFFICULTY: / / / / /

TIME TO MAKE: ⌛⌛⌛⌛⌛

I came up with this design for my mum's birthday. She is a spiritual lady who practises yoga and meditation every day, and while she is very health conscious, she doesn't mind a piece of cake every now and then … especially chocolate! So here I combined a few of her favourite things.

OPTION ALERT! This cake can easily be made with an eggless cake recipe and buttercream replacement based on vegetable fats to suit dietary restrictions

WHAT IS CHAKRA?

An ancient Sanskrit word and understanding that the body, along the spine has 7 chakra points, all represented by symbols and color, the base being red and representing our base human needs and working through to the violet color at the crown, our understanding and connectivity to divinity and enlightenment. The colors in order are red, orange, yellow, green, blue, purple and violet. The idea and understanding of Chakras have evolved over time and are better explained and represented in texts other than here in a cake book—if you are interested I highly recommend researching it and its relationship to the human body, or ask your local yoga teacher!

YOU WILL NEED

15 cm/6 inch round shallow cake tin (pan)

3 batches white cake batter of your choice (mud, Madeira or sponge)

7 gel food colors; I have used red, orange, lemon yellow, leaf green, royal blue and electric blue combination, regal purple and electric purple combination, and violet and electric purple combination

White royal icing (see page 39)

Small cranked handle spatula

22-gauge wires

Sugar glue

Gum paste

Edible metallic gold paint, or gold dust and rose spirit

Paring knife or small sharp kitchen knife

Wheel tool (optional)

1 cake board for base of cake

1 display board/plate/wooden stump

Before we start: A note on tins for layer cakes

I have used specific rainbow cake tins for this recipe. These are very shallow so I can fill them three-quarters full knowing that I will get a small, thin layer out of each. I have these tins in 15 cm/ 6 inch and 23 cm/9 inch sizes. I can fit three of the smaller tins in my oven at any one time, which cuts my baking time significantly but, of course, lengthens my cooking time by a little.

These tins are great but if you don't have a regular use for them, you don't need to buy them to make a rainbow or any multi layer cake. With a suitably sized round tin you already have at home, only partially fill it with batter. This is a little less exact and to get consistent, even layers you have two choices: you can be exact and put your tin on the kitchen scales and stop adding batter when the scales reach a specific predetermined weight or you can do it by eye.

HOT TIP! If you are using a deeper tin to make thin rainbow layer, grease and line your tin with baking paper. This makes it easier to get out of the tin when its baked. Also, if your tin is very deep, the heat trapped in the top of tin in the vacant space may cause the top of the layer to crust and go brown. If this happens place a round of foil on top of the cake once it has risen just as it starts to brown to help protect it.

MAKING THE CAKE LAYERS

1 Preheat the oven to 120–130°C/250–265°F for mud cake, or 180°C/350°F for a sponge cake batter. If you are using packet mix cakes, follow the instructions on the packet for temperature. Grease and flour or line your baking tin(s).

2 Make up the cake batter and decant equal measures of it into seven bowls, for the seven colors. Add the color to each bowl, using a teaspoon or small whisk to thoroughly mix the color through the whole batter.

HOT TIP! Making it with sponge cake? Check out the helpful hints to get a flat top and avoid trimming on page 14

3 Pour in the batter and bake until cooked through, 17–25 minutes, depending on your cake recipe. When the top of the cakes spring back when gently touched, test them with skewer—if it comes out clean it is ready; invert onto a wire rack to cool, then wrap in cling film (plastic wrap) and refrigerate until cold.

TRIMMING THE CAKE LAYERS

1 I try really hard not to trim these cakes. Trimming creates major cake crumb and I am putting them together with a thin layer of pure white royal icing, royal icing is stiff and will drag cake crumb, and because the cake is very brightly colored, it will be very, very noticeable.

2 If you have to trim these cakes, do so when they are refrigerated cold and one at a time, thoroughly cleaning your bench of bright colored cake crumb in between each layer so that there is less risk of cross contamination.

You can apply sugar syrup to the cut area of the cake to help reduce its crumb drop amount. I tend not to do this with bright colors and white royal icing because if you make a mistake and add too much and it leaks out, it can ruin your entire design.

ICING THE CAKE

1 To contain the cake crumb and minimise the risk of color cross contamination, coat each layer of cake entirely in royal icing. Whisk a batch of royal until it forms peak that bends over slightly/ This is more liquid and smooth than a standard royal icing and will smooth across the rough surface of your cake easily.

2 Allow the royal icing to air dry just a little—this will be enough to contain the crumb—then stack them, adding a little more royal icing between each layer. Allow the stack to air dry a little (not too much) and add a layer of stiffer peaked royal icing to the outside of the stack with the flat edge of a cranked handle spatula. To get a smooth finish use long smooth strokes with the flat blade of the spatula around the cake. To create a rough, peaked texture use small back and forth motions with the flat edge of the spatula and by flicking your wrist, twist the spatula at the end of the stroke to cause a peak.

NOTE: if you are making this for home, the royal icing should be enough to stick the layers together and keep them stable. If you plan to travel with this cake you should really put support dowels into the cake before icing the outside of it.

MAKING THE TOPPER

1 Find an Om symbol (or any of the symbols from the Chakra chart) and print it out onto A4 paper and cut around it to make as paper template.

2 Roll out some gum paste to 2.5 mm/$\frac{1}{10}$ inch thick, and using a wheel tool, scalpel, or a small kitchen/paring knife, cut out the shape. I find that a scalpel or sharp paring provides the cleanest cut and holds the shape, then I tidy up with a wheel tool.

Make two if you have time in case of breakages. I cannot stress enough how helpful a back up piece will be. Thin, flat structures with a lot of negative space are fragile!

3 Move the cut shape to a flat, non-stick surface dusted with cornflour, for drying.

4 Cut the 22-gauge wires to appropriate lengths and apply sugar glue to the ends. Insert the wire into the shape at various points to create stability. I start with the base of the larger piece

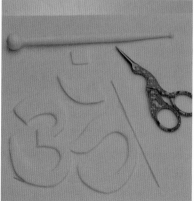

first to avoid movement in the smaller pieces once they are attached.

5 Repeat this for any smaller pieces and once the wires have been inserted, insert the wires sticking out of the base of the small shape into the top of the larger shape to connect them. Set aside to dry. Depending on the weather this can take days, so plan ahead!

6 When the shape is dry you can paint it. Start painting on the back to get a feel for the paint. For this structure I used pre-made edible metallic gold paint. You can also use a gold dust that you mix with rose spirit (see page 27 for information).

Once the paint has dried it is ready to placed on top of the cake, simply insert the wires gently into the iced cake until the topper is sitting just above the icing, or slightly pushed into it for more stability if you like.

Gelato Rainbow and Raindrops

DIFFICULTY: ✏️✏️✏️✏️✏️
TIME TO MAKE: ⏳⏳⏳⏳⏳

I love rainbow cakes and this one is just so fun, especially as a birthday cake for a weather-obsessed child, a get well gift, or as a fun surprise for anyone whose song is 'You are my Sunshine'.

YOU WILL NEED

Round cake tin (pan) (I used an 18 cm/7 inch diameter round tin and filled it to half its capacity)

Note: I have made thicker layers of cake and less of them, if you wish to have thinner layers follow the layer advice for Rainbow Bright or Om Chakra cake

5 batches sponge cake batter (you could also use mud or Madeira cake)

7 gel food colors (for figurines and cake batter), egg yellow, mint green, sky blue, electric pink, regal purple, orange and black

Butter and icing (confectioners') sugar, for the buttercream

Small cranked handle spatula

Black edible ink pen

22-gauge wires

Sugar glue

Gum paste

Clay extruder (optional)

1 cake board, for the base of cake

1 display board/cake plate/wooden stump

Royal icing

Piping bag

233 grass tip/nozzle

Small blossom cutter

Circle cutter (small enough to fit inside small star cutter)

Star cutters in small medium & large

White edible paint food color, for the eyes (optional)

Black gum paste or fondant, for the sunshine eyes

MAKING THE CAKE LAYERS

1 Preheat the oven to 120–130°C/250–265°F for mud cake, or 180°C/350°F for a sponge cake batter. Grease and flour or line the cake tin(s).

2 Make up a batch of cake batter and decant equal measures into five bowls—for the five colors. Add the color to each bowl, using a teaspoon or small whisk to thoroughly mix the color through the whole batter. Color one bowl with each of the following colors: egg yellow, mint green, sky blue, electric pink, and regal purple. See page 25 about using sky blue gel food color.

3 Tip each batter into a cake tin and bake for 25–40 minutes, depending on the cake recipe and layer height. When the top of the cakes spring back when gently touched, test them with skewer—if it comes out clean it is done. Be flexible with your cooking time, cooking times vary based on your tin size, amount of cake in the tin, recipe, chocolate and sugar content and a variety of other factors … keep an eye on it.

TRIMMING THE CAKE LAYERS

1 When your cakes have cooled, wrap each cake individually in cling film (plastic wrap) and refrigerate until cold. It is a lot easier to trim a cold cake.

I did not trim this cake. The light crust was very moist so I chose to keep it for color differentiation between the layers. If you have to trim these cakes, do so when they are refrigerator cold and thoroughly clean your bench of cake crumb between each layer so that there is less risk of cross contamination of color.

ICING THE CAKE

1 Make your buttercream and add whitener before adding the sky blue color, to avoid it throwing a green shade. Keep a quarter of this aside, to be used between layers.

2 Ice the base layer cake to the board of the same size. Cover the entire cake with blue icing and stack the next cake layer on top and repeat the process. Don't worry that the sides look like rolls; you will fill this in and make it even.

3 Once all of the cakes are stacked together put them in the refrigerator so that the buttercream can cool and set a little.

4 While the cake is the fridge, color up a small amount of fondant green, roll it out and use it to cover the display board (see page 18) ready to place the iced cake on.

5 Remove the cake from the refrigerator and apply the rest of the room temperature blue buttercream to the outside and top of the cold cake. Using a large cranked handle spatula and working from the base up, smooth the buttercream in long lines, working upward to create the rustic, rough rendering with long vertical lines visible in the finish.

When the buttercream has set place it onto the green fondant covered board

TROUBLESHOOT: Travelling with this cake? Layer cakes should have a board every second layer and dowels to support them. Without a support structure inside the cake, the finished design is not as stable. If you have to transport this cake a long way I would suggest one, thick central dowel in the centre of the cake. If you are making this to enjoy at home, you don't need to bother with this step!

MAKING THE RAINBOW

1 Make gum paste from your fondant and divide your gum paste and color each lot in the corresponding colors you have chosen.

2 To shape the rainbow, I secure a drinking glass to a non-stick surface using a roll of gum paste so it won't move.

3 There are two ways to make the rounded sausage-shaped colors that stick together to make a 3D rainbow.

You can roll each gum paste color by hand on a small scale version of what is required for the side of the rainbow bright cake, see page 24 for details on gum paste. This is a good option if you plan to do this only once and don't need a tool.

The second way—which gives you a more even finish and is a lot easier (for me)—is using a clay extruder. You still roll your colored gum paste into a rough sausage shape so it fits into the clay extruder and then you simply plunge out the perfectly cylindrical shape.

4 Before inserting the gum paste, put the round shaped tip in the end and fill the extruder with cornflour and plunge it out through the tip to ensure the gum paste won't stick to the inside of tool. I do this in-between each and every use. Additionally, to assist the plunging process, warm up the gum paste in your hands, so that is is easier, and more pliable to work with.

Continuous pressure will create a blemish-free cylindrical shape. Place the cylindrical shape around the glass in step 4 immediately before extruding any more colors. Repeat until rainbow is complete.

4 Wrap the first sausage around the outside of the glass, and then wrap each subsequent sausage around the last one, sticking them together with sugar glue.

5 Once you have done this for all of the colors you are going to add, using the glass as my guide and a sharp long kitchen knife, cut the ragged ends of the rainbow off in a straight line.

6 Cut the 22-gauge wires long enough to sit in the cake to a depth that will stabilise the size and weight of the rainbow—the bigger it is, the longer the wire. Cut one wire for each end of each color. Apply sugar glue to the end of the wire and insert it into the color sausage as far as it will go—your aim is to get this inside the straight length of the color and stop before it curves. This means the outside colors will have more wire inside than the smaller ones on the inside.

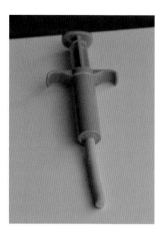 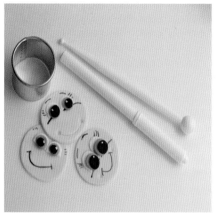 

7 Allow the rainbow to dry on a flat non-stick surface. This will mean the back of the rainbow is a little flatter than the front but this will not be noticeable.

MAKING THE SUN

1 Color up some gum paste yellow and orange. Roll it out the yellow on a non-stick, cornflour-dusted surface, then using star and a circle cutters, cut out 1 large star, 1 small star and 1 circle. The circle cutter should be small enough to fit inside the centre of the small star.

2 Roll out the orange gum paste and cut out 1 medium star.

3 While the circle is still soft, use a small circle cutter to imprint a smile by inserting half of the cutter, at a 45-degree angle, into the base of the circle.

4 Use your small ball tool to make indents each end of the semi circle smile; this creates dimples and cuteness in equal measure.

5 Allow the stars and the circle to dry hard, then stick them together with sugar glue or royal icing if you have any to hand.

6 To make the eyes for the sun, roll out some white gum paste quite thin then using an oval cutter, cut out two whites of the eyes and stick these to the sun's face with sugar glue.

7 Next, color some gum paste blue, make a small ball of it, and cut it in half. Roll these two halves into balls and ensure they are of equal size. On a non-stick surface (dust with cornflour and cornflour your fingers) using a forefinger, press directly down onto the blue ball to make it a flat disc shape. Adding sugar glue to the back of the disc, stuck it to the bottom part of the white of the eye. Repeat with a smaller amount of black gum paste to make the pupil.

9 With a toothpick/cocktail stick or fine paintbrush, put a white dot in the top right-hand corner of each pupil to create a cute light reflection effect.

10 Using a black edible pen draw on eyebrows and eyelashes.

11 To attach the sun to the rainbow, use a little royal icing and leave laying flat to set hard.

TROUBLESHOOT: I didn't cut my rainbow straight and I didn't notice until I put it into my cake, and now it's crooked. Don't panic! Simply pull the rainbow out slightly so it's straight and insert it into the cake until the longer edge of your rainbow touches the royal icing. Leave it there and make slightly larger clouds, the clouds are going to sit in front and behind the rainbow and will cover your mechanics and mistakes.

MAKING THE CLOUDS

1 To make the clouds that will sit in front of the rainbow, make round balls from gum paste about the size of a Malteser. Using sugar glue, arrange these into a base and stack some on top of the base to create a second layer. You are making the base slightly wider than the width of one side of the rainbow base. Make four and allow them to dry.

2 Roll out some white gum paste quite thin, and make it wide and long enough to cover the stack and have some left over. Cover the stack with a thin layer of sugar glue and place the gum paste over the stack. Using clean, dry, cornflour-dusted fingers, smooth the layer of gum paste over the stack and push it into the crevices around the balls to create a ball-cloud shape. With the excess left over tuck it under the cloud and trim away as required.

3 Place the clouds into the blue buttercream before it dries so that they are affixed in place. If you need to travel with the cake, affix in place with royal icing.

MAKING THE CLOUD BUNTING

1 Roll out the white gum paste quite thin on a non-stick, cornflour-dusted surface. Use a cloud cutter, a cloud-shaped object, or paper template to cut out clouds.

2 Cut out enough thin, flat clouds to go all the way around the top of the cake and then cut an extra five, just in case. Set aside to dry hard, then stick in place with buttercream.

MAKING THE RAINDROPS

1 Color some gum paste grey using black gel food coloring. Add a drop of pale pink to give it some warmth and vibrancy.

2 Roll it out quite thin on a non-stick, cornflour-dusted surface. Use a teardrop cutter (frangipani cutters are the perfect shape and size) or a paper template, cut out enough raindrops to go all the way around the sides of the cake. Cut out enough raindrops to go all the way around the sides of the cake at the density you prefer. Then cut an extra 5–10 just in case.

3 Wait for the raindrops to dry hard and using an edible black pen, draw a smile, two eyes and some eye lashes on each to create a happy face.

4 Add them to the buttercream while it is still soft—as the butter firms up again it should hold the clouds and raindrops in place.

MAKING THE GRASS AND FLOWERS

1 Color up some gum paste whatever color you would like your flowers and their centres to be. Roll out the gum paste and using a small blossom cutter, cut out flowers.

Use a ball tool in the centre of the flower to remove it from the cutter, this will give it a 3D shape.

2 Roll a small amount of colored gum paste into little balls then stick to the flower centres with sugar glue.

3 Part fill a piping bag, fitted with a 233 grass tip/nozzle, with a small amount of green buttercream and pipe small tufts of grass across the green fondant-covered board. Add flowers to the tufts as you go so they set in place as the buttercream hardens.

TROUBLESHOOT: If you live in a hot climate or are experiencing hot weather, replace your buttercream with royal icing to avoid your designs sliding off the cake because the butter in the buttercream has a low melting point.

Rainbow Bright Cake

DIFFICULTY: /////
TIME TO MAKE: ⏳⏳⏳⏳⏳

I love rainbow cakes, they are so bright and happy. This is such a versatile design—suitable for children and adults birthdays, baby showers, christenings and leaving celebrations.

The idea of a rainbow cake is flexible, it can be a combination of as many colors as you like and whatever shades you like; over the page you will see I have included a rainbow cake in gelato shades of color. If you are strapped for time or don't have that many people coming, drop a few colors from the rainbow cake to reduce the number of layers and voila, right size cake, still nailing the rainbow design.

OPTION ALERT!

To make this a good luck theme, follow the instructions for the Gelato Rainbow Cake on page 155 and the Shamrock for Good Luck on page 179 and add a 4 leaf clover to the end of the rainbow!

YOU WILL NEED

Shallow round cake tin (pan) (I used seven tins each 23 cm/9 inch diameter)

4 batches white cake batter of your choice (mud or sponge) (see page 35)

7 gel food colors, for the fondant and cake batter: red, orange, lemon yellow, leaf green, sky blue and electric blue combination, regal purple and electric purple combination, and rose pink and electric pink combination

Chocolate ganache (see page 17)

Fondant

Small cranked handle spatula

22-gauge wires

Sugar glue

Gum paste

Clay extruder (optional)

1 cake board, for base of cake

1 display board/plate/wooden stump.

Royal icing

MAKING THE CAKE LAYERS

1. Preheat the oven to 120–130°C/250–265°F for mud cake or 180°C/350°F for a sponge cake batter. Grease and flour or line the cake tin(s).

2. Make the cake batter and decant equal measures of it into 7 bowls—for each of the 7 colors. Add a color to each bowl, then use a teaspoon or small whisk to thoroughly mix the color through the whole batter. Tip each batch of batter into a prepared cake tin.

3. Bake for 17–25 minutes depending on your cake recipe and layer height. Insert a skewer into the centre of the cake and if it comes out clean it is cooked through.

TRIMMING THE CAKE LAYERS

If you need to trim these bright cake layers, see the advice provided in the Om Chakra cake recipe on page 149.

ICING THE CAKE

1 To contain the cake crumb drop and minimise the risk of color cross contamination, I coat each layer of cake entirely in a soupy consistency chocolate ganache.

2 Return the cakes to the refrigerator to let the ganache shell set and bring back out and return to room temperature.

3 Stack the layers with usual, peanut butter consistency ganache. Once you have completed ganaching the layers together, return to the fridge and let the ganache set. Once set, bring it back out and when the ganache and cake are close to room temperature, ganache the outside of the cake, see page 41 for ganaching technique tips.

This is a lot of in and out of the fridge and it takes some time but it is worth it—getting chocolate to perform the way you want it to ensures your cake will hold its shape … remember you are not supporting this cake with boards or dowels. If you are travelling with this cake, see the trouble shooting notes in the gelato rainbow cake section.

4 Now the ganache has been applied and set appropriately, you can add your fondant. Color up equal amounts of fondant bright rainbow colors. On a clean, non stick, cornflour dusted surface, section off a portion of fondant in your first color.

NOTE: the portion size of your fondant will depend on two factors: firstly on the circumference of your cake—you need it to make it all the way around when you roll it into a sausage shape; secondly you need to decide how thick you want each sausage round. I have gone with larger sausages so I only need 2 of each color to cover each layer of cake. The thicker rolls suit the large tall size of the cake—it keeps the proportion of the overall design. Remember, if you opt for smaller thickness of the rolls you need to make more!

5 Roll it between your palms to make a general sausage shape out of it. Then place it on the surface and roll it with flat fingers against the surface to gently elongate the sausage shape— work from the centre of the sausage shape outwards, this elongates and thins. Making the same movements from the outside in thickens the shape! (Remember this if you accidently rolled your sausage shape too much in one spot and it goes all thin in just one area!)

6 Keep rolling until it is an even size all along the shape and long enough to reach around the circumference of your cake (I keep a piece of kitchen string stuck to my bench to measure the length I need) cut off the ragged ends and wrap around your cake. Secure it together at the back with sugar glue.

7 Repeat for the next roll. When it is the correct length and thickness, apply sugar glue to the top of the first roll. Place the second roll on top of the first, wrapping it around the cake and securing at the back with sugar glue. Repeat this until you have covered the sides of your cake, alternating the colors as you like.

8 Just before you place the rainbow topper on the cake, make a batch of royal icing and apply it to the top of the cake using a small clean cranked handle spatula to smooth it to the edges so it neatly sits on top of the last roll. This serves two purposes—it looks like a cloud mass for the rainbow to sit on, and the hard nature of royal icing (when it is dry) helps to hold the topper and the last roll in place.

TROUBLESHOOT: I accidently stuck my finger into my cake and it's right at the front! What do I do? Don't worry and don't try and remove a sausage of fondant from the cake and then replace it—this will not end well. You can do a patch-job by covering it with a little yellow sugar-star motif cut out of your left over gum paste. Attach with sugar glue and voila! Note: if you have done this on the yellow rolls, make the star a different color. Cake decorators patch things all the time, now you know it you will be looking for it, just have the grace not to ask or mention it.

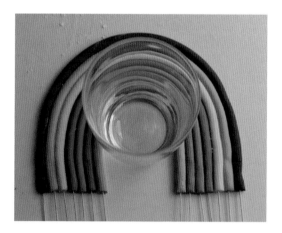

MAKING THE RAINBOW TOPPER & CLOUDS

1 Before you even start the topper, decide how big you need it to be. I have used 9 inch tins and added thick rolls of fondant to the side so the top of my cake has significant room. As such I have chosen a wide drinking glass, which I have to hand, and have secured this with a roll of gum paste to a non-stick work surface so it won't move. I am going to add the first color around this glass in a deep horseshoe shape and continue to add colors next to it until I reach my desired number of colors.

If you don't have the same space I do, try using the small end of the drinking glass, or a round salt shaker—as long as it is round and you can affix it to the work surface to shape your rainbow.

Follow the advice provided in the Gelato Rainbow section on page 155.

Rita's Beehive and Cupcakes

DIFFICULTY: / / / / /
TIME TO MAKE: ⏳⏳⏳⏳⏳

This is my favourite cake. When I first start to think about cakes with a surprise inside I thought of my Aunty Rita and her obsession with bees and beehives. The result was this beehive cake in rich honey and caramel flavors that is cute as a button.

YOU WILL NEED

Dolly Varden/crinoline lady cake tin (pan) (19 cm diameter x 15 cm deep/7½ inch diameter x 6 deep (or smaller, depending on how many people you need to feed)

1 batch caramel mud cake batter (see page 34)

½ batch white chocolate mud cake batter, for the cake balls (see page 35)

250 ml/8 fl oz/¼ cup honey, for the cake balls

Cake ball tray

Gel food color, egg yellow, and pink

White fondant

Black fondant

CMC powder, to turn the fondant into gum paste

Hexagon cutter (a pentagon or octagon cutter will also work if you already have them)

Fondant or kitchen knife

Non-stick mat

Cornflour (corn starch) and icing (confectioners') sugar, for dusting

Chocolate or caramel chocolate ganache

Sugar glue

Royal icing

Cupcake cases

Cupcake tray

Cake board for display (I have used a textured black board. Alternatively you can cover a standard board with black fondant)

Piping (pastry) bag

1M piping tip/nozzle or piping tip/nozzle of your choice

20 or 22-gauge wires

Heart cutters: large and small

Modelling tools: wheel cutter and ball tool

MAKING THE CAKE BALLS

First things first, you need to make honey flavored, yellow colored cake balls from white chocolate mud cake and then freeze them. You can do this a week or more in advance.

1 Preheat the oven to 150 °C/300 °F. Grease both sides of the cake ball tray.

2 Mix up one batch of white mud cake batter as per the recipe section and add the honey to the mix. As the mix starts to combine add a little egg yellow color to make the batter a deep, rich golden yellow color. Spoon the batter into the ball tray. Bake for 17–20 minutes. Test to see if the cake balls are cooked (see page 13). Set aside to cool.

3 Once you have cooked all of the cake batter and all of the cake balls have cooled, you need to freeze them. Individually wrap each cake ball using freezer wrap or 'go-between' between each cake ball in a sealable plastic container to ensure they don't stick together and to avoid icicles forming on them. Remember the cake balls need to be frozen so they don't disappear into the mud cake batter when we re-bake them, so don't skip this step!

MAKING THE CAKES

1 Preheat the oven to 120–130°C/250–265°F for caramel mud cake.

2 Stand the small tip of the Dolly Varden tin (that you have already greased and floured, or lined) inside a round cake tin that is small enough to cradle the Dolly Varden, this will help keep it stable while in the oven. Half filling the supporting cake tin with water will help stop the lower part of the cake from overcooking. If you have an egg ring, place this at the bottom of the round tin for additional support. Grease and flour the Dolly Varden tin.

3 Make the caramel mud cake batter. Place a small amount of caramel mud cake batter in the narrow base of the tin and add one frozen cake ball. Cover the cake ball with mud cake and continue to add frozen cake balls at equal distances apart and repeat in layers until the tin is almost full. Leave one thumb-width of space between the level of batter and the top of the tin to allow for the cake to rise.

4 If you can see cake balls atop of the batter, smooth the caramel mud cake batter over the top of the balls with a damp spatula and bake immediately.

Bake for the time required for the size tin you have chosen, remembering the batter you have chosen and your oven may vary cooking times.

Test to see if the cake is cooked by inserting a skewer at three different points across the cake, to ensure you are accurately checking the cake batter not the cake balls. If the skewer comes out clean, the cake is ready.

NOTE: Dense, slow cooking mud cake in this odd shaped tin takes a long while to cook so be patient and expect it to be baked 'long and low'. I have an incredibly hot oven so I set my temperature gauge for 120°C /250°F and it took me 3¼ hours to cook it.

ICING THE CAKE

1 I find using a Dolly Varden tin, like the hemisphere tin, gives me a perfect curve, and applying a standard layer of ganache makes it less smooth. So to keep the shape and provide a perfectly smooth surface I heat the ganache until it is pumpkin soup consistency and pour it over the cake—the ganache is thin enough to coat the cake and take on the cake's shape rather than

 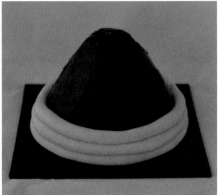

help to shape the cake. This way I get to cover and moisture-seal my cake with chocolate, give the fondant something to stick to and still keep the perfectly smooth curved shape. Do this and leave the ganache to set.

2 Color the fondant yellow. On a clean, non-stick, cornflour-dusted surface, roll out a portion into a sausage shape. See notes on how to achieve this in the Rainbow Bright cake recipe on page 143. The portion size of your fondant will depend on two factors: first on the circumference of your cake (which gets smaller as you go up) you need it to make it all the way around when you roll it into a sausage shape; secondly you need to decide how thick you want each sausage round. I have gone with larger sausages so I don't need to make as many. Also, the thicker rolls suit the large size of the cake; it keeps proportion of the overall design.

3 Keep rolling until it is an even size all along the shape and long enough to reach around its circumference.

4 Cut off the ragged ends and wrap around the cake. Secure the ends together at the back with sugar glue.

5 Repeat this for the next roll. When it is the correct length and thickness, apply sugar glue to the top of the first roll and overlap the first roll with the second roll, wrapping it around the cake and securing at the back with sugar glue. Repeat until the cake sides are covered.

6 At the top there will be little dip between the last layer of fondant roll and the top of the cake. Make a ball of yellow fondant and squash it between your palms. Sit it on top of the cake.

OPTION ALERT! You don't have to roll out fondant sausages! You can cover the entire Dolly Varden cake shape with yellow fondant, smoothing it down as you go, and then use a texture mat to imprint a honeycomb pattern all over it.

MAKING THE BEE

NOTE: It is best to do this days in advance to allow ample drying time. As with other fragile structures, if you have time and resources, always make two just in case.

1 Make gum paste from your yellow and black fondant if required, following advice on page 24.

2 For the body, make a ball with the black gum paste and taper each end slightly so it makes a very subtle oval shape.

3 Roll out the yellow gum paste quite thin and using a wheel tool (or a small sharp knife) cut small thin yellow stripes. Apply sugar glue to the back and wrap them around the body. Secure neatly at the back, cutting away any excess.

4 Roll out the yellow gum paste slightly thicker this time and cut out 2 large love hearts for wings. Trim the pointed base of each so that they fit together neatly. Apply sugar glue to the smallest third of the hearts, then centre the bee body on top of the hearts.

5 Roll out some black gum paste and cut out two small hearts. Trim one-third of the length off the point of each heart. Applying sugar glue to the back and stick them to the yellow wings, flat edge tucked under the body of the bee.

OPTION ALERT! You can use a piece of material or texture mat to imprint a design on the wings for effect.

6 Using black gum paste, roll a small ball for the head, the size should be in proportion to the body size you have made. Before I attach my bee head to the body, I detail the face. That way if I get it horribly wrong and have to start again, I'm not risking damage to the body/head connection with excessive wiring in and out.

7 To make the face, use a small circle cutter (or a small heart) at a 45-degree angle to indent a smile. Using the small end of the ball tool, make small indents at each end of the embossed smile to make dimples for maximum cuteness.

8 To make the eyes, stack a large black ball under a medium white ball under a small black ball and push down with the index finger squashing them together—this gives an all-in-one large bug eye. For the eye detail, add very small balls of white gum paste at the top right-hand sides of the pupil (optional). Stick each eye in place with sugar glue.

9 Attach the head to the body using a small amount of sugar glue to secure the head and body together. You can ensure stability by using a cut-to-size piece of raw spaghetti or cake decorating wire. Use a small amount of sugar glue to secure the head and body together.

10 For the antennae, roll two small balls of yellow gum paste and cut two small pieces of wire, apply sugar glue to both ends and insert the wires into the head of the bee. Once inserted, gently add the balls to the end of the exposed wires and leave to dry.

11 Apply sugar glue to one long wire. Holding the bee gently by the body to secure it, insert the wire into the base of the bee as far as you can, ideally this will make it into the head. Apply sugar glue around the hole that the wire has made and thread a small yellow ball of gum paste onto the wire and up to the base of the bee. Once this yellow ball has been secured, pinch the end to a point down the wire for a yellow stinger.

IMPORTANT NOTE: Keep a record of the number of wires that are inserted into the cake; they must come out of the cake and be accounted for before you cut up the cake and serve it.

12 Allow the bee to dry. This time will vary dependent on the weather where you live.

13 Insert the bee into the cake top.

To finish the board, roll out whatever yellow gum paste or fondant you have left and cut out a few honeycomb shapes and place them sporadically across the black board like honeycomb pieces.

Busy Bee Cupcakes

Making the mini bee

Note: if your bee is laying flat on top of the cupcakes it is ideal but not necessary to make the mini bees from gum paste; fondant will work because the figures are completely supported. It is important to note that no inedible material is to be used in the cupcake toppers, as people are more likely to eat these!

1 Following the instructions above for making the bee—make a body by forming some black gum paste into an oval shape and pulling one end into a point to make a black stinger.

2 Add two small thin yellow gum paste stripes to the body.

3 Attach a round fondant head using sugar glue—the royal icing on the top of the cupcake will help keep this in place.

4 Attach two round yellow balls directly to the head with sugar glue for antennae.

5 Use a small round cutter to indent the smiling mouth.

6 Make the white and black parts of the eyes and attach with sugar glue.

7 Follow the steps above for the wings on a smaller scale. If you don't have cutters the right sizes simply use a wheel tool to cut out the shapes of the wings freehand.

Making the cupcakes

1 Preheat the oven to 120–130°C/250–265°F for mud cake.

2 Make the caramel mud cake batter (otherwise use the left over from your cake batter if you made enough) and line the cupcake tray with cupcake papers.

3 Place approximately one-tenth of the batter into the cupcake cases. Add one frozen cake ball to each cupcake case, pushing them firmly to the base of the liner so that they don't rise too much.

4 Part fill a piping (pastry) bag with the rest of the batter and pipe around the cake ball. The batter will not cover the cake ball. Smooth some batter over the cake ball to create a join between the batter and the top of the ball to guide the direction of the rising batter, which will also help to keep the frozen ball down.

5 Bake immediately for 25–35 minutes, or until skewer comes out clean. Leave to cool completely.

6 Once the cupcakes are cooked and have cooled completely, you can pipe royal icing or buttercream in a spiral motion using a 1M tip or similar. For these cupcakes I wanted a soft swirl that sat low, to make a bed for my mini bee so I used royal icing and beat it until it formed a peak that folded over slightly.

7 Add your pre made mini bee immediately before the royal icing sets. When the royal icing dried it secures the bee to your cupcake.

OPTION ALERT! Instead of icing you could simply apply a layer of ganache the cupcake tops and add a pentagon/hexagon shape to the top in yellow fondant. Add a mini bee to this, if you like. You could also put small amounts of real honeycomb on top of the ganache-topped cupcake. Or, make a large flower topper for the cupcake and add a small bee to the centre of the flower for maximum cuteness.

Good Luck

Shamrock For Good Luck

DIFFICULTY: //// /
TIME TO MAKE: ⧗⧗⧗⧗⧗

The four-leaf clover motif conjures up images of the Emerald Isle. It's a symbol of wishing someone all the luck in the world. I made this cake for a 'farewell, and good luck on your new adventure' cake for a work colleague who was moving onward and upward. This cake is quaint, simple and conveys obvious sentiment. It is easy to make, so the effort for reward return is high.

YOU WILL NEED

Loaf tin (pan) (10 x 24 x 7 cm/5 ½ x 9½ x 2¾ inch)
Round tin, 15 cm/6 inch diameter
1 batch chocolate mud cake batter or chocolate sponge
1 batch white chocolate mud cake batter (see page 35)
Gel food coloring: forest green
Kitchen knife
Shamrock/four-leaf clover cutter
Chocolate buttercream (see page 38)
Cake comb
Gum paste

Sugar glue
22-gauge wires (18 or 20 gauge will also work)
Display/cake board
Food flavoring of your choice for the shamrock (optional)
Set-up board (or baking paper on your bench)
Modelling tools: Dresden tool
Paint brush, rose spirit and edible gold dust, OR edible metallic gold paint with pen or brush
Print of the words 'good luck' in your preferred font in an appropriate size.

MAKING THE SHAMROCK CAKE

1 Preheat the oven to 120–130°C/250–265°F. Grease and flour or line the loaf tin.

2 For the four-leaf clover, make one batch of white chocolate mud cake and color it with forest green gel food coloring. You may also like to flavor the cake so that the green shamrock cake inside the chocolate cake brings additional flavor, consider mint or marshmallow food flavoring, or leave it plain.

3 Tip the cake batter into the prepared tin and bake until cooked through. Invert onto a wire rack and set aside to cool.

4 Once cooled, wrap the loaf in cling film (plastic wrap) and put it in the refrigerator. Once at refrigerator temperature, bring it out and, using a bread knife, cut the loaf into 2–2.5 cm/ 1 inch thick slices. If it has started to come to room temperature as you have cut it, put it back in the refrigerator—you need these slices as cold as possible without being frozen to get the best cut out.

5 Spray the clover cutter lightly with vegetable oil—this makes the cut cake run past the shape easier without causing crumbs or breaks. Position it over the slice and cut out a shape. Remove the excess cake from around the edges and gently use your finger to push out the shape a little at a time working your way around evenly so it doesn't crack.

Cut out as many clovers as you can just in case you need them for spares.

Hot tip! Frozen cake crumbs will keep well in the freezer so put aside all your spare clovers and scrap green colored cake that was cut away from the crust edge. You can crumb these left over pieces with your fingers into a bowl and make cake pops or pound cake with it.

6 Wrap each shape individually and put them in the freezer. We need the clover to be frozen so they don't over bake, dry out or liquefy when we re-bake them in the chocolate mud cake.

MAKING THE CAKE

1 Heat the oven to 120–130°C/250–265°F and grease and flour or line the round cake tin. Make one batch of chocolate mud cake. If you are filling a 15 cm/6 inch round tin you will have batter left over. Either make these into spare cupcakes and freeze until required or reduce the recipe by approximately one-third.

Alternatively you can use a lighter chocolate cake such as sponge for this step if you prefer, because the decoration is very lightweight, a dense cake is not required.

2 Place one-fifth of the batter into the loaf tin, use this as base to secure the clovers. I put my clover in upside down, so that the base of the cake in the tin becomes the cake top, this gives me a perfectly flat top, with clean sharp edges. Any doming I need to cut away is underneath the cake and therefore less work for me to straighten out and make smooth.

3 Whichever way you decide to put in your clover, place them no less than 2 cm/¾ inches apart. Push the clover into the batter but try not to connect them all the way to the base of the tin, we want them to ideally be hovering in the centre of the cake. Remember, even though this is a round tin, we are still lining these up in a straight row of clover for maximum effect when we cut the cake.

4 Once all of the clover is in place, disperse the rest of the batter into the cake tin between the clovers. Again, I highly recommend using a piping (pastry) bag for this—you really want to make sure there are no pockets of air where you have missed pushing batter between the clovers and make sure the batter is even. When piping I work in a loop, around the edges and zigzag through the clover and repeat. You may need to keep propping your clover up—don't worry, the more batter you put in the more they will stay in place.

5 If your clovers are visible after all of the batter is in the tin, use a dampened cranked handle spatula to smooth the batter over the top of the clovers. Use a kitchen knife or skewer markers if your oven will allow it, to mark where the clover so you know where to cut it for maximum impact.

6 Bake immediately for 45–60 minutes, or as per the time required for the recipe you used. When it comes time to check your batter, be sure to check the cake with skewer at three different points across the cake, to ensure you are accurately checking the cake batter not the clover parts!

7 Invert the cake onto a wire rack to cool and note where the markers for the end of the clover rows are and mark the inverted cake in the same places using a dab of plain (all-purpose) flour.

Once the cake is cooked and cooled completely, it is ready to decorate!

ICING AND DECORATING THE CAKE

1 Mix up the chocolate buttercream. Using a cranked handle spatula (or butter knife), liberally apply the buttercream over the surface of the cake. Use the spatula to shape the buttercream so it reflects the general, neat shape of the cake.

2 Next use a cake comb to create a pattern of interest around the cake. Hold the comb at a 45-degree angle to the cake, and touch the side of the cake with it, resist the temptation to push the comb in. Once you have the angle, slide the cake comb around the cake to create a pattern in the buttercream. Even pressure equals even lines. Refrigerate the buttercream until set.

3 For this design I have finished off with an over-sized gold satin ribbon. Gold and deep green are royal, opulent colors and the gold ties in the gold lettering of 'good luck' on the shamrock topper. The oversized nature of the ribbon on such a small cake is a statement piece—the cake is the present, the present is little in size and large in gesture and good will. Be very gentle when you add a ribbon and do so when the cake is as cold as possible to avoid staining and damage.

OPTION ALERT! The rustic look is really fashionable at the moment, if you want to achieve this you only need to slightly adjust the recipe. The chocolate buttercream recipe in this book is simply cocoa powder and milk added to standard buttercream—the milk is added

to counterbalance the drying nature of the cocoa powder. If you add cocoa powder without milk, the buttercream will be very stiff and a little dryer. This makes it harder to put on the cake so you may need to use a warm spatula/knife to create a little melting of the butter to smooth it out, let it come to room temperature and then cake-comb it—the dryness will drag the buttercream and give it a rough, rustic texture. (As a cake designer, I 'get' this look, but as a cake decorator it always feels like I have not finished the cake properly!) Conversely if you want it super smooth and shiny check out the chocolate Swiss meringue frosting, or Italian buttercream on page 40!

MAKING THE SHAMROCK TOPPER

It is a good idea to make this ahead of time so it has time to dry. Also, make more than one if you have the time and resources, just in case.

1 Roll out the green gum paste 25mm/¹⁄₂₅ inch thick and using the shamrock cutter, cut out the shape. Use a cranked handle spatula to move the shamrock to a non-stick surface such as baking paper, to dry. If there are ragged bits around the edges, use the edge of your finger and the heat of your hands to smooth it over, otherwise a wheel tool works well.

2 Cut the wires to length and dip one end of each in sugar glue, removing the excess glue with your fingers. Insert the end covered in sugar glue two-thirds of the way into the shamrock.

3 Place a print out of the words 'good luck' over the shamrock and secure in place—it is a small area so you can use your hand or sticky tape it to the bench. Using the flat side of a Dresden

tool, gently trace over the letters to emboss the font style onto the shamrock.

4 Once the words have been gently embossed I allow my shamrock to dry completely hard before applying the gold paint/paint pen. I do this because I find gum paste accepts paint a lot easier and it is neater to work on a hardened surface

5 Trace over the letters with the edible gold pen/paint brush. Place the topper on the cake by inserting the wires.

NOTE: It is important you know exactly how may wires have gone into the cake and count exactly that many when you remove the topper before cutting it up to serve.

OPTION ALERT! Making a small cake for someone but suspect there will be quite a few people attending? Make chocolate cupcakes and use the 233 grass tip to pipe green buttercream grass on top and adorn them with a small shamrock made from your left over green gum paste, you can team this up with shamrock cookies … and voila! Everyone is fed something sweet and the recipient gets to take their cake away with them!

happy birthd

Splat Graffiti and Cupcakes

DIFFICULTY: / / / / /

TIME TO MAKE: ⧗ ⧗ ⧗ ⧗ ⧗

Channel your inner child and prepare to have fun—this cake is a blast to make and decorate. My best advice is to cover all of surfaces and walls with baking paper or aluminium foil before you get carried away!

I have used a hemisphere tin here because the unexpected shape is a surprise in itself, however the cake and decorating techniques can be applied to any shape tin you have and it will be just as effective.

YOU WILL NEED

Hemisphere tin, 20 cm/8 inches round,
  10 cm/4 inches deep
7 piping bags, for the batter
7 teaspoons
Gel food coloring (see guide below)
Batter whitener
White gum paste
Black fondant
Ganache, 500 g/1 lb 2 oz
Royal icing
2 batches white chocolate mud cake batter
  (divided into 7 equal amounts, each a different
  color) (see page 34)

Ball tool
Letter cutters (optional)
Small blossom cutter
Sugar glue
Cupcake cases
Cupcake tray
Cake board
Cornflour (corn starch) and icing (confectioners')
  sugar, for dusting
Non-stick mat
Rolling pin
New cleaning cloth

COLORS

This cake is very bright. I used the same gel food color in the cake batter as I did in the royal icing and they are as follows. Note that I added batter whitener to the batter to reduce the yellow color base—this allows the batter to better take on the bright shades of gel food color.

ORANGE: I used the Americolor brand of orange because it is really bright. If you have an orange that is more sedate, add a few drops of electric orange to increase the vibrancy. Electric orange on its own tends to lack depth.

RED: I used standard red gel food coloring after I had already dyed the batter orange. Always color the base orange first, it reflects red really well, and you use less red dye and avoid moving through the pink scale to achieve a red with depth.

YELLOW: I used the Americolor brand of lemon yellow because it is really bright. If you have a yellow that is more sedate, add a few drops of electric yellow to increase the vibrancy. Like electric orange, electric yellow on its own tends to lack depth.

GREEN: I have used leaf green—bright, vibrant and a real depth to the color

BLUE: For this I have used electric blue with several drops of royal blue to ensure the blue color. Electric blue and sky blue are vulnerable to taking on a greenish tinge due to the off-white/cream colored base of cake batter or buttercream—as such a few drops of royal blue with its darker pigment added before the electric or sky color secures that blue base.

PINK: I have used electric pink, or as I like to call it, flamingo-pink. This color works for this cake and flamingos, however it is also useful to add vibrancy to all of the other pink colors (1–2 drops only) so a good one to have in your tool kit.

PURPLE: I have used a 50/50 mix of electric purple and Americolor regal purple. Electric purple on its own is a horrible shade but any other purple by itself is very muted. Like pink, electric purple is a must have for your tool kit as 1–2 drops added to other purple shades increase their vibrancy without changing their shade. With purple being the most unstable color on the spectrum when it comes to heat, light and time, this is a super handy color to have.

MAKING THE CAKE

The idea is for the cake inside to match the splattered bright coloring of the super impressive decoration on the outside, carrying the theme throughout the entire cake. I have used a mud cake recipe because it is dense enough to take the weight of the decoration without bowing at the sides and will stay fresh for longer which allows me more decorating time without worry.

1 Preheat the oven to 120–130°C/250–265°F. Grease and flour, or line, the hemisphere tin. Stabilise the hemisphere tin atop of a small round tin cake tin one-fifth filled with water. Ensure the water doesn't touch the tin. (If you don't have one, use an egg ring on a tray in the oven.)

2 Make up a batch of white chocolate mud cake and distribute the batter evenly between seven bowls. If you want to be exact, weigh the mixing bowl before and after you make the batter, subtract the bowl weight and divide the batter weight by 7. Place each bowl on the scales as you add batter to a specific weight amount. Otherwise, eyeball it. Add gel food color per the table above, to one bowl at a time and stir through with a teaspoon or small whisk. Repeat this for all seven colors, making sure they are mixed thoroughly.

3 Fill seven piping bags with the seven different colored cake batters and clip off the end of each with a piping bag clip or several clothes pegs. Have two or three high-sided deep bowls handy so that you can rest the larger end of the piping bags into them without losing batter when you need to swap bags.

4 Cut the ends off the piping bags, small end up so you don't lose any batter! Start piping

round bulbs of batter into the hemisphere tin. When you have done one layer, try and put different colored batter on top of the base later and so on, to ensure an even distribution of the colors. This part gets really fun, keep filling until you reach about a thumbs width from the top of the tin.

TROUBLESHOOT! Help my batter is too runny and the blobs are not holding their shape! If this happens, place your batter in the fridge for a while until the batter becomes cold. This will help the batter to stay in shape—it will spread a little but we don't want it to spread too much before it goes in the oven.

5 Bake for 60–75 minutes, for the mud cake, or until a skewer, when inserted in the centre, comes out clean. Test your cake 10 minutes before the timer is due to go off and get an idea of where it is up to, adjust your timing from there. Depending on your oven, the type of chocolate used and the size of your hemisphere tin (or tin of your choice) your cooking time may vary. When it is cooked, invert the cake onto a wire rack (rounded side up) and allow it to cool.

COVERING THE CAKE

1 First we need to ganache the cake. If you have gone for a traditional round or square shaped tin, follow the instructions on page 41. I find that the hemisphere tin gives me a perfect curve, ganaching it like a usual cake actually makes it less smooth, so for a perfectly smooth hemisphere I heat my ganache until it is pumpkin soup consistency and pour it over the cake— the ganache is thin enough to coat the cake and take on the cake's shape rather than help to shape the cake. This way I get to cover and moisture seal my cake with yummy chocolate, give the fondant something to stick to and still keep my perfectly smooth curve. Allow the ganache to set before moving into step 2.

2 Roll out your black fondant onto a non stick, dusted surface. Lay it over your hemisphere cake and using your hands smooth it down over the cake immediately. Tuck it in at the bottom edges and cut away the excess with your fondant or kitchen knife. If this excess doesn't have any ganache or moisture on it, you can use it again. Place the cake onto the display board, securing it in place with a small amount of ganache underneath and let this layer of fondant set a little (it will form a crust that is firmer to a light touch than freshly applied fondant—this gives the royal icing something more solid to stick to.

3 Follow the instructions in the How To section to cut out letters. Use sugar glue or royal icing to secure the letters to your board. Note: I have used a black display board, you can simply cover a standard display board with black fondant—see page 18.

OPTION ALERT! I have added the words happy birthday in small, simple lower case font for maximum impact. The other option for this style of cake is to write the birthday person's name in graffiti-style lettering on the board—you can do this with royal icing, a fondant/gum paste cut out or if you are like me and can't draw and have minimal time you can print out the name or message on black paper and stick it to the black board with royal icing.

MAKING A SPLAT! HOW TO DECORATE THE CAKE

1 For this cake I made the equivalent of 3 batches of royal icing from the recipe section. Make the icing and divide it into seven bowls, then using a teaspoon for each bowl mix the colors through each portion of royal icing.

IMPORTANT NOTE! Royal icing dries quickly. You need to take steps to avoid this because there will be some time between coloring and finishing the cake. I like to cut a new cleaning cloth slightly larger than my bowl top, I then wet and wring out the cloth so it is adequately damp and lay it across the top of my royal icing—this retains moisture and prevents the air from drying it out. Take caution not to use too much water though, as water added to the mix will reduce its consistency and therefore its ability to hold shape upon impact.

2 Before you begin applying the graffiti splats you need to cover your work area. You will be

flicking royal icing which dries like cement—you don't want to be trying to remove that from your kitchen walls! If you have already attached your cake to the display board, use foil around and slightly under the cake so you cover the display board. Tape up baking paper to the wall or window behind the cake also.

3 Stand about 30–60 cm/11–23 inches away from your cake, take about ¾ of a teaspoon full of your first color. With the rounded, full part of the spoon facing away from you, hold the spoon in one hand, place the index finger of your free hand onto the top point of the teaspoon, pull the top point of the teaspoon back towards you, keeping your hand firm (like you are trying to physically bend the spoon and then let your index finger go) this should sling shot the royal icing toward the cake. Upon impact the round bulb of royal icing will splat on the cake and even drip down a little giving the effect in the picture. Repeat this with your first color at even points over the cake—this is setting up your guide points. Remember you have SIX more colors to go so don't get carried away and apply too much.

Work through your colors. I tend to do about six sling shots of each color and then move on and keep repeating until my cake is evenly covered.

4 Once you are happy with your cake, allow the air to set the royal icing so it becomes dry and hard. Once is has dried you can remove the protective baking paper and aluminium foil and throw it away!

Note: it's a good idea to get your bowls and spoons in hot water as soon as you are finished with them to avoid having to scrape off dry hard royal icing!

Why all the Royal fuss? If Royal icing sets so hard, why do I use it? Why not use gel or buttercream? I use royal icing because it sets. It is a stiff consistency and sticky when I splat it onto the cake so it holds its shape and sticks there. Because air at room temperature dries it, I don't need to worry about it melting if the temperature rises or being smudged. The butter in buttercream has a low melting point and is prone to becoming soft, which can lead to it sliding down the cake. Also buttercream by nature is heavy so layers of it on top of each other without the consistency of royal icing can cause it to slide down the cake too, ruining the overall look. As for gel, it never sets and is very liquid which I find does not reflect color well when applied to a dark surface.

OPTION ALERT! If you don't want to use royal icing, simply color white chocolate and follow the exact same steps. Just be sure to use an oil-based food color (usually comes in powder form) as the water base of gel food color doesn't emulsify well into the oil base of chocolate.

MAKING THE CUPCAKES

1 Preheat oven to 120°C/250°F for mud cake. Line the cupcake tray with cupcake cases.

2 Use the cake batter leftover from making the main cake to fill the cupcake cases. Pipe a blob of each color into the cupcake case. Continue again until the cupcake cases are full to one finger-width lower than the top of the paper cases, to allow for rise.

3 Bake for 25–35 minutes for the mud cake, or until skewer comes out clean.

DECORATING THE CUPCAKES

1 Apply a layer of ganache or buttercream the top of the cupcake, to keep it moist on top and to gives the fondant something to stick to.

2 Roll out the black fondant about 4 mm/0.16 inch thick. Use a circle cutter that is big enough to fit over your entire cupcake. This allows for depth as well as diameter. If you don't have big circle cutters you can use an egg ring, they work for smaller cupcakes when you're caught out. Using the right sized circle cutter, cut out your black fondant topper and lay it over the top of you cupcake. Using clean dry hands smooth out the topper. You may also use an acetate square if you have it, this will give a nice shiny smooth finish. Smooth down the sides so they cover and tuck under the edges of the cupcake. Do this for all of the cupcakes.

3 Roll out the white gum paste and using a small blossom cutter, cut out as many flowers as you need for your cupcakes. If your gum paste is sticky, make sure the non-stick surface you use is dusted with cornflour. You may need to dust your cutter with cornflour too. When you cut out the flower, rub the cutter back and forth on the board/mat to ensure the flower is cleanly cut,

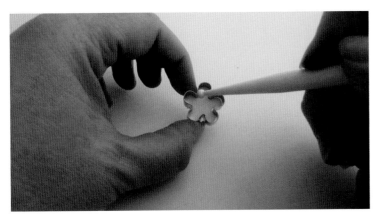
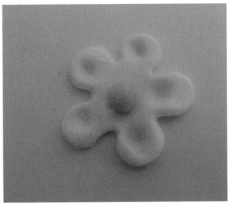

remove the cutter from the rolled out gum paste and on another non-stick surface, use the small end of your ball tool in the top part of each petal of the flower to push it out of the cutter. This will cause a dimple in each petal to create interest and texture.

4 Color a smaller amount of gum paste in a contrasting tone and make little balls for the flower centres, attaching them with sugar glue. Stick the flowers to the tops of the cupcakes using sugar glue.

OPTION ALERT! These do not need to be flowers, a really good alternative is brightly colored stars, but don't be limited by these two choices—make it personalised to the recipient with little skateboards or whatever their favorite thing is at the time.

The Fairy Door

DIFFICULTY: ∕ ∕ ∕ ∕ ∕

TIME TO MAKE: ⧗ ⧗ ⧗ ⧗ ⧗

Incredibly popular at the moment is the idea of a little wooden fairy door attached to your skirting boards 'to allow fairies access to your home' and delight little girls everywhere with the all of the stories you can possibly conjure up about fairies. I just love the idea of this and so does my little cousin Hallie and so drawing inspiration from this I created a fairy door cake—when you open the door to the fairy house cake—out pops all of her favorite lollies! Surprise and excitement awaits.

You can make a fairy out of gum paste, there are so many free tutorials online for this and the creative work is just stunning. The other option, which I have taken, is to use a fairy doll so that it becomes part of the present that she can keep and continue to play with long after the birthday cake has been eaten.

YOU WILL NEED

Hemisphere tin 20 cm/8 inch and 10 cm/4 inch deep (or oven safe soup bowl)

1 batch white chocolate mud cake or sponge cake (see page 35)

Food flavouring (I used strawberry and cotton candy)

Buttercream (see page 38)

Gel food coloring (rose pink, avocado green, forest green, bush green, mint and leaf green)

CMC powder and fondant or gum paste

Rose leaf cutter

Leaf veiner

Sugar glue

Wood grain embosser (or similar)

Edible gold paint

Black edible pen

Lollies, for the centre of the cake

Cornflour (corn starch) and icing (confectioners') sugar, for dusting

Fairy toy for the cake (optional)

MAKING THE CAKE

1 Preheat the oven to 120–130°C/250–265°F for mud cake, or 180°C/350°F for sponge cake batter. If you are using packet mix cakes, follow the instructions on the packet for temperature but be flexible with your cooking time, this tin is a different shape and may take a little longer than a standard round tin.

2 Grease and flour, or line, the hemisphere tin. Stabilise the hemisphere tin atop of a small round tin cake tin one-fifth filled with water. Ensure the water doesn't touch the tin. (If you don't have one, use an egg ring on a tray in the oven).

3 Make the cake batter, adding your color and flavour. I have dyed the cake rose pink to provide a feminine contrast to the muted green of the leaves. I also added strawberry and cotton candy food flavouring to give the dense mud cake a light, sweet, berry flavour.

TIP: You may notice in the step-by-step photographs that this cake domed slightly on the top and I have not cut this away. This was because the top of my cake was nice and moist when I took it out of the oven and I wanted to use it to my advantage—it gives me height and structural integrity, the base was covered in buttercream to retain moisture and any gaps are filled with buttercream and covered by my leaves! When the cake is cut this will not be very noticeable and provides slightly larger slices of cake.

4 Bake for 60–75 minutes for the mud cake, or 30–40 minutes for a sponge cake, or until a skewer, when inserted in the centre, comes out clean. Be sure to test your cake 10 minutes

before the timer is due to go off and reassess and adjust your timing from there. Turn out onto a wire rack and leave to cool.

5 Wrap the cake in cling film (plastic wrap) and put it in the refrigerator until cold. Cake carving is always easier with a cold cake.

6 Once cold, take the cake out and using a sharp knife, cut away the slice of cake that will be the door. My door was approximately 2 cm/¾ inch thick. Wrap this piece and put in the refrigerator.

7 Using a teaspoon, hollow out the centre of the cake as deep as the middle of the dome, or further, if you prefer. Note: Mud cake is denser and therefore more structurally stable than sponge cake and as such will cope better with a deeper/larger hole. Remember you will be adding decoration to the top of the cake so if you have opted for a sponge recipe—keep the hole for lollies more conservative in size.

8 Once you are happy with the depth and size of the hole, fill the cavity with lollies. I do this by holding the cake in one hand and filling it, gently, with the other. Be gentle and resist the temptation to over fill the cake, especially a sponge as it may crack.

TROUBLESHOOT: I was too rough with my cake and it cracked. What do I do? This depends on the size and location of the crack and whether or not you have lollies in it yet. The top of the cake coming off or breaks around the door are harder to fix. First things first, I would put both pieces on the display board and using buttercream, stick the two pieces back together. Refrigerate the cake until set, then cover it completely in buttercream and put it back in the refrigerator. If that works you may have saved the day. If the problem is with the door area, depending on the size of your cake, you can always start carving again on the other side; assess the damage and don't panic.

OPTION ALERT! I prefer buttercream for this one because the leaves are small individual pieces that don't require the sturdiness of ganache to secure them in place. You can use ganache if you prefer it but be careful not to seal the replaced cake wedge in place. If you do, recut the cake wedge through the ganache before you apply the gum paste door front.

10 Secure the cake to the display board using buttercream and replace the door into the slot it was cut from. Secure it with a small amount of buttercream on the outside of the cake around the cut marks. Don't use too much—you don't want resistance when you open the fairy door!

MAKING THE FAIRY DOOR

1 This one has to be made ahead of time so it can dry hard and hold its shape.

2 Make up some gum paste by adding 1 teaspoon of CMC powder to 100 g/3½ oz of fondant: we are using this ratio because we need the door to set quite firm to avoid the risk of breaking. Color up the gum paste as required. I used the same rose pink that I used in the cake batter to carry the theme throughout the design.

3 Roll out the gum paste to 25mm/¹⁄₁₀ inch, and cut out the shape of the door—make this slightly larger than the door piece you cut from the cake.

4 Using a wood grain embossing tool press into the gum paste door. Depending on the weather and your gum paste, you may need to dust the embosser with cornflour to avoiding stickiness.

5 Roll out the gum paste for the lintel above the door. Cut a long rectangle and using a cranked handle spatula, transfer it to cornflour-dusted surface and allow it to dry with the door.

6 If you are going to paint the lintel, do so when it is dry. I used edible gold metallic paint. Allow this paint to dry before using an edible ink pen (I used black) write 'Fairy Door' on the lintel.

OPTION ALERT! Personalise the name plate above the door to include the recipient's name or the fairy name in their favorite story.

7 Attach the lintel to the top of the door with sugar glue and allow it to dry.

8 To make the doorknob, roll a small amount of gum paste into a ball and lightly squash it with your index finger so it is slightly flat on both sides but still rounded. Allow to dry and paint it to match the lintel. When the paint is dry, secure it to the fairy door with sugar glue.

TROUBLESHOOT: My lintel and doorknob won't stick to the door with sugar glue! If this happens, make up a small amount of royal icing and use that.

MAKING THE LEAVES

I suggest making the leaves ahead of time as well, as these are the most time consuming element to this cake design.

1 Add 2 teaspoons of CMC powder to 500 g/1 lb 2 oz of fondant; we want the leaves to be soft to bite into when the cake is eaten but slightly stiffer than standard fondant so they hold their shape and texture.

2 Color the gum paste as required. I have used a combination of five different greens to give the impression of leaves on the forest floor at various stages of decomposition. If you don't want to go that far, buy one dark green color and make a light, medium and dark shade of the one green, giving at least 3 different shades will create depth and interest to the design.

OPTION ALERT! Make the leaves brown green and orange and even use a maple leaf cutter for a real Autumn feel.

3 Roll out the gum paste to 25mm/¹⁄₁₀ inch thick and using a rose leaf cutter, cut out the leaf shapes. Cut 5–10 at a time and emboss with the veiner before they start to dray to avoid cracks and wrinkles.

4 Place the leaf shape onto/into the cornflour-dusted leaf veiner and press down lightly to emboss the leaf texture. Remove it from the veiner and place it onto a dusted flat surface to dry a little. Make as many leaves as you can. If you are making these well in advance, set the leaves aside in covered trays to dry but not completely dry out.

HELPFUL HINT: You need to make a lot of leaves to cover a cake. Get a head start a week or more in advance and cut some out each night while you watch TV.

DECORATING THE CAKE

1 Make and color one batch of buttercream. Apply a layer over the cake and the display board. I have used a heart shaped cake board because it creates interest and gives me space at the front of the fairy house to apply leaves to the ground as well, which carries the 'house under the hill on the forest floor' theme throughout the design. If you have time and resources you can make a neat little path to the fairy's door out of gum paste, color it a swirly brown or grey to make it look like rock paving.

2 Using a small amount of melted chocolate on the cake wedge, secure the door in place first, that way you can position leaves over and around the joins of the door with the cake to give it complete look and hide your work.

3 After securing leaves to the section around and above the door, work across the cake from there, evenly distributing each color.

4 Place or secure you fairy topper to the cake if you choose to have one and you are done!

East Meets West
Battenberg-Style
Celebration Cake

DIFFICULTY: / / / / /

TIME TO MAKE: ⧗⧗⧗⧗⧗

Reportedly designed in the late 1800s for the wedding of an English princess to a German prince of Battenberg, the cake was designed in the German style to represent the bringing together of two people, two cultures and the unity of both. The traditional Battenberg cake is a sponge in pink and white and is wrapped plainly in a thin sheet of marzipan.

It remains a beautiful celebration cake respectfully representing the union of two cultures; with this in mind I have helped a few DIY brides design a few modern variations of the Battenberg for their wedding cakes, my favorite of which has to be the Anglo-Chinese wedding. Red and gold are both auspicious colors in the Chinese culture and the symbolism of the Battenberg style cake makes it the perfect sentimental choice for an Anglo-Chinese wedding. The red and gold individual cakes in this design, finished with a small gold bow are so delicate. Take heed, although these individual cakes are a great touch for a wedding dessert they are small and fiddly and take a long time to construct, so consider your time plan and number of guests before committing to making them yourself!

YOU WILL NEED

Square cake tin; size will depend on how many you need to make (I used an 18 cm/7 inch square, 7.5 cm/3 inch deep cake tin)

2 batches white chocolate mud cake batter (see page 35)

Gel food color: egg yellow, gold, orange and red

Red fondant

CMC powder, to turn the fondant into gum paste

Silicon mould, for a bow (optional)

Wheel tool cutter

Kitchen knife

Rolling pin

Non-stick mat

Cornflour (corn starch) and icing (confectioners') sugar, for dusting

White chocolate ganache

Sugar glue

MAKING THE CAKE

1 Preheat the oven to 120–130°C/250–265°F for mud cake. Grease the square tin and dust it with flour, or line the tin with baking paper.

2 Make up the white chocolate mud cake, or your own favorite recipe or packet mix. Be sure to add your gel food color early and ensure it has been emulsified into the cake batter mix. When making red, I dye the batter orange first. To make the gold batter, add the gold and egg yellow food color at a 1:1 ratio.

NOTE: If you make an 18 cm/7 inch square tin you will have batter left over; either make these into spare cupcakes to freeze for lunch boxes or reduce the recipe by one-quarter.

3 Bake immediately for 45–60 minutes or according to the recipe you used. Insert a skewer into the cake to test if it is cooked through—when it comes out clean it is ready.

4 Allow the cake to cool to room temperature then wrap it in cling film (plastic wrapl) and put it in the refrigerator.

5 Repeat steps 1–4 to make a second cake in the alternate color.

CUTTING THE CAKES

We need to cut the cakes into long, thin, equalled sized rectangles to be stacked on top of each other. This is not as easy as it looks; if you are slightly out in your measurements you will notice it when you put the cakes together.

1 Trim the square cakes so that all of the brown crusts on the top, bottom and sides have been removed.

2 Next we need to cut the Battenberg rectangles out. There are many ways to do this (check it out online). I cut my square cake into equal widths creating long square-ended rectangles. I then cut these rectangles in half making them shorter. Cut each rectangle into four quarters. Repeat for the second color cake.

3 Stack the cakes Battenberg style. Trim to make sure that all cakes are level.

4 With the perfect rectangles, you can now 'glue' the cakes together using white chocolate ganache at a thick soupy consistency. I have chosen white chocolate for this because it matches and complements the chocolate of the mud cake and the white color disappears from sight taking on the tonal value of the darker cake.

5 Coat the outside of cake in peanut butter consistency ganache, following the techniques outlined in the How To section to ensure a smooth, square-edged finish on the cake. Refrigerate to set.

6 Remove the cakes from the refrigerator and allow them to come close to room temperature.

Roll out the red fondant on a non-stick surface. Cut it to the same length as the Battenberg and ensure that one side is cut very straight.

7 Apply ganache to the straight edge of the fondant to act as glue. Align the long edge of the cake with the straight edge of fondant and smooth into place. Picking up the other side of the fondant, wrap it up and over the cake, smoothing it into place as you go to avoid air pockets. Both ends should be free, uncovered and aligned with the red fondant.

Once the fondant is in place, cut away any excess and either pinch the edges of fondant together, or seal them in place hiding the seam line on the underside of the cake.

TROUBLESHOOT

If you're fondant is too long and flops over the end of the Battenberg, don't fret! Simply take a small, sharp pair of embroidery scissors and gently trim the excess the fondant away using the cake as a guide. If you have fallen short you can try and smooth the fondant toward the short edge relying on its elasticity and stretching properties to get it to the edge (Note: if you do this it will look thinner in some places than others when you look closely at it).

MAKING THE BOW

1 Depending on budget and time, you could tie a real, satin ribbon around these cakes making them little presents. Allow the ganache and fondant to set a little before you do this.

2 To make edible bows, measure the width of the top of the cake and the height of both sides, add these three numbers together and this is the length of gum paste you will need to cut into ribbon strips.

3 Cut the edible ribbon and apply sugar glue to the back of it before securing it in place over the cake.

4 For this bow I used a silicon mould because it is so quick and super effective. Dust the mould first with cornflour and push a small ball of gum paste into the silicon mould. Bend the mould backwards and gently coax out the bow. Repeat to make as many bows as you need.

5 To paint the ribbon on the bow gold, use either edible metallic gold paint, or mix gold edible dust and rose spirit (see page 27).

Paint the bow separately and when both are dry, secure the bow in place with sugar glue.

Battenberg-Style Christmas

DIFFICULTY: / / / / /

TIME TO MAKE: ⏳⏳⏳⏳⏳

Try this modern Christmas twist on the old favourite Battenberg design. White chocolate mud cakes colored red and green put together and smothered in white chocolate ganache and topped with festive little sugar holly leaves. Simple, effective and made into single portions for plating up dessert.

VARIATION

White chocolate mud cake, like vanilla and butter sponge cakes take on other flavors really well. Why not try raspberry and cheesecake flavors, or strawberry and marshmallow. Try traditional rum and raisin or honeycomb and butterscotch. You can even serve it up with ice cream to match the flavor.

YOU WILL NEED

Square cake tin (pan) (I used an 18 cm/7 inch, 7.5 cm/3 inch deep tin)

2 batches white chocolate mud cake batter (see page 35)

Gel food color, to color the batter (I used orange as a base color and added red to achieve a deep red color, and forest green)

CMC powder, to turn fondant into gum paste

Holly leaf cutters or silicon mould

Kitchen knife

White chocolate ganache

Sugar glue

MAKING THE CAKE

1 Preheat the oven to 120–130°C/250–265°F for mud cake. Grease the tin and dust with flour, or line with baking paper.

2 Make up the white chocolate mud cake, or your own favourite recipe or packet mix. Be sure to add your gel food color early and ensure it has been emulsified into the cake batter mix.

NOTE: If you make an 18 cm/7 inch square tin you will have batter left over. Either make these into spare cupcakes to freeze for lunch boxes or reduce the recipe by approximately one-quarter.

3 Bake immediately for 45–60 minutes, or according to the time required for your recipe. Test to ensure the cake is baked through by inserting a skewer into the centre of the cake. If the skewer comes out clean, the cake is ready.

4 Allow to cool to room temperature, then wrap in cling film (plastic wrap) and refrigerate until cold.

5 Make a second cake.

NOTE: Make these cakes in advance and freeze them.

CUTTING THE CAKE

1 Trim the square cakes so that all of the brown crusts are removed. Cut the cakes into long, thin, equally size rectangles. This is not as easy as it looks; if you are slightly out in your measurements you will notice it when you put the cakes together.

2 Now I have shorter square-ended rectangles of equal width, I cut all of these into four quarters.

3 Stack the cakes into a Battenberg design. Trim the paired up lengths to make sure there is no excess sticking out.

4 Using white chocolate ganache 'glue' the cakes together. Refrigerate to set. Coat the outside of the cakes in ganache, following the techniques outlined on page 41. Refrigerate to set.

5 Remove the cakes from the refrigerator and allow them to come close to room temperature.

MAKING THE HOLLY

1 To make edible holly, add CMC powder to the green and red fondants or color some gum paste.

2 If you are using a cutter, roll out the gum paste and cut out holly leaves. These should stick to the ganache, if they do not you can use a small amount of sugar glue to secure them.

3 If you are using a silicon mould, dust it inside with cornflour. Using a small amount of green gum paste, push a small amount of it into the silicon mould, bend the mould backwards and gently coax out the leaves. Repeat these steps for as many leaves as you need. Secure the leaves to the cakes.

4 To make the holly berries, roll three little red balls per cake and secure them onto the joining point of the holly leaves with sugar glue.

High Tea Cupcakes

DIFFICULTY: 〰️〰️〰️〰️〰️

TIME TO MAKE: ⏳⏳⏳⏳⏳

Want to make cupcakes for an afternoon tea but feel they have been over-done and a bit blah? Want to jazz them up and make them a bit different? Me too. Try these!

These are caramel mud cake cupcakes; the centres have been hollowed out with an apple corer and filled with yummy, creamy chocolate ganache of different flavors and the tops detailed with fine gold stencilling. Bring out the good china, it's time to have afternoon tea like ladies!

HOT TIP

When I need my mud cake cupcakes to rise with a flat top to maximise decorating space, I add an extra 30 seconds of mixing to the batter and like my sponge cake trick, I let the batter sit in the cases, on my bench for 15 minutes before putting them into the oven. This allows time for the air to leave and the batter to settle, which is your best chance of getting a flat top cupcake

YOU WILL NEED

1 batch mud cake batter (see page 34)

White chocolate ganache (see page 41)

Food flavoring (I have used salted caramel, butterscotch and coffee)

Apple corer

Black fondant

Circle cutter

Cupcake stencils

Edible gold paint, or dust and rose spirit

Cupcake cases

Cupcake tray

Piping bag

Round piping tip/nozzle (medium sized, must be smaller than the apple corer)

Crank handled spatula

MAKING THE CUPCAKES

1 Preheat the oven to 120–130°C/250–265°F for mud cake batter.

2 Line a cupcake tray with cupcake cases. Fill three-quarters full with batter.

3 Bake for 25–35 minutes for the mud cake, or until a skewer comes out clean when inserted into the centre. Keep an eye on your cupcakes and be flexible with the time, depending on your oven, the type of chocolate you used or a different recipe—the cooking time may vary.

4 Allow to cool, then refrigerate until cold.

5 Using an apple corer, remove the centre of each cupcake.

6 Divide the white chocolate ganache evenly between three bowls. Before flavoring ganache I like to warm it up so it becomes a little closer to soup consistency, the heat and the liquidity help the flavor to disperse through the ganache easily and more evenly.

You can do this ahead of time because you need this ganache to be at normal consistency when you pipe it into the cupcakes.

7 To add the color and flavor to your ganache, measure it out as required and then stir with a teaspoon, you can use a whisk however this will add more air to the ganache and may cause air pockets in your piping later.

8 Flavor the color ganache as desired and allow it too cool back to a peanut butter consistency, then part fill a piping bag with one ganache flavor. Pipe the ganache into the core of the cupcake by inserting the tip as far as you can without putting pressure on the top of the

cupcake. Once it is full, apply a small amount of ganache to the top of the cupcake and smooth it over the top evenly with a crank handled spatula (or knife).

DECORATING THE CUPCAKES

1 Roll out the black fondant about 4 mm/0.16 inch thick. Use a circle cutter that is big enough to fit over your entire cupcake. This allows for depth as well as diameter. If you don't have big circle cutters you can use an egg ring; they work for smaller cupcakes when you're caught out. Using the right sized circle cutter, cut out your black fondant topper and lay it over the top of you cupcake. Using clean dry hands smooth out the topper. You may also use an acetate square if you have it, this will give a nice shiny smooth finish. Smooth down the sides so they cover and tuck under the edges of the cupcake. Do this for all of the cupcakes.

2 Prepare the gold paint (For dust and rose spirit usages see page 27).

3 Place the first stencil over the cupcake and hold in place with your hand. Paint over the stencil with the gold paint on a paintbrush with your other hand. Try and do this with as few strokes as possible and always work in just one direction. Gently remove the stencil, either by picking it directly up or peeling it back slowly. Repeat for each cupcake, washing/cleaning the back of the stencil between each use if required.

Party Cupcakes

DIFFICULTY: /////
TIME TO MAKE: ⏳⏳⏳⏳⏳

Had a request for 'just cupcakes'? Make party-worthy and fun cupcakes with this twist on the classic cupcake—birthday message included! These are chocolate mud cake cupcakes; the centres have been hollowed out with an apple corer and replaced with creamy white chocolate ganache that has been flavored in unexpected ways!

Take this idea a step further by mixing small lolly pieces into the ganache when you flavor and color it to give it an extra zing! Popping candy, chocolate rocks and the humble 100s&1000s make a huge impact in color, flavor, texture and surprise!

YOU WILL NEED

1 batch mud cake batter (see page 34)
White chocolate ganache
Food flavoring of your choice (I used tutti-fruitti, bubblegum, Strawberry, Nutella and Peanut butter)
White fondant (or colored fondant),
Gel food color: orange, red, royal blue, forest green, lemon yellow, regal purple

Circle cutter
Blossom cutter
Bunting mould OR triangle cutters
Edible black ink pen
Cupcake cases
Cupcake tray
Piping bag
Round piping tip/nozzle, medium

MAKING THE CUPCAKES

1 Preheat the oven to 120–130°C/250–265°F. Line the cupcake tray with cupcake cases.

2 Three-quarters fill the cupcake cases with batter.

HOT TIP: See page 15 for how to get flat top cupcakes

3 Bake for 25–35 minutes or until a skewer, when inserted into the centre, comes out clean. Keep an eye on them and be flexible with your baking times.

4 Turn out onto a wire rack to cool, then refrigerate until cold.

5 Using an apple corer, remove the centre of each cupcake.

6 Warm the white chocolate ganache to the consistency of soup, then divide it evenly into separate bowls. Add a different color and flavor to each bowl and mix it through with a teaspoon. Do this ahead of time because the ganache needs to cool back to a peanut butter type consistency before you pipe it into the cupcakes.

NOTE: if you are adding lolly pieces to each flavor, add them at this step.

7 Pipe the ganache into the core of the cupcake by inserting the tip as far as you can without putting pressure on the top of the cupcake. Once it is full, apply a small amount of ganache to the top of the cupcake and smooth it over the top evenly with a cranked handle spatula (or knife).

DECORATING THE CUPCAKES

1 Roll out the colored fondant about 4 mm/0.16 inches thick. Use a circle cutter that is big enough to fit over your entire cupcake. This allows for depth as well as diameter. If you don't have big circle cutters you can use an egg ring, they work for smaller cupcakes when you're caught out. Using the right sized circle cutter, cut out your fondant topper and lay it over the top of you cupcake. Using clean dry hands smooth out the topper. You may also use an acetate square if you have it, this will give a nice shiny smooth finish. Smooth down the sides so they cover and tuck under the edges of the cupcake. Do this for all of the cupcakes.

2 Using leftover colored fondant, roll out each in turn and cut out blossoms. Arrange on the top of each cupcake, contrasting the colors.

3 To make bunting, if you are using a silicon mould, dust it with cornflour and place a small ball of white fondant into the bunting mould, smoothing it out with your fingers. Use a rolling pin cautiously to flatten the back but beware that some moulds cause the fondant to stick.

Alternatively, use a triangle cutter to roll out the fondant thinly, cut out the desired number of triangles and use a Dresden tool to emboss the stitching detail by hand.

4 Using your edible black-ink pen, carefully trace over the embossed stitching and lettering on the bunting. If you have not used a mould you may write the letters freehand.

Repeat for each cupcake, keep the filling a secret and enjoy the party-goer's surprise!

Adult Jelly Shot Cupcakes

DIFFICULTY: / / / / /

TIME TO MAKE: ⏳⏳⏳⏳⏳

Having a party for adults and want all the fun of kids' cupcakes with an adult party twist? Jelly shot sponge cupcakes are easy to make and delicious to eat.

OPTION ALERT! Try soaking gummy lollies (gummy bears) in alcohol and then mixing them in with the jelly for an extra alcohol kick!

IMPORTANT NOTE

Take care in calculating how much alcohol ends up in each cupcake, this can be hard to gauge, especially if you add alcohol soaked lolly pieces to your jelly but it is very important, especially for the designated drivers.

YOU WILL NEED

1 batch sponge cake batter

Frosting of your choice (I used: buttercream with
   chocolate page 38)

1 pack of jelly crystals

200 ml/7 fl oz alcohol of your choice

Cupcake cases

Cupcake tray

Apple corer

Piping bag

Round piping tip, medium

MAKING THE JELLY

I simply used my favourite packet jelly mix for this recipe. Most packet mixes will call for boiling water to dissolve the gelatine crystals, then once it starts to cool, the addition of cool/cold water before being put in the refrigerator to set. Instead of the cool water component I simply add alcohol instead. If you are making your jelly from scratch you can simply follow this step at the point you add the cold liquid component. Easy.

MAKING THE CUPCAKES

1 Preheat the oven to 180°C/350°F for a sponge cake batter. I use vanilla/white cake batter because it contrasts better with the color of the jelly for a more impressive finish. Line the cupcake tray with cupcake cases.

2 Fill the cupcake cases three-quarters full with batter and bake for 20 minutes, or until cooked through. Your oven, the recipe and the size of your cupcake cases means the cooking time may vary. The cakes are ready when a skewer comes out clean.

3 Allow to cool, then refrigerate to chill, as it is always easier to cut a cold cake—especially a sponge which is very crumbly by nature.

4 Using an apple corer, core out the centre of the cupcake. Carefully remove the cored piece of cake and set it aside on a plate, we will need this again later. Repeat this for all of the cupcakes.

5 Using a spoon, scoop your jelly into a piping bag with a rounded tip in it. I don't break up the jelly too much before putting it into the piping bag because it is a soft product that will break

down as I pipe it into the cake, I try and keep the break down to a minimum to reduce the chances of it dissolving into the cake, which will still taste great but lack the same texture, color and effect. Fill the core with jelly by inserting the tip as far as you can without putting pressure on the top of the cupcake and piping it in. Stop before the jelly protrudes from the top.

6 After the jelly has been piped, cut a small piece-off of the top of the core you removed earlier and stick it back into the cupcake to seal the jelly and protect it from the frosting.

Jelly starts to dissolve at room temperature so you want to get the cakes back into the refrigerator as soon as you can and bring them out again when you are ready to serve them for the best effect.

DECORATING THE CUPCAKES

I always consider the need for refrigeration when choosing your frosting options: royal icing will go very hard and fondant will be wet and waxy so neither of these are good choices for this sort of cupcake. Consider a dusting of icing sugar to allow the cake and jelly flavors dominate, or just a small cover of thin icing/buttercream. If you want to go big, like I have here with the purple swirl, make the buttercream recipe on page 38 with the chocolate option and color it with regal purple. You can even add 5-15ml of a flavored liquor (if it goes too runny add more icing sugar as needed) and pipe it on with a 1M piping tip/nozzle or similar.

Rum Baubles

DIFFICULTY: ✎✎✎✎✎

TIME TO MAKE: ⧖⧖⧖⧖⧖

Surprise the adult family members this Christmas with rum balls disguised as edible baubles—pretty enough to be seen on the tree!

This is where fresh-frozen cake left over from other projects comes in handy, use that or cake crumb from other projects for this recipe if you can.

OPTION ALERT

For an extra rum-kick, soak the raisins in rum before adding them to the mixture.

You could dip half of the bauble in cake confetti and make gold sparkle pattern on red and green baubles, or leave off the confetti entirely and go for the smooth bauble look, both patterned and completely gold. Why not try silver?

YOU WILL NEED

Makes: 12 rum balls

Half of a 15 cm/6 inch round chocolate mud cake, crumbed

½–⅔ cup/ 125 g of chocolate ganache

30–50 g (1–1¾ oz) sultanas (golden raisins) or raisins

125 ml/4 fl oz dark rum, or alcohol of your choice

Green cooking/cake pop chocolate, or color of your choice

Cake confetti

Edible gold paint (I used edible gold dust and rose spirit)

Paintbrush

Plate that can be put in the freezer

MAKING AND CRUMBING THE CAKE

To crumb the cake, first cut the crust off of all of the sides of the cake, so only soft cake crumb is visible, discard this crust. Holding the cake over a large bowl break it into pieces with your hands, keep picking up pieces of cake rubbing gently between your fingers until all of the cake has been reduced to a fine crumb. Pour in 125 ml of rum and stir through the cake crumb evenly. If you have time, let it soak overnight.

MAKING THE RUM BAUBLES

1 Heat up ganache to a thick soupy consistency and add it and your raisins to the cake crumb and rum mix and stir through thoroughly, I like to use my hands for this step to ensure an even mixture. Set aside mix in the refrigerator for at least 20 minutes, to give the ganache a chance to harden back to thicker consistency. At this point you want to put a plate in the freezer to get very cold.

2 When your ganache is thicker and the mix is cool, remove the mixture from the refrigerator. Make the rum balls by removing equal portions from the bowl, kneading it very slightly and rolling it between my palms. When the ball is formed place the ball directly onto the frozen plate—this extreme cold will help the ball retain its shape.

TROUBLESHOOT: If your mix is falling apart, first check the ganache—is it cold and thick enough or does it need longer in the refrigerator? Is there enough of it? If these two factors are fine, check the size of your fruit compared with the size of the balls you are rolling, lastly, there may be too much rum to cake ratio, try adding more cake crumbs.

  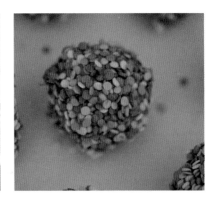

DECORATING THE RUM BAUBLES

1 Working quickly, melt the chocolate in a bowl set over a pot of hot water. Keep moving the chocolate until it is liquid and take it off the heat immediately. Do not overheat the chocolate and resist the temptation to melt it quicker by boiling the water in the pot—if your chocolate changes color, looks granular and dry and tends to clump you have overheated the chocolate and you need to start again.

2 Using a spoon and your fingers, dip each rum ball into the bowl of melted chocolate, turning it over and over until it has an even coat of chocolate. Move the ball immediately to step 3.

3 Drop the cake ball into the bowl of cake confetti and turn it over and over immediately to coat the wet chocolate in the confetti, once coated place the rum bauble on a frozen plate to set.

Repeat this for all of the rum baubles. You may need to reheat the chocolate slightly. If you have a lot of rum balls I suggest melting small batches of chocolate at a time, while it will take a little longer it is more likely to preserve your chocolate and avoid any wastage.

Allow these to set for several hours. On a hot day I set my rum baubles in the refrigerator however, if you do this, make sure they have fully come back to room temperature before proceeding to the next step.

4 To paint the baubles gold you have two options, pre-made edible gold paint or mixing edible gold dust with rose spirit (in an egg cup) and painting it onto the bauble. Regardless of the option, always start at the bottom, paint the bottoms of all of them and when dry turn them over and paint the rest. These look great nestled together on a plate in the middle of the table, serve as petit fours with tea and coffee, or anytime, and watch the delighted surprise when your guests realise they have a nice rummy-treat!

Chalkboard Heart

I adore the chalkboard effect on cakes, I have no idea which cake designer first came up with it but I completely understand its rise in popularity. The simplicity and the romance of this design is especially popular for engagement and wedding cakes – so what could be more fitting than a red love heart surprise inside!

I have kept my decoration for this one simple for the sake of explanation but if you are thinking about making this cake I implore you to do a little internet research on the multitude of design ideas, it really is one of those ideas that can be so easily customised for the recipients.

OPTION ALERT

The heart requires two cakes. I have used three for height. So what do you do with the third, plain cake? You can tort it, which means cut it in half and put one layer over the top and the other on the bottom so the cake has an even amount of plain chocolate above and below the heart or, as I have chosen, you can put the third (plain) cake as the base layer so that the heart is sitting toward the top of the cake like it is rising. To make this a balloon heart, simply cut a very small circle from the centre of the bottom cake and fill it with a different color cake mix. (If you do, be sure to make it a color that contrasts so it is visible i.e. light blue or bright green not brown.)

YOU WILL NEED

Round cake tin (pan) 18 cm/7 inch round, 7.5 cm/3 inch deep cake tin (size is dependent on size of your design and how may you need to feed)

Square cake tin (pan) 18 cm/7 inch square cake tin (you can use whatever size and shape you like, I find for cakes I am going to crumb, a square cake gives me more cake, less crust and is easier to cut crust away)

3 batches mud cake batter (see page 34)

1 batch white cake mix (mud, sponge or Madeira) dyed red

Gel food coloring: orange and red

Chocolate ganache, 750 g–1.25kg/1 lb 10 oz–2¾ lb

White chocolate ganache (see page 41)

Black fondant, 1.25–1.5 kg/2¾–3 lb 5 oz

Fondant or kitchen knife

Rolling pin

Non-stick mat

Acetate square

Modelling tool: Dresden tool, ball tool

Cornflour (corn starch) and icing (confectioners') sugar, for dusting

2 cake boards the same size as your cakes

Edible white paint, or dust and rose spirit.

Paintbrush

Peony (large flower of your choice)

MAKING THE CAKES

1 Preheat the oven to 120–130°C/250–265°F. Grease and flour, or line the cake tin with baking paper.

2 Make the chocolate mud cake batter, pour into the prepared tin and bake for the time specified for the tin size. Repeat again for the second and third cakes. Allow cakes to cool completely. When cool, wrap each in cling film (plastic wrap) and refrigerate until chilled.

3 Once cold, I return the cakes, one at a time to my cake tin and use my cake tin as a guide to cut off the dome top/level the cake evenly, using a sharp bread knife. Otherwise if you own a cake level, use that. Level all three cakes.

THE RED HEART CAKE MIX

1 Make the white cake mix of your choice, dye it orange first and then add red food color to make sure you get a really nice deep red tone.

2 Bake it in a smaller tin and cut the baking paper so it comes above the top of the tin to allow for extra rise of the cake. I baked my batter (enough for an 8 inch) in a 7 inch square tin. This creates a lot of cake with very little crust, which is what you are after.

3 Once it has been baked and cooled, cut all of the sides off of the cake so there is absolutely no cake crust at all—just bright red soft cake crumb. This will be very messy.

4 Place your remaining cake into a large bowl and crumb it, first by breaking it into pieces and then by rubbing the small parts through your fingers until you have a fine cake crumb mix.

5 For one sponge cake I add ⅔ of a cup of white chocolate ganache (I use white chocolate ganache because it will take on the color of the cake crumb). You can use buttercream but I find it doesn't set as dense inside the cake or cut as well as ganache, which is also easy to mix through the crumbs evenly. Set this aside but do not refrigerate it yet.

CARVING ROOM FOR A HEART

1 Let's call the base cake #3, the middle cake #2 and the top layer of cake #1. Start with cake 2. This is going to be the bottom half of the heart. Using a circle cutter, carefully line with up with the centre of your cake and insert it as far into the cake as it will go, this is simply your guide shape and a loosened point for your knife to start accessing the cake. Remove the circle cutter.

2 Using a small kitchen (paring) knife, insert it into the slit made by the circle cutter at a 45-degree angle. Insert the knife as deep as you wish the point of the heart to be—do not go all the way down to the bottom of the cake.

3 Maintaining a 45-degree angle, start to cut the cake by moving the knife up and down in a sawing motion, gently working your way around the circle shape made by the cutter, do this gently and slowly—what you are doing is cutting a cone shape out of the centre of the cake, you are going to need this so be careful with it. Do not change the angle of the knife or your heart will be lopsided.

4 Once you have moved all the way around the circle, use your knife to gently guide out the cone shape. Place it aside somewhere safe.

5 Now, for the top of the heart, choose which side of cake #1 is going to be the top—I would choose the side that was in the bottom of the cake tin because it's usually very flat with square edges and will make the decorating of the cake a lot easier. Once you know what side of the cake will be the top, flip it upside down so the cake-top is on your table-top.

6 Repeat the exact same process you did for cake #2 to make the bottom of the heart put the cone aside with the other one (this is your back up cone).

7 Now we need to make the top part of the heart bigger. Using the side edge of the teaspoon (little one from the cutlery draw, not metric), scrape it gently across the cake and remove a little at a time. Have a small bowl handy to deposit the cake crumb; you first want to make the circle all one size, so it is cylindrical hole.

8 Once you have done this, start to carve the cake away at the base of the hole. What you want to see when you look into this hole is the sides of it sloping down like the pyramids. Once you achieve this, stop. Resist all urge to keep digging and never carve to the top of the cake.

NOTE: This is not as easy as it seems and the first few times you do it, it will not look 'right' like it's going to make a heart, remember getting a shape by carving the centre of a cake means working with circles

FILL UP YOUR HEART

1 Using the red sponge cake crumb, fill up the hole that is the base of the heart first— cake #2. Make sure you compact the cake mix in there.

2 Next, place the best of the two cake cones into the centre of the hole you carved for the top of the heart in cake #1. Ganache the base of the cone (with the chocolate ganache to color match) so it sticks down well. This cone shape is going to be point that makes the top of the love heart shape.

3 Once the cone is in place, fill up the hole with red cake mix. Start with the lowest, deepest parts and make sure it is well compacted.

STACK, GANACHE AND CHILL

1 Apply ganache to the tops of cakes, around the red cake mix but never on the red cake mix.

2 Flip cake #1, the top of your heart, back over so the hole is facing downward and attach it over the top of cake #2.

3 Using ganache, secure cake #2 on top of cake #3 and apply a light ganache over the entire cake to seal it.

NOTE: if you decided to torte cake #3 so you have an equal amount of blank cake above and below the heart, ganache the two cake halves to the top and bottom of cakes #1 and #2, using the flattest sides as the base and top to make ganaching and covering with fondant easier.

4 Refrigerate to set. Bring it out and let it come back to room temperature, and apply a coat of peanut butter-consistency ganache over the cake using the double board method on page 18 of the techniques section to get it very straight. Allow the ganache to set.

BUT I CAN'T WAIT! Can't wait to see if it turned out? Worried it won't have turned out and you don't want to find out on the big day when you cut it? Yes you can cheat! Make sure the cake is fridge-cold, when you have your ganache and boards ready to go cut one neat wedge out of the top two layers of the cake and check it. Put the wedge back into the cake and ganache it back together. When you make the cake be sure to mark this area with design detail so you know where it is—get the recipient to cut in a different spot and re-cut your cheat spot later when you are dishing up the cake.

While it is unprofessional to use this method, I would be inclined to check it if you are making this for wedding or an engagement—these are not events you want to make a mistake on! If it didn't work out, don't worry, my first few looked dreadful. Don't be disheartened… try again.

ALL WRAPPED UP IN FONDANT

1 To attach the fondant I use a lid and wrap method for this sort of tall cylinder cake. First, rollout your black fondant and cut it into a circle to fit the top of the cake. I usually use my clean dry cake tin to do this.

2 Place the fondant circle on top of the cake.

3 Measure the height and the circumference of your cake. You need to roll out your black fondant fairly close to these dimensions. Don't be afraid to use a cornflour/icing sugar combination to dust your roll out surface—white dusty marks on a matt black finish is what we are after, it gives an authentic chalkboard feel.

4 You can do this next step this one of two ways; (i) Pick up the fondant, draping it over your forearms and gently wrap it around the cake starting with the centre of the black fondant sheet at the front of the cake, wrapping it around the cake like a towel. Be sure the straight edge lines up with the lid at the top. If you have excess it will splay out across the board at the base of the cake like a skirt. After completing step 9 you can come back and cut away this excess with a fondant or kitchen knife. OR (ii) Be sure the straight edge lines up with the base of the cake and if you have any excess it will peek over the top of the cake and can be neatly cut away and moulded in with the heat of your hand and acetate square after you have completed step 9.

Choose whichever way feels more comfortable for you. If this is your first time wrapping a cylindrical cake shape, it is likely you will end up with a combination of both.

5 Join the fondant edges at the back of the cake together to make a seam, trimming away any excess. Use a little bit of sugar glue to secure the seam at the top if you really need to, then quickly set about using acetate square over the seam. If you don't have hot hands you may need to alternate the acetate sheet with the palm of your hand or fingers so your body heat will help melt the fondant back together. Work the acetate in a circular motion, with that and the heat of your hands the seam should all but disappear.

6 Repeat the same for the top edge.

TROUBLESHOOT: Don't despair if you have underestimated the fondant length and your seam doesn't meet up, just work quickly—smoothing the fondant with the warmth of your hands around the cake, stretching the elasticity of it to reach further and further around until your two seams meet. Having to do this may cause you two problems: the fondant may rip in one spot if

you smooth from the same point too much so try and smooth from up and down the cake. The other issue is that smoothing the fondant edges forward to meet each other may pick up some ganache and cause chocolate smudges on your fondant, again, if this isn't too large you may be able to remove it with a ball of black fondant like an eraser, dark on dark isn't as noticeable.

DECORATE ME DARLING

1 Determine what you want your design to look like. Print out some ideas and trace them on baking paper (you can combine several) to make the design to shape. Ensure it fits on the cake.

2 When the fondant has set a little you can use small pins to secure the baking paper in place over the front of the cake. Note: you don't want to use fresh fondant as it is too soft but if it has set too hard it won't emboss with your tools.

3 Using a combination of your Dresden and ball tools, trace over your design to emboss it onto the front of your cake—you are going to want to work in good sunlight for this and the next step!

4 Once you have finished tracing, remove the baking paper and inspect your embossing, if you are happy with it proceed to paint within the lines.

5 To mix up the paint, I use edible white dust and rose spirit, I use a watery mix to give a chalky effect—it means you may need to repaint over some areas but the extra effort is worth the final product. Paint within the lines. Once you have completed your design, allow it to dry.

6 Lastly, add a large sugar or fresh flower to the top of the cake, positioned slightly off centre and you are ready to go.

Oscar Owl Cake and Frankie Fox-Face Cupcakes

DIFFICULTY: ////

TIME TO MAKE: ⧗⧗⧗⧗

My husband and I love owls! We are fortunate enough to have quite a few where we live, and one cheeky fellow who takes up residence on our clothesline inspired me to make Oscar the Owl. Naturally, like all woodland creature stories, where there is an owl, there is fox, and we have dubbed our local pair Frannie and Frankie, and while they are not exactly orange foxes, most woodland creature stories feature them this way and what a nice contrast the orange cupcakes make with the brown owl feature cake on a party table. The best thing is, when you bite into the fox faces you are surprised with crumbled honeycomb and Oscar's belly is full of malt balls (Maltesers) and honeycomb pieces … YUM!!

OPTION ALERT!

Want to go all-out cute for a child's birthday and make a pink or blue owl? Match this up with light brown fox faces and consider a bow on one ear of each to make them girly.

YOU WILL NEED

Dolly Varden cake tin, 19 x 15 cm/7 ½ x 6 inch
1 batch caramel or chocolate mud cake batter
  (see page 34)
White fondant
Small amount of black fondant
Gel food color to color your fondant (I have used
  chocolate brown, warm brown and orange for
  the beak and fox and egg yellow for the owl
  eyes. Also forest green, mint green, bush green
  and bottle green for the forest floor effect)
CMC powder, to turn fondant into gum paste
Rose leaf cutters (at least 2 sizes)
Leaf texture mat/silicon mould/or a dried corn
  husk
Large heart cutter
Triangle cutter
2 round cutters of different sizes, suitable for eyes

Peony rose cutters (optional)
Edible black ink pen
Fondant or kitchen knife
Non-stick mat
Cornflour (corn starch) and icing (confectioners')
  sugar, for dusting
Chocolate or caramel chocolate ganache
Sugar glue
Cupcake cases
Cupcake tray
Cake board for display
Foam ball (this is for the head, choose a size that
  is in proportion to the size of your cake body)
1 wooden dowel
Aluminium foil
Modelling tools:
  wheel cutter and ball tool

MAKING THE HEAD IN ADVANCE

Allow time to make this and have parts of it dry before the baking and decorating of the cake.

Beak and ears first

1 First, make the beak. Color a small amount of gum paste—I used orange first and then added a touch of brown to make it a more muted color.

Fold some aluminium foil into the shape of the beak. Form a triangle that will stand upright in a peak. Make sure there is foil leftover to bend upwards and take the shape of the foam ball.

2 Roll out your orange gum paste quite thin and lay it over the shape of the foil template you made. Use small embroidery scissors to cut away any excess. Try not to smooth the gum paste onto the foil with your fingers because this will create a rippled, textured beak rather than a smooth one. Lastly, secure the ball in place on the table top and using pearl head pins, secure the gum paste covered foil onto the foam ball (the beak should point outwards). This ensures that that gum paste will dry in the shape of the owl head and fit on perfectly when it is dried.

Allow this to dry into shape (it's OK if it is a little soft and malleable, as long as it holds its shape).

Don't worry if the non-triangle part of the beak is big and ugly—this is the part of the gum paste that will attach the beak to the ball head, it's large to give a better anchor point. The more of it you have the more secure your beak will be and it will be covered with feathers.

When you attach the beak and feathers around it, line up where the nostrils will go, parallel to each other at the top of the beak and using your edible black-ink pen draw two dots or lines.

3 OK, so most owls don't have 'ears' in the traditional sense but this looked so cute that I couldn't resist. To make them I simply rolled out light brown and dark brown gum paste and laid them on top of each other. I then cut out two triangles.

Using my cornflour dusted fingers I shaped the ears to be more 3D by pushing into the base and pinching the tip of the triangle. For one ear I twisted it at the halfway point so that it looks like Oscar is listening to something behind him. The base of the triangle I bent backwards to create an anchor to the foam head. Allow the ears the same time to dry as the beak and be sure to have the anchor points drying in the shape of the ball. Using the foam ball or having a spare is always the best option.

Heads up

The head can be fragile and as you won't be eating it, you can use gum paste to make the feathers that cover it so that they set hard to help protect its shape.

1 Insert the wooden dowel into the base of the foam ball. This should fit snugly and not move. Secure with hot glue, if you like, but be sure to cover the glued area with gum paste so it doesn't come into contact with the top of the cake.

2 To work on the head you need to secure the wooden dowel into something; I use leftover pieces of Styrofoam, improvise with what you have.

3 First step is to cover the base of the head with feathers, and up the front of the face one-third of the way. This places the feathers under the beak that would otherwise be too tricky to apply later.

4 Then attach the beak and ears, once they are in place you can then add the rest of the feathers.

Making the feathers

1 Color up your gum paste several slightly different shades of brown for color contrast. To cut

out the feathers I used a small rose leaf cutter for the head feathers and medium rose leaf cutter for the body feathers. The serrated edge of the leaf cutter gives the impression of feathering.

2 Cut out 6–10 leaves at a time and place each into a (rose) leaf veiner, which is a dual sided silicon mat. Any veiner you have will do, we are aiming to give the feathers texture, which adds depth and interest to the finished design. If you do not have a veiner, dry up a corn husk, attach it to small wooden block and use that, corn husks give a great veining effect.

3 Attach the feathers in lines around the shape using sugar glue for the head. Cover the base of the head with feathers, and up the front of the face one-third of the way. Attach the beak and ears. Once they are in place, add the rest of the feathers.

4 For the front of the face I used a fanning effect from the beak so that the feathers look like their bases are in the centre of the face and the tapered ends point outwards, this adds character and interest to the face.

PSST!

Make extra feathers for the body, just in case you break one while finishing the cake, you will have spares at the ready to patch it up!

The eyes make it

To make the eyes, I have used two different size round cutters. If you do not have cutters, follow the eye instructions for Daisy Cow and work on a larger scale.

1 Roll out white fondant quite thinly and cut two circle shapes. Using your fingers pinch the sides of the circle so they are very flat.

Oscar Owl Cake and Frankie Fox-Face Cupcakes

2 Roll out yellow fondant and cut out two yellow circles with the same cutter and place the yellow circles on top of the white ones, affixing in place with sugar glue. The pinched edges of the white circle should make the white of the eye fractionally larger than the yellow.

3 For the pupils, roll out the black fondant quite thin and cut out two circles using the smaller circle cutter and attach them to the centre of the eyes with sugar glue.

4 Lastly add white dots to the top right-hand corners of the pupils using edible white paint, white dust and rose spirit, or batter whitener. Use a fine paintbrush, a cocktail stick or the tip of a Dresden or ball tools. If you have none of these, use small balls of white fondant squashed flat with your finger and attached with sugar glue. Remember they must both point the same way to look like light reflections.

5 Attach the eyes gently to the face with sugar glue, positioning them above and to each side of the beak.

MAKING THE CAKES

1 Preheat the oven to 120–130°C/250–265°F for mud cake. Grease and flour your Dolly Varden cake tin. You can use cake release/ vegetable oil spray.

2 Stand the small tip of the Dolly Varden tin inside a round cake tin that is small enough to cradle the Dolly Varden, this will help keep it stable while in the oven. Half filling the supporting cake tin with water will help stop the lower part of the cake from overcooking. If you have an egg ring, place this at the bottom of the round tin for additional support. Grease flour the Dolly Varden tin.

3 Make the mud cake batter and pour into the tin. Once the batter is in the tin, smooth over the top with a spatula or knife (slightly dampen it to avoid batter sticking to it) and put into the oven right away. Bake for the time required for the size tin you have, remembering your oven and batter recipe may vary the cooking times.

NOTE: Dense, slow cooking mud cake in this odd shaped tin takes a long while to cook so be patient and expect it to be baked 'long and low'. I have an incredibly hot oven so I set my temperature gauge for 120°C/248 °F and it took me 3 hours to cook it.

4 Check your cake about 10 minutes before the timer is due to go off to be sure of its progress. Test to ensure the cake is baked through by inserting a skewer into the centre. If it comes out

clean, the cake is ready. Turn out to cool on a wire rack. When the cake has cooled completely you need to refrigerate it, as it is also easier to carve a cold cake.

DECORATING THE BODY

1 To fill the cake, I cut off the top third of the cake in a clean straight cut and using a spoon, scoop out the centre of the cake to the required depth.

NOTE: You can cut and scoop where you like, I cut off the top third and work downwards because I find leaving the heavier base of the cake and majority of the cake uncut assists with the structural integrity of it when you apply the head. Do not scoop out the cake all the way to the bottom; you not only need it intact for structural support, but to anchor the wooden dowel from the head. As a general rule I cut off one-third, scoop one-third, and leave one-third

2 Fill the hollow centre of your cake with malt balls and crumbled chocolate honeycomb pieces. Spread ganache on the cut part of the cake on both pieces and place the top one-third back onto the cake. Refrigerate to allow the ganache to set the seam together.

3 Apply a layer of ganache to the cake.

4 Follow the instructions above for cutting and texturing the feathers for the head, but this time using fondant instead of gum paste. I use the larger rose leaf cutter for this because the body is large and it gives a better sense of proportion as well as a lot less feathers to cut out!

5 Be sure to make extra feathers for the body, just in case you break one while finishing the cake, you then have spares at the ready to patch it up

OPTION ALERT! Why not use two or three shades of brown to make the feathers and arrange in a color sequence to create patterns, or even just one color arranged to make a love heart on the belly. If you do this, don't make the colors too dissimilar. The color difference between three balls in front of you versus how it looks on the cake is very different.

6 When you attach the feathers to the body, do so in lines around the cake and start from thebase up. Some feathers will change shape a little in the veining process, which gives different shapes and directions to the tapered ends so you won't end up with obvious rings of feathers.

7 Once you have placed the feathers all the way to the top, attach the head. I do this by guiding the wooden dowel down into the cake and through the centre of it. Make sure you have measured the length of the dowel first, if it is too tall, cut it to length accordingly.

MAKING WINGS AND FEET

1 For the wings, I used a darker brown fondant so they are a more obvious. Rolling out my fondant a little thicker than the feathers, I have achieved the shape by using my peony rose cutters. You can also achieve this shape by cutting it out free hand using a small knife. Add texture with the leaf veiner. Layer the shapes, ruffled ends pointing outward to give a feathered wing effect.

OPTION ALERT! For a more defined wing, make a teardrop shape out of gum paste (moulded over the Dolly Varden tin and cover it in a combination of smaller and larger 'feathers'. Or, if you want to build up the wing to give a defined, 3D effect, you can make the gum paste teardrop shape domed, be sure the edges are flat to the shape of the tin to enable you to secure it. If you chose this option use a lot ganache and let it set before applying a multitude of little feathers in a slightly different color to the wings. Prepare your gum paste wing base ahead of time with the beak and ears and be sure to make more than two just in case, a breakage is hard to patch up!

2 Using my left over gum paste from the beak, my largest peony cutter, and leaf veiner, I cut out and textured two webbed looking feet—biologically inaccurate but very cute none the less.

MAKING THE FOREST FLOOR

1 You can now transfer your cake to your cake board. Before you do, add the feet to the board so that when you position the cake the ends of the feet disappear underneath the body and give the effect of being attached.

NOTE: I decorated the cake already on the display board to avoid having to move it because I knew no matter what mess I made, I was going to cover the board with leaves.

2 To get the forest floor effect I simply used the same cutters and veiners on gum paste colored four different shades of green and using my ganache, attached them to the board to look like scattered leaves. While autumn colors work, they tend to blend into the owl color, decide early if you are going to make the cake realistic or cute, the latter lends itself to more contrasting colors.

MAKING THE FOX FACE CUPCAKES

1 Preheat oven to 120–130°C/250–265°F for mud cake. Line the cupcake tray with cupcake cases.

2 Make a batch of mud cake batter. Fill the cupcake cases three-quarters full.

PSST! See page 14 for tips on how to get a flat top cupcake – this will come in handy when we have to decorate the faces!

3 Bake in oven for 25–35 minutes for the mud cake or until skewer comes out clean. Depending on your oven, the type of chocolate used and the size of your cupcake cases your cooking time may vary.

4 Allow the cupcakes to cool and put them into the refrigerator to get cold. It is always easier to cut a cold cake.

5 Using an apple core, remove the centre of each cupcake. Carefully remove the cored piece of cake and set it aside on a plate, we will need this again later. Repeat this for all of the cupcakes.

6 Crumble the chocolate-coated honeycomb pieces into a bowl and using clean, dry hands, gradually add the honeycomb crumbles to the hollowed out centre of each cupcake. Fill to just below the top and use the top portion of the cored out centre pop plug the hole and press down lightly to secure it – this will prevent the honeycomb from escaping and the ganache from making the honeycomb gooey.

7 Apply a layer of ganache to the top of your cupcake.

Making the fox face

1 Roll out the orange fondant about 4 mm/⅛ inch thick.

2 Use a circle cutter that is big enough to fit over your entire cupcake. This allows for depth as well as diameter. If you don't have big circle cutters you can use an egg ring, they work for smaller cupcakes when you're caught out. Using the right sized circle cutter, cut out your

fondant topper and lay it over the top of you cupcake. Using clean dry hands smooth out the topper. You may also use an acetate square if you have it, this will give a nice shiny smooth finish. Smooth down the sides so they cover and tuck under the edges of the cupcake. Do this for all of the cupcakes.

3 Add a small amount of CMC powder to the leftover orange fondant. Roll it out and using triangle cutters cut out two triangular ears per fox face cupcake. Leave them on a cornflour-dusted surface to slightly stiffen before adding them to the cupcakes, that way the ears will retain their shape when they stick out off the top of the cupcake.

4 Using your white fondant and large heart cutter, roll out and cut one love heart for each cupcake. Cut each love heart in half with a kitchen or fondant knife. Once cut add each half of the love heart to either side of the fox face, straight edges facing outwards to the edge of the cupcake and shaped edges pointing inwards. Position them at such an angle to ensure the two pointed ends meet at the base of the cupcake – this will be the fox's long nose. Repeat for each cupcake, securing in place with sugar glue.

5 Using black fondant, roll two small balls for the eyes and one slightly larger ball for the nose. Using sugar glue – attach the eyes on the inside edge of the top of each heart and secure the nose at the point where the two white ends of the hearts meet.

Checkerboard Baby Shower Cake

DIFFICULTY: ✏✏✏✏✏

TIME TO MAKE: ⧗⧗⧗⧗⧗

With the advent of technology being able to show and tell us so much before the baby is born, many people still opt for the ultimate surprise and choose not to know the sex of their baby before he or she is born. This is sweet, and gives the perfect opportunity to make everything at the baby shower pink and blue! While the choice not to find out the sex of the baby is often it is met with cries of 'How can you not know?' or, 'It makes it so hard to buy for you' at the baby shower, the expecting Mum (and Dad) are often heard to say, 'As long as the baby is healthy and happy.' It is a beautiful sentiment and is what anyone wishes for themselves and friends having a baby, being able to capture this on the cake itself is a lovely touch.

OPTION ALERT!

If you have a religious blessing or cultural sentiment for an expectant mum and her bub, the plaque idea is a nice way to incorporate that into the baby shower cake too!

YOU WILL NEED

Checkerboard Cake Set (I used a set that contains 3 x 23cm/9 inch shallow round cake pans and a checkerboard batter divider, see notes)

OR

Shallow round cake tin

AND

Baking paper, a ruler and a compass to create templates (see notes)

2 batches white cake batter of your choice (mud, sponge or Madeira – see page 35)

Batter whitener

White chocolate ganache*

Buttercream replacement and icing (confectioners') sugar (or use buttercream or royal icing)

Cake comb

2 gel food colors, for gum paste and cake batter (I used soft pink and sky blue)

Gum paste, or fondant and CMC powder

Edible pink and blue metallic paint

Small cranked handle spatula

Sugar glue

1 cake board, for base of cake

1 display board/plate/wooden stump

Plaque cutter

Edible image of desired saying or blessing, to scale

Bootie cutters (or purchased booties)

Bib cutter /small circle and small pastry cutter, ribbon and blossom cutter

(or purchased bib)

Rattle cutters (or purchased rattle)

Modelling tools: Ball tool, frilling tool (optional)

Silicon mould: flower face

MAKING THE CAKE LAYERS

There are several ways to approach baking a checkerboard cake. The first is using a specific tin set. These are fantastic because they come with a divide, perfectly shaped for the tins in the set. The divider splits the cake into three circles, small in the centre, medium that surrounds the small and large on the outside.

The idea is that you insert the divider into the greased tin and pour batter color 1 into the small and large circle slots and batter color 2 into the medium circle slot, you then remove the divider and bake immediately. Repeating the process for the next layer of cake but reversing the order so that batter color 2 is now poured into the small and large circles and batter color 1 only poured into the medium circle. When you stack the cakes, color 1 and 2 are always on top of each other no matter how many layers you bake. This alternating color gives you a checkerboard effect when you cut the cake. If you are using a cake recipe that gives you incredibly thick batter, give this way a try—it makes the process of baking a checkerboard cake so much easier.

Checkerboard Baby Shower Cake

Alternatively, bake two layers of solid blue and two layers of solid pink cake. (Remember these are low-sided cake tins so one batter mix will fill two tins). Once I have baked my cakes and cooled them to refrigerator temperature, I use a checkerboard divider to cut out the three circle sizes I need, and then I construct my own checkerboard. I use this method each time because the cake recipes I prefer to use produce quite runny batters and if I were to put them into the one tin with the batter divider, I get wobbly lines of colors.

*If you use this option you will need an additional white chocolate ganache top stick the circles together securely.

1 Preheat the oven to 120–130°C/250–265°F for mud cake, or 180°C/350°F for a sponge cake batter. Grease the cake tin(s) that you will be using with vegetable oil / cake tin release spray or grease and flour, or line the tray. Add batter and bake.

2 Make up the cake batter for colors 1 and 2. Pour into the tins, smooth the top level and bake immediately for 17–25 minutes depending on your cake recipe and layer height. Test the cakes by inserting a skewer in the centre. If it comes out clean, the cake is ready. Leave to cool on a wire rack.

TRIMMING THE CAKE LAYERS

1 Trim the top of each cake level. I try really hard not to have to trim cakes but you really need flat, flat tops on the checkerboard design so for me, it's unavoidable. If, like me you prefer a trimmed cake for this design so you have better control over the exact nature of the squares, over fill the tin slightly so when the cake rises, it rises above the tin, that way when you trim the cake, you can do it with the cake inside the tin again, using a sharp bread knife and the top of your tin as a guide. See page 14 for top tips on how to do this.

If you have used the first method, and baked the two colors in the one tin, stick each layer together with frosting and proceed to icing the outside of the cake as instructed below. If you have used the alternate method, follow steps 2–9.

2 Wrap each cake individually in cling film (plastic wrap) and chill in the refrigerator. Once cold I bring the cakes out and using the divider that has been greased lightly with vegetable oil, cut the cake layer into circles. You must do this very gently and ease the cutter in to avoid cake breakages.

3 When you have cut the cake, you need to gently ease the medium and small cake circles out of the cutter by working around both edges of the circle a little at a time with gentle fingers.

4 Have the cake board ready and cover it with runny chocolate ganache.

5 Place a large cake circle of color 1 first. Using a spoon, coat the inside of the circle with ganache. This ganache is going to allow the next circle to slot into place and act as a glue to stick them together.

6 Insert the medium cake circle of color 2 inside. Using a spoon, coat the inside of the circle with ganache as before.

7 Add the small circle of color 1 into the centre of the medium circle. Cover the top of all three cake circles with ganache.

8 Repeat this process with alternate colors as another layer of cakes on top of the first. Repeat for as many layers as you have accounted (baked) for.

OPTION ALERT! You could also trace around the base of the tin onto baking paper. Cut out the tracing and fold it in half. Mark the halfway point. Measure the distance between the diameter and the edge of the circle. Divide that measurement by 3 and make a mark at each of these points. Using a pair of compasses anchored at the halfway mark, fix the pencil in place over the first mark and draw an arc. Repeat for the second mark. You should now have a half circle with two half circles drawn on it. Keeping the paper folded, cut out the along the lines, then iron the pieces flat. Use these as a template to cut out your cakes with a knife.

ICING THE CAKE

1 I wanted pure white icing for this gender-neutral cake so when you cut it the pale tone of the pastel pink and blue POP rather than getting lost in contrast with the icing.

To get pure white icing you have four choices: royal icing, Swiss/Italian meringue, batter whitener in buttercream (can taste funny if you need to add a lot), or buttercream replacement (this is based on vegetable fat and used in place of butter at the same quantities as the buttercream recipe).

Royal icing holds its shape but it sets hard and can crack when you cut it. I prefer the meringue icing, however egg whites, even if cooked properly, always make me uneasy for pregnant women, who have to be super careful of eggs (and everything else!) For this cake I used the super-white buttercream replacement.

2 Using a long, cranked handle spatula, apply a generous layer of icing to the top and sides of the cake. I have added a generous layer because I am going to be taking some back off the cake with the cake comb and I don't want to risk getting down to the cake level. If you are leaving the top of the cake smooth, use the spatula to make it so at this point.

3 Once applied, take your cake comb, placing it flush with the side of the cake and angling it at a 45-degree angle, apply a small amount of pressure and moved the cake comb around the cake. You may need to wipe off the excess icing that has built up on your cake comb and repeat the process. If you have patches or holes, fill these in and try again. The trick to an even pattern is consistent movement and pressure.

MAKING THE CAKE TOPPERS

1 For the bib, roll out some gum paste, and cut out the shape. If you don't have a bib cutter, use pastry cutters (with the scalloped edges) to cut out a circle. Use a smaller circle cutter to take out a chunk at the top for the neck of the bib.

2 Using the ball tool in a circular motion, massage each scallop on the bib—this will make each larger and thinner and, if you do it on the edge of the scallop, frilly. I have opted for indents so I can add blue and pink balls of fondant in an alternating pattern, securing them with sugar glue.

3 Using blue and pink gum paste, I have used a silicone mould to make the flower face as the main motif for the bib. Alternatively, cut a flower using a small blossom cutter or pipe an appropriate word in the space.

4 Using the pointy end of a frilling tool/cell pin/toothpick, make two holes at the pointy end of the bib large enough to thread through ribbon when the gum paste has dried completely.

Note: This is a fragile point of the shape. You need to be very gentle; making sure the hole is wide enough otherwise it will break. I highly advise making 2 to allow for breakages.

Making the booties

These take a little longer. If you don't have cutters, download templates from the Internet; for this one you can't really improvise with other cutters as they have very specific shapes.

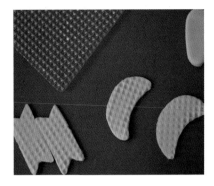  

1 For the sole, roll out some gum paste to 3 mm/⅛ inch thick, and using the base of a shoe cutter or template, cut out the shapes (they should look like a little like a kidney or peanut shape). Always make extra just in case. Allow these to dry and set hard—this may take a day or two as they are very thick. You need the thickness to give the base show height; it provides a more secure anchor point for the front and back of the shoe to be glued to and it needs to be set hard so it provides resistance to the front and back of the shoe which is better support for the shape.

2 Roll your gum paste very thin and cut out the front and back of the shoe. Apply sugar glue around the edges of your shoe base and add the back of the shoes first and the front of the shoes second—the front of the shoe should slightly overlap the back part of the shoe. Remember when applying the front part of the shoe, the convex (larger side) goes at the base and the concave (indented part) becomes the top of the shoe, so when it is attached you get that horseshoe shape on top of the foot. The back of the shoe should look like a rectangular banner.

You can decorate the shoe however you like. There are some amazing piped detail options out there. I have used a texture mat on my gum paste before I cut out the shapes, and this gives the booties a knitted effect. In terms of the top of the shoe you can leave the top open, and following the instructions for the bib, make two holes to feed ribbon through when it has dried or, you can bend them inwards so they almost touch and when they are dry, affix a blue and a pink bow. To make the bow I have used a silicon mould.

Making the rattle

1 Cut out the body of the rattle and set it aside to dry.

2 Cut out two circles, these need to be larger than the holes in the rattle cutter because you need to allow for the doming.

3 Use a small blossom cutter to make pretty 'holes' in the rattle. Dry the circles over a spherical object. I used golf balls.

4 Make several balls of gum paste and set aside to dry.

5 Assemble the components when they are dry using royal icing. Attach one side of the circle and allow that to dry. Put the dry balls inside the dry circle and prop the rattle up on its side, against a mini wall of aluminium foil and apply royal icing to the edges of the second circle then attach it to the rattle, holding it in place with scrunched up aluminium foil until the royal icing sets.

6 Use royal icing to pipe small dots or patterns around the join to both hide your mechanics and add detail. You can also decorate the handle, my original one had an 'it's a girl' ribbon to contrast with the boy ribbon.

TROUBLESHOOT: What do I do if I broke my rattle and didn't make a spare? If it is broken on just one side, you can lay the rattle flat on the cake, it will still look like a rattle with the good side facing upwards.

Making the plaque

I have used a special plaque cutter for this. You can use templates from the internet cut out of paper and simply cut around your desired shape with a small knife.

1 Roll out some gum paste and cut out a shape using a plaque cutter. Allow to dry on a non-stick surface.

2 Apply a coat of sugar glue to the front. Detach the edible image from its backing paper and roughly cut around it making it larger than is needed. Very gently hold it above the plaque, and line up where the words will sit ensuring it is straight.

3 Place the image down over the plaque and using your embroidery scissors, trim it to fit the plaque. Smooth down the edges with your fingers and allow to dry.

4 Add edible pink or blue metallic paint to the edges. Leave to dry then add it to the cake. I used a small ball of gum paste behind the plaque to prop it up, both secured in place by the icing.

OPTION ALERT! You can attach your edible image to your rolled out gum paste and use your cutter over both at once. I am heavy handed so this tends to cause wrinkling and ripping of my edible image, which is why I haven't used that option here. If you are using a template and very sharp knife, you could use this option for optimal results. I tend not to cut out both separately and fit together because sometimes pressure on one end of a cutter can cause the gum paste to take on a slightly different shape or angle, not noticeable to the eye but very notable why you try to line up an image over the top. Use whichever option works best for you.

Checkerboard Chess Cake

DIFFICULTY: ╱ ╱ ╱ ╱ ╱
TIME TO MAKE: ⧗ ⧗ ⧗ ⧗ ⧗

I have helped a lot of people design a chess-themed cake for their chess-obsessed child's birthday. If you have the time, you can hand make all of the chess pieces and incorporate characters from their favourite comics, movies or games. For this design I kept it simple and made a checkerboard cake the same color as the chess board it is displayed on, using the same colored chess pieces to continue the cream and brown theme throughout the design. You can use smaller squares and make a full chess set or a cut down version like I have here. Either way, it is always nice to place the remaining chess pieces on the board in the same position as their latest or greatest win.

OPTION ALERT!

Have an edible image made up of your message and attach it as a plaque to the side of the cake, follow the instructions included in the Checkerboard Baby Shower Cake and use gold and cream colors of the cake.

YOU WILL NEED

Checkerboard Cake Set (I used a set that contains 3 x 23cm/9 inch shallow round cake pans and a checkerboard batter divider, see notes)

OR

Shallow round cake tin (pan) (whatever size suits you, adjust quantities and bake time accordingly)

AND

Baking paper, a ruler and a compass to create templates (see notes)

1 batch vanilla flavored white chocolate mud cake batter (see page 35)

1 batch chocolate mud cake batter (see page 34)
Ganache (see page 41)
Chocolate brown fondant
White fondant
Small cranked handle spatula
Sugar glue
Square cutter
Letter cutters
1 cake board for base of cake
1 display board/plate/chess board

MAKING, BAKING, TRIMMING AND ASSEMBLING THE CAKE

See the notes given in the baby shower checkerboard cake on page 249

Note for this cake I have added vanilla extract to the white chocolate mud cake batter to give it a richer, creamier flavor.

ICING THE CAKE

I have opted for chocolate brown fondant as my cake cover.

1 Apply a layer of ganache to the cake following the instructions on page 16. Leave to set then cover the cake with chocolate brown fondant, following the instructions on page 20.

2 Transfer the cake to your display board before decorating.

DECORATING THE CAKE

1 For the chessboard, roll out some white fondant and cut out white squares, the brown of the cake will act as the dark squares on the chessboard. Stick in place with sugar glue. Make the first square you add one of your corner squares, for your second square add it on the diagonal

and for the third add it to the same first row—having its bottom corner touching the top corner of the second square. This makes spacing easy and even as now you have a framework you can continue to place squares.

Note: the size of your squares will depend on how large the top of your cake is and how big you want your mock chess board decoration to be. I have used larger squares and mini board and real chess pieces to give the idea of chess—if you are making this to celebrate a particular winning move the squares will need to be significantly smaller to fit on the top of the cake. In this instance I suggest using travel-chess sized playing pieces.

2 I have used 1970s-style bubble writing letter cutters for the message on the side of the cake and attached them with sugar glue.

3 Lastly, I have displayed my cake atop a real wooden chess board for effect. If you do not have one, you can cover a masonite board with swirly brown fondant and emboss a wooden grain pattern or cut many squares and make a chess board on the display board as well.

Checkerboard Race Track Cake

DIFFICULTY: ✎✎✎✎✎

TIME TO MAKE: ⧖⧖⧖⧖⧖

Race car cakes have no age limit and are just so fun. The decoration on this design is just so simple and quick to do but has such a great impact; it's great to carry the surprise through to the cake itself and make a black and white checkered flag cake!

Bikes and cars are very similar when it comes to race track cakes, follow the instructions below and use a racing bike instead to change up the design to suit your recipient.

YOU WILL NEED

Checkerboard Cake Set (I used a set that contains 3 x 23cm/9 in shallow round cake pans and a checkerboard batter divider)

OR

Shallow round cake tin (pan) (whatever size suits you – adjust quantities and bake time accordingly)

AND

Baking paper, a ruler and a compass to create templates (see notes)

1 batch white chocolate mud cake batter

1 batch chocolate mud cake batter

Gel food color: black for the chocolate cake batter, green for the buttercream grass

Batter whitener for the white chocolate mud cake

Ganache

Black and white fondant

233 Grass tip/nozzle

Piping bag

Coupler

Small (paring) kitchen knife

2 plates or circle templates of different sizes

Small cranked handle spatula

Sugar glue

Rectangle cutters (if you have them other see notes for knife use)

Letter cutters

1 cake board, for the base of the cake

1 display board (I used black)

2 checkered flags

1 race car

4x A4 edible images of black and white checkered flags

Non stick mat

Rolling pin

MAKING, BAKING, TRIMMING AND ASSEMBLING THE CAKE

See the notes given in the baby shower checkerboard cake on page 249.

When making the white chocolate mud cake batter, use batter whitener so make it very light/white in color. When you make the chocolate mud cake, add the black gel food coloring to get black cake batter. This will give us the base colors to build the checkered flag cake.

DECORATING THE CAKE

1 Before you start anything else, make a black race track out of black fondant so it has time to air dry a little before moving it to the top of the cake.

To make a race track, roll out 300 g/10½ oz of black fondant, quite thick, on a cornflour-dusted non-stick mat. Sizing up the top of my cake, I was able to use a dinner plate to cut around as a

template for the outside of the circuit, this allowed room between the outside of the circuit and the edge of the cake to provide emphasis. I then used a small saucer as a template to cut out the centre. Use a sharp knife to do this. If you don't have cutters and your plates don't match up—make and use paper templates. Remove the excess black fondant and leave the track to dry. If you are in really hot or humid weather conditions you may consider adding CMC Powder to your black fondant before you start, you don't want it to be too hard though as it will be eaten when you cut the cake.

2 I have used plain buttercream that has been lightened with the same batter whitener to ice the sides of the cake only. Smooth the buttercream as flat as you can and make sure it is even all the way around. Use and additional board on top of the cakes if you need a guide.

NOTE: I need to use a light color buttercream, almost white, so it does not show through the edible image I will place over the top of it.

3 Refrigerate the cake until the buttercream has hardened, then place the cake on its black display board.

4 Once the buttercream has come back to room temperature you can gently apply the edible images to the side of the cake. I would advise starting at the front of the cake so you have less visible seams from front on, then carefully line up the black and white squares to help hide the seams of the images. Once in place, trim any excess off of the top of your image with a small, sharp pair of embroidery scissors.

4 Carefully place the race track on top of the cake.

5 Thinly roll out the white fondant. Using rectangle cutters, cut out rectangles for the white lines on the road to signal a road divide (these are not always present on a race track but helps give it character). If you don't have cutters, simply use a knife to cut several at a time by making a grid pattern of rectangles. Attach the white lines with sugar glue.

6 Color a small amount of buttercream green and put it in a piping bag with your 233 grass tip/nozzle and coupler attached. Following the grass piping instructions from the Daisy Cow Cake, pipe grass around the edge and in the centre of the race track. Also pipe around the base of the cake, this will help secure it if you haven't lined up your image very well.

7 Add the checkered flags and race car to the top of the cake. Note: you can secure the car with royal icing or ganache but it is best not to secure it all, and place it on top when the cake is in situ. That way the car is clean and ready to be played with and not damaged in any way by washing off of the edible food products.

OPTION ALERT! Why not go all out and put signs, a pit stop or even a plaque that looks like an advertising board with the recipient's name on it—edible images are super handy for this.

I have used letter cutters to cut out the recipient's name. You can add these to the grass area or board, if you like.

TROUBLESHOOT: Oops! I have ripped my edible image and it is visible, what should I do? If it rips toward the top or the base, simply pipe the grass up/down toward it and cover it—make it look like the grass is starting grow up/down the wall. Once you have covered the tear, repeat this design at equal spaces around the cake so it looks intentional.

Ring in the Rose Cupcake

DIFFICULTY: 🥄🥄🥄🥄🥄

TIME TO MAKE: ⏳⏳⏳⏳⏳

I am a huge fan of cake designer, decorator and teacher Debbie Brown, literally the only time I have been star struck was meeting her. Naturally I have all of her books and have drawn inspiration from her amazing creations over the years. In her wedding cake book there are mini cakes that are entire rose heads—divine—and ever since seeing them I have been hoping for a wedding proposal cake order as an excuse to make my own version of the design idea. Instead I will share it here with you. If you use it, let me know—I am a hopeless romantic.

YOU WILL NEED

1 ring

1 batch cake batter of your choice, I have used white chocolate mud cake batter (see page 35)

White fondant

Gel food color to color the fondant for the rose and leaves; I have used soft pink and Forrest green

Non-stick mat

Cornflour (corn starch) and icing (confectioners') sugar, for dusting

Chocolate ganache(see page 41)

Sugar glue

Cupcake cases

Cupcake tray

Cake box for display (optional)

Aluminium foil

Modelling tools: ball tool

Rose petal and leaf cutters (set of 5 sizes)

Leaf texture mat/silicon mould/or a dried corn husk

MAKING THE CUPCAKES

1 Preheat the oven to 120°C/250°F for mud cake, or 180°C/350°F for a sponge cake batter or follow the instructions on your packet cake mix. Line the cupcake tray with cupcake cases.

2 Make a batch of cake batter and fill the cupcake cases three-quarters full. Bake for 25–35 minutes for the mud cake, or 17–20 minutes for a sponge cake, or until a skewer, when inserted into the centre, comes out clean.

3 Allow the cupcakes to cool.

MAKING A RING IN A ROSE

1 Color the fondant light pink. I added ¼ of a teaspoon of CMC powder to 250 g/9 oz of fondant, to make it stiffer and hold its shape better. If you are in a hot or humid climate, add ½ to 1 teaspoon.

2 Apply a coat of ganache to the top of each cupcake.

3 Make a ball of fondant to sit in the centre of the cupcake. Push the ring into the ball of fondant so it sits upright by itself.

4 Make a long thin sausage of fondant and use your rolling pin to roll it out flat so you have one long, thin, flat oval shape. Start to roll one end to create the start of a spiral; you want the inside

to be going downward not sticking out. Once you have started this, position it next to the ring so the lowest point of the spiral sits above the ring. Continue the spiral, wrapping the ring in the fondant tightly so it is covered by the spiral. If your spiral starts to bend and fold at the top, let it—this looks more natural. Bend it to the shape and angle that best suits your rose and covers the ring.

5 After the initial ring wrap, you need to start adding petals. I start with my smallest rose petal cutters, and work my way through the 5 petal sizes in the set as I work my way outward to the edge of the rose. A rose usually has 5 petals per layer. If you find you have made them too big or small and need more or less, don't worry, they will blend in. Cut out 5 small petals for the first layer, on a cornflour-dusted non-stick surface, then roll over them gently with a rolling pin to flatten them a little more and create a more natural shape.

6 Using the ball tool, gently rub the ball in a circular motion just inside the edge of the petal, working your way around the petal—this makes the petal larger and thinner on the edges, and they will start to curl slightly which gives them a real garden-rose look.

7 Once you have shaped the petals, apply the petals with sugar glue. I work in an anti-clockwise circle adding one petal at a time. When you add a petal, gently pull back the petal using one finger in the centre of the top edge—make these bends more pronounced the further out you work. If the bends look too rounded, simply pinch them to a point; you will notice garden rose petals have a slight point when they are fully open.

8 After you have the first two rows, allow them to set a little before adding any more. In this time you can make the leaves.

TROUBLESHOOT: If the petals start to droop or fall off, you may have rolled the fondant too thick. Start again with thinner petals and allow more drying time between every second layer of petals.

MAKING THE LEAVES

1 To make the leaves, use the leaf side of your largest petal cutter. Add a small amount of CMC powder to the green fondant, and roll and cut it out.

2 Cut out 5–6 leaves per cupcake. I place each leaf, one at a time, into my rose leaf veiner, which is a dual-sided silicon mat. If you don't specifically have rose leaf veiners, use whatever veiner you do have—dried corn husk gives a great veining effect.

3 Attach the leaves around the edge of the cupcake at an angle to give a fanning effect. I attach half of each leaf to the cake and have half hanging over the edge—this makes them fragile and they may need support until they dry. I create a large cup of scrunched up aluminium foil—this is light and easy to spin around to work on my cupcake and also provides a make-shift shelf for my drying leaves.

OPTION ALERT! You can always make the leaves ahead of time and have them dried before adding them to the cupcake. If you take this option they will be very stiff and not malleable to the shape of the cupcake and may require additional ganache to secure them in place. Make a few more than you will need in case of breakages.

4 Continue adding the petals, allowing some drying time after every second row. After 3 or 4 rows start to position your petals at more of an angle to create a full bloom and fill in the space between the centre of the rose and the cupcake top.

5 The last layer is always the trickiest to add. Do it while the layer below it is fresh so that the petals are malleable. You may need to use a modelling tool to gently lift petals in order to gently slide the last row into place. Allow the petals time to dry before putting into a box.

6 Decorate the rest of the cupcakes in the same way but make sure you remember which one has the ring in it, or try and make the one special cupcake a different color rose to the rest. If you really only need the one cupcake, freeze the rest of the batch (un-iced) for lunch box treats at a later date.

Jack the Pumpkin Lantern and Halloween Cupcakes

DIFFICULTY: ✏✏✏✏✏

TIME TO MAKE: ⧗⧗⧗⧗⧗

Who doesn't love Halloween? It's an excuse to dress up and eat lots of sweet treats! And nothing says Halloween like a Jack o'lantern. With all the leftover pumpkin from lantern carving, steam it up, mash it down and make a sweet spiced pumpkin cake full of lollies! Team it up with Halloween-themed cupcakes with bright purple cake batter filled with an orange jelly surprise under a swirl of bright orange buttercream—a few simple decorating tricks and it is definitely a holiday treat!

MAKING THE JELLY

I use my favorite packet jelly mix and follow the manufacturer's instructions. If you can't find orange or you don't like the flavor, choose a lemonade flavor that is clear and add orange coloring. Allow time for the jelly to set really well before using it to pipe into the cupcakes.

YOU WILL NEED

1 batch spiced pumpkin cake

1 batch white mud cake batter

Ball tin 16 x 7 cm/6¼ x 2¾ inch

White chocolate ganache

Gel food coloring: regal purple for the cupcake batter and ganache, orange for the buttercream and fondant, forest green (or brown) for Jack's stalk

1 pack of orange jelly (jello)

Buttercream

2D piping tip (nozzle)

Round piping tip (nozzle) (medium)

Piping bag

Gum paste or fondant & CMC powder: white and black

Orange fondant

Edible black-ink pen

Sugar glue

Cupcake cases

Cupcake tray

Circle cutter

Oval cutter

Teaspoon

Lollies

Wooden skewer or dowel, to make indents

MAKING THE CAKE

1 Preheat the oven to 150°C/300°F for spiced pumpkin cake.

2 Grease both sides of the ball tin and place them in their ring holders on a flat cookie tray on your bench top. If you don't have a ball tin, use oven-safe soup bowls instead.

3 Pour an even amount of batter into each half of the ball and place the entire tray in the oven to bake. Bake for approximately 30–40 minutes, until cooked through.

4 Once cooked, turn the cakes out onto a wire rack to cool, wrap in cling film (plastic wrap) and refrigerate until cold, as it is always easier to cut a cold cake.

5 When it comes time to trim a ball cake, I like to return it to its tin, securing it on the ring it was baking on and using a sharp bread knife and gentle sawing action, cut the top off of the cake using the top of the tin as my height guide. This will help you achieve two halves of a perfect sphere to create a real 'ball shape'.

I actually constructed this cake with the help of my friend Sarah who cleverly suggested taking and extra 1.5-2cm/½–¾ inches off of each layer, which would make the two halves form an elliptical shape which looks more like a real pumpkin.

6 Using a circle cutter, mark the position of the hole in the cake, aim for the centre. Remember you don't want the hole to be so big it destabilises the structure. Using a teaspoon, follow the

cut made by the circle cutter and remove the cake centre. Repeat on the second half.

HOT TIP: To make sure the holes are the same depth on both size I place my index finger in the centre of the hole and note where the line of the cake hole comes to. Match it up on both sides. Note: If these don't match it isn't the end of the world. If you have one that is significantly larger than the other—make that the bottom one.

7 Fill both halves with lollies; I have used chocolate-coated pineapple nougat, worms, caramel popcorn, marshmallows and freckles.

8 Apply a small amount of chocolate ganache to the cake surrounding the holes on both sides. Stick them together by holding one sphere in each hand and gently pushing them together, starting at the bottom and quickly closing the gap to avoid lollies falling out—any lollies that do fall out don't count and can be eaten by the decorator. Note: if you use purple ganache for this step, it is OK and will look funky. I have used the white ganache before coloring because over time it will take on the color of the cake and not be as noticeable, if you really want to make the seam invisible, use white chocolate ganache, or melted chocolate.

9 Color up the rest of the chocolate ganache bright purple and using a cranked handle spatula, apply the ganache to the cake. I start at the bottom of the cake and when the bottom one-third is done I flip it over touching only the naked cake and place it onto its display board. I then apply ganache to the rest of the cake. Allow to set before adding the fondant.

DECORATING JACK

1 Color up your white fondant orange.

2 On a well dusted non-stick surface, roll out the orange fondant into an elliptical shape.

3 Using clean, dry hands transfer the fondant onto the cake so it lies over the top (you can use the rolling pin method here, if you prefer). Once the fondant is on the cake, smooth it across the top and down the sides. Cut away any excess and smooth it in to a neat point at the base.

4 Using the end of your small rolling pin make an indent in the top of the cake, this indent will secure the stalk later, but needs to be made now while the orange fondant is still supple.

5 Line up a wooden skewer or dowel against the side of the cake and make a small impression in the side. Line up the bottom end of it with the base of the cake and the impression on the side and using a little bit of pressure, push it into the cake—you should now have a straight line from the base of the cake up to the side of the cake. To continue it, line the top of the skewer with the top of the cake and the impression in the side of the cake, starting at the point of the side impression, apply pressure to the skewer, moving it upwards to indent the fondant all the way to the top. Now you have your first indent you can see how deep it should be and plan out how many you would like and how many can fit, evenly spaced around the cake. Continue this process until you have as many segments as suits your cake.

6 To add the stalk, add some CMC powder to some green or brown fondant and roll it into a short, fat sausage shape. Apply some sugar glue or leftover ganache to the indent and insert the stalk, bend it over slightly to give a natural, off-the-vine look. Note: if it isn't holding its shape, allow the stalk to dry a little before adding it to the cake. If it is really a problem, secure it in place with a stick of raw spaghetti for added structural support.

Happy lantern eyes, nose and smile

So you have you Jack-a-happy-lantern shape. All the personality of your pumpkin is in the eyes and mouth, so get creative, check out jack-o'-lantern faces on the internet, mix and match expressions and make him your own.

The mouth

1 To make the mouth roll out a thin layer of white fondant (it doesn't need to be gum paste), and using a little knife cut freehand a crescent shape that would indicate a smile.

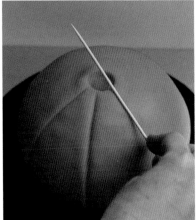

2 Apply a small amount of sugar glue to the back of the mouth and stick in place.

3 For the teeth: roll out a thin layer of black fondant and cut out little squares with either a square cutter or a small knife. Attach to the mouth in a random-gap-toothed manner, top and bottom. Affix them in place with sugar glue.

Eyes

1 To make the eyes use one round cutter and an oval cutter. If you do not have cutters, follow the eye making instructions for Daisy Cow, on a larger scale, and to achieve the oval shape, simply start with an oval ball.

2 First roll out your white fondant and cut two oval shapes. Then, using your circle cutter, roll out your black fondant and cut two circles for the pupil of the eye. Attach the black circles at the base of the white ovals with a small amount of sugar glue.

3 If you have edible white paint, white dust and rose spirit or batter whitener to hand, you can add white dots to the top right hand corners of the pupils to give the eye a cute look. You can apply this as a small dot with a paintbrush, a toothpick or the tip of your Dresden or ball tools. Alternatively, you can achieve this with tiny balls of white fondant.

4 Once you have made the eyes, attach them gently to the face.

5 Decide on the nose size and shape, once the eyes and mouth are in place. You may not need one at all. Roll out some white fondant and cut out a shape using a triangle cutter. Stick in place with sugar glue.

TO MAKE THE CUPCAKES

1 Preheat the oven to 120°C/250°F for mud cake. Line the cupcake tray with cupcake papers.

2 Make the batter, adding your purple food color at the start of the mixing process.

3 Fill the cupcake cases three-quarters full with batter. Bake for 25–35 minutes for the mud cake, or until a skewer, when inserted in the centre, comes out clean.

4 Allow the cupcakes to cool and put them into the refrigerator to get cold. It is always easier to cut a cold cake.

5 Using an apple corer, remove the centre of each cupcake carefully and set it aside for later. Repeat this for all of the cupcakes.

6 Using a spoon, scoop the jelly into a piping bag fitted with a rounded tip/nozzle. I don't break up the jelly too much before putting it into the piping bag because it is a soft product that will break down as I pipe it into the cake. Fill the core with jelly by inserting the tip as far as you can without putting pressure on the top of the cupcake and piping it in. Stop before the jelly protrudes from the top.

7 After the jelly has been piped, cut a small piece-off of the top of the core you removed earlier and stick it back into the cupcake to seal the jelly and protect it from the frosting.

Jelly starts to dissolve at room temperature so you want to get the cakes back into the refrigerator as soon as you can and bring them out again when you are ready to serve them for the best effect.

DECORATING THE CUPCAKES

1 Make up the buttercream, coloring it orange.

2 Scoop the buttercream into a piping bag fitted with a 2D tip/nozzle.

3 For the big ice cream swirl look, using a swirling motion, apply the buttercream, starting with a circle tracing the circumference of the cupcake top and spiralling in towards the centre. Repeat for a second layer, starting further in. Repeat again for a thin layer starting further in again and finally, a small swirl on top as layer 4.

If the big ice cream swirl look isn't to your taste, you can change the design, height and amount to suit.

OPTION ALERT! Use brightly colored sprinkles or add a Halloween-themed sugar topper to the cupcakes like bats or witches, if you like. For a vampire theme, pipe black food gel coloring and red jelly into the cupcakes.

Christmas Tree Fruit Loaf

DIFFICULTY: / / / / /

TIME TO MAKE: ⧗ ⧗ ⧗ ⧗ ⧗

Want to breathe some new life into the old favorite Christmas fruit cake? Me too! That's why I designed this one … quick, simple and very effective! A nice light, sweet fruit cake baked into a loaf for easy cutting and sneaky extra slices, with a festive green tree surprise when you cut it!

OPTION ALERT!

Add an interesting flavor to your green cake mix, so when it is re-baked into the fruit cake you get a combination of flavors—try adding festive cake spices or butterscotch. Or why not use a gingerbread man cutter and flavor the white cake with ginger, nutmeg and mixed spice!

YOU WILL NEED

Loaf tin (pan) (10 x 24 x 7 cm/5⅓ x 9½ x 2¾ inch)
1 batch white chocolate mud (see page 35)
1 batch light fruit cake batter (see page 36)
Christmas tree or festive cookie cutter
Gel food coloring: forest green
White chocolate ganache
White fondant

Green and red gum paste/ fondant and CMC powder
Holly leaf cutter(s)
Sugar glue
Cranked handle spatula
Display board

MAKING THE GREEN CHRISTMAS TREES AND FRUIT LOAF

1 Preheat the oven to 120–130°C/250–265°F for mud cake. Grease and flour, or line the loaf tin.

2 Once the loaf has cooled completely, wrap it in cling film (plastic wrap) and put it in the refrigerator. When chilled, using a bread knife, cut the loaf into 2–2.5 cm/¾–1 inch thick slices. If your cake has started to come to room temperature as you have cut it, put it back in the refrigerator—you need these slices as cold as possible without being frozen to get the best cut out.

3 Lightly spray the Christmas tree cutter with vegetable oil and use to cut out trees from the cake slices. Remove the excess cake from around the edges, then gently using your finger to push it out a little at a time working your way around the shape evenly so it does not crack. Make as many trees as you can.

4 Wrap each tree individually and freeze. The trees must be frozen so that they don't over bake, dry out or liquefy when we re-bake them in the fruit cake.

5 Preheat the oven to 180°C/350°F for light fruit cake (lower if you have a hot oven). Grease and flour the loaf tin.

6 Place approximately one-fifth of the batter into the loaf tin and use this as base to secure the frozen trees. Space the trees no less than 2 cm/¾ inches apart. When you put the trees into the batter, push them down to the base of the tin to secure them.

7 Once all of the trees are in place, disperse the rest of the batter into the cake tin between them. The fruit may make it difficult to use a piping bag. Make sure there are no pockets of air

where you may have missed pushing batter between the trees and make sure the batter is even. You may need to

keep propping your trees up—don't worry, the more batter you put in the more they will stay in place.

8 Once the batter is in the tin, you don't want to see trees sticking out of the batter, use your cranked handle spatula (slightly wet to avoid batter sticking to it) to smooth the batter over the top of the trees.

9 Bake immediately for at least 50 minutes or according to the recipe you have used. When it comes time to check your cake, be sure to check the cake is cooked through by inserting a skewer at three different points across the cake to ensure you are accurately checking the cake batter and not the trees!

Leave to cool on a wire rack. Once the cake is cooked and cooled completely—it is ready to decorate!

DECORATING THE CAKE

1 Smooth a thin layer of white chocolate ganache over the top of the cake.

TROUBLESHOOT: Does your cake look a bit dry on the top? Make a sugar syrup or reduce some apricot jam and brush a layer or two of it over the top of the cake—this will help moisten and seal the top of the cake as well as act as glue for the fondant.

2 Roll out approximately 250 g/9 oz white fondant into a rough rectangle slightly larger than the top of the cake. Once you have rolled it out, gently pull the edges at different intervals all the way around to form mini rounded balloons; these will be the fondant parts that hang down the side of the loaf to look like melting snow.

3 Apply the fondant to the top of the loaf and smooth it gently, pulling the 'melting snow' sides into shape.

MAKING THE HOLLY

1 Thinly roll out the green gum paste. Using your holly leaf cutter cut out you three holly leaf shape note: if you have single cutters, just cut out three leaves of the same size. Make two—lay one on a flat surface to dry. With the second, place it into a shallow dish or scrunch up aluminium foil to make a small well to lay in it to dry—the desired effect we want to achieve is leaves that point upwards ever so slightly.

2 Make three small, equally sized red balls for the holly berries with your red gum paste. Attach them to the centre of the second holly leaf shape (or if you have single leaf cutters add them directly to the cake when it is time).

3 When you apply the holly to the cake, apply the flat one first and then the shaped one directly above it. The flat one below looks like shadowing and gives a great effect for very little extra effort.

OPTION ALERT! Feeling confident with your gum paste and cutters? Why not cut out many holly leaves and arrange them, over lapping to form a wreath on top? Add red berries with sugar glue around the wreath and finish with a bow. See Rum Baubles cake on page 227 and painting with edible gold dust.

Individual Fruit Cakes

DIFFICULTY: ✎ ✎ ✎ ✎ ✎
TIME TO MAKE: ⏳ ⏳ ⏳ ⏳ ⏳

Want to serve up a Christmas dessert with a surprise that looks fancy but is easy to make? These individual fruit cakes with a hidden cake bauble inside are a delight to behold, with all the glamour of an al a carte meal that is not only easy to make but can be made ahead of time to take the stress out of your Christmas soirée.

OPTION ALERT!

Add an interesting flavor to your green/red cake mix, so when it is re-baked into the fruit cake you get a combination of flavors; try adding festive cake spices, apple pie mixed spice with ginger, butterscotch or even dried plum and cranberries for sharp taste.

YOU WILL NEED

1 batch light fruit cake batter (makes 24) (see page 36)

1 batch mud cake batter for cake balls (see page 34)

Spices, to flavor the cake (optional – I have used apple pie spice and ginger)

Cake ball trays

Tray (pan) of individual mini cakes OR use large individual Dariole moulds

Gel food color: I have used forest green, orange and Christmas red

White chocolate ganache

White fondant

CMC powder, to turn fondant into gum paste

Edible gold paint / gold dust with rose spirit

Paintbrush

Edible red glitter

Cake confetti

Sugar glue

Large circle cutter

Rolling pin

Non-stick mat

Cornflour (corn starch) and icing (confectioners') sugar, for dusting

Green and red gum paste / fondant and CMC powder

Holly Leaf Cutter(s)

MAKING THE CAKE BALLS

First you need to make red and green colored cake balls from white chocolate mud cake.

1 Mix one batch of white chocolate mud cake batter. Flavor it if you like.

2 Once mixed, divide the batter equally between two bowls and color one batch with forest green and the other batch first with orange and then with red to make the tone an intense red.

3 Preheat the oven to 150°C/300°F. Grease both sides of your cake ball tray with cake release agent/vegetable oil. Spoon your batter into the base tray.

4 Bake for 17–20 minutes. Depending on your oven and the cake batter recipe you use the cooking time may vary. As a general rule the cake batter should come out of the top of the cake ball tray a little or at least be visible and when you put a skewer in it, the skewer should come out clean. I always sacrifice one cake ball from the centre of the tray to cut open and check—this also means you get to eat it!

5 Once you have cooked all of the batter and the cake balls have cooled, individually wrap the cold cake balls in cling film (plastic wrap) and freeze them. I put freezer wrap or 'go-between'

between each cake ball to ensure they don't stick together and to avoid icicles forming on them. Remember, the balls need to be frozen when we bake them again, so they don't dissolve and disappear into the fruit cake batter so don't skip this step.

MAKING THE LOAF CAKES

1 Preheat the oven to 180°C/350°F. Grease and flour the mini cake tray (pan) (or large Dariole moulds).

2 Make one batch of light fruit cake batter.

3 Place batter in each mini cake slot filling it approximately one-fifth full of batter. Remove the frozen cake balls from the freezer, unwrap them and add frozen cake balls to each loaf pan, anchoring them in the batter. Cover the baubles with batter leaving enough space for the cakes to rise.

For some of my individual cakes, I filled them right to the top, knowing they would ride over the cake pan, this created a muffin top/toadstool shape that I could decorate for a very different snow capped mountain effect.

4 Bake immediately for 20–25 minutes, or until cooked through. Test the cakes by inserting a skewer into them. If the skewer comes out clean then the cakes are ready. Invert onto a wire rack to cool.

MAKING SNOW-CAPPED FRUIT MOUNTAINS

For some of my individual cakes, I filled them right to the top, knowing they would rise over the cake pan, this created a mushroom top that I could decorate with white fondant like snow melting down over the sides and a little holly on top.

1 To achieve its look, simply ganache the top of your cake, roll out your white fondant and using a circle cutter, cut out the top of your cake. Before applying the circle topper, gently pull at the edges of the circle to create peaks of snow than can gently hang over the sides of the individual cake. To create the holly, see instructions on page 284)

PSST! Make sure you don't roll the white fondant out too thick—if you do you may experience the melting snow drooping lower than expected or the smaller stem of the cake may buckle under the weight and fall over or start to crack.

MAKING LITTLE DOMES OF DELIGHT

These are three cakes, covered the same way with slightly different decorations for radially different effects.

1 First, place the cake upside down and using a kitchen knife, trim any excess cake away so there is no mushroom head.

I like to leave the base of the cake facing upwards because with my individual cake tin the base is slightly narrower than the top is this gives me a very slight dome.

2 Apply ganache to each cake.

3 Roll out your white fondant thinly and to size and cover the individual cake the same way you would a round cake, however be very gentle when smoothing down the sides.

4 To make the holly—see the instructions in the Christmas fruit loaf.

5 To make the golden coins for luck, put a handful of cake confetti into a small bowl. Add some edible gold dust on top then 1 teaspoon of rose spirit. Using a teaspoon, turn the cake confetti over and over, allowing the gold dust and liquid to coat them thoroughly. Set aside

on the bench, uncovered, for at least 2 hours to allow the rose spirit to evaporate, turn it over again a few more times with the teaspoon to ensure the confetti is thoroughly coated in gold and then attach a spoon full of it to the top of your individual cake, securing in place with a small amount of melted green chocolate which will act as glue. Note: you do not need a lot of chocolate for this!

6 To make gold cakes, mix edible gold dust with rose spirit to form a soupy liquid consistency. Working quickly, with a paintbrush coat the white fondant with gold. You may need to apply two coats to ensure the gold is opaque. Set aside for the rose spirit to evaporate before applying the second coat.

7 When the gold is touch dry, add a small amount of sugar glue to the top of the cake and dust the glue spot with red glitter.

Banana Star

DIFFICULTY: / / / / /

TIME TO MAKE: ⏳⏳⏳⏳⏳

If, like me, you frequently have leftover, over-ripe bananas that you freeze with the intention of making something later and never do … try this! I decided to bake my banana cake into a loaf tin shape, colored brightly and when cooled to fridge temperature, I cut out fun shapes from it and freeze the shapes. Then, the next time I have leftover bananas, I bring out the frozen banana cake shapes and bake them into a banana bread, top this with cream cheese frosting and cut that into slices that easily fit into a lunch box and voila … an exciting lunch snack that gets eaten.

Get your fussy eater to cut this otherwise boring-looking-loaf to reveal the star surprise and see how quickly they want some more!

OPTION ALERT!

Add an interesting flavor to your cake mix, so when it is re-baked into the banana bread you get a combination of flavors—try caramel or honey.

YOU WILL NEED

Loaf tin (pan) (10 x 24 x 7 cm/5⅓ x 9½ x 2¾ inch)
1 batch banana cake batter (see page 33)
1 batch banana bread batter (see page 33)
Star cutter
Gel food color: egg yellow

Cream cheese, butter and icing (confectioners')
  sugar, for the cream cheese frosting
Crank-handled spatula
Display board

MAKING STAR SHAPES

1 Grease and flour, or line, the loaf tin. Preheat oven set at 190°C/375°F.

2 Make one batch of the banana cake. Color the batter with egg yellow food color. Pour batter into the prepared loaf tin and bake immediately for 40 minutes. Insert a skewer into the centre. If the skewer comes out clean the cake is baked. Invert onto a wire rack to cool.

3 Wrap the cold cake with cling film (plastic wrap) and refrigerate until chilled. Using a bread knife, cut the loaf into 2–2.5 cm/¾–1 inch thick slices. Spray your star-shaped cookie cutter lightly with vegetable oil to help glide it through the cake slices. Cut out as many stars as you can from each slice. Try to plan ahead to minimise waste.

4 Wrap each star individually and freeze. The stars must be frozen so that they don't over bake, dry out or liquefy when we re-bake them in the banana bread.

MAKING THE BANANA BREAD

1 Following your favorite banana bread recipe or following the banana cake recipe again, preheat your oven, grease and flour the loaf tin and prepare your cake batter.

2 Add approximately one-fifth of the batter in the loaf tin. Use this as base to secure the frozen stars. Space the stars no less than 2 cm/¾ inches apart. Be sure to push the stars all the way to the base of the tin.

3 Disperse the rest of the batter into the cake tin between the stars. Use a piping bag fitted with a large round tip/nozzle to do this. Make sure there are no pockets of air between the

stars. Don't worry if the stars don't align. Using a cranked handle spatula, ensure the cake batter covers the tops of the stars.

4 Bake immediately in accordance with the recipe you have chosen. To check that the cake is cooked through, insert a skewer at three different points across the cake to ensure you are not testing the pre-baked stars. If the skewer comes out clean, the cake is ready. Leave to set in the tin for a few minutes then turn out onto a wire rack to cool.

5 Make one batch of cream cheese frosting and spread over the top of the loaf.

OPTION ALERT! Got any sprinkles in the cupboard? Dust over the frosting for added interest. To dress up the cake for any of the holidays like Valentine's day or Easter, add cut out fondant shapes or little figurines or any of the Christmas details on previous pages. Add some gold confetti on top for instant glam!

Duck Pond Cupcakes

DIFFICULTY: / / / / /
TIME TO MAKE: ⏳⏳⏳⏳⏳

YOU WILL NEED

1 batch mud cake batter (see page 34)
1 pack of jelly (jello) of your choice
Blue chocolate or white chocolate (or white
    chocolate ganache) and blue food color
Gum paste or white fondant and CMC powder
Gel food color: gold, lemon yellow, orange, blue
Edible black-ink pen

Sugar glue
Cupcake cases
Cupcake tray
Piping bag
Round piping tip/nozzle (medium size)
Small embroidery scissors

FIRST MAKE THE JELLY

1 Make one batch of packet jelly mix—if you can't find blue, choose a lemonade variety that has a clear color and color it with edible blue color. Leave to set well before using it to pipe into the cupcakes.

MAKING THE CUPCAKES

1 Preheat the oven to 120°C/250°F for mud cake batter. Line the cupcake tray with cupcake cases.

2 Make up one batch of your chosen mud cake batter. Three-quarters fill the cupcake cases with batter.

3 Bake for 25–35 minutes for the mud cake, or until a skewer, when inserted into the centre, comes out clean.

4 Allow the cupcakes to cool and then refrigerate them until cold, as it is always easier to cut a cold cake.

5 Using an apple corer, remove out the centre of each cupcake carefully and set it aside for later. Repeat this for all of the cupcakes.

6 Using a spoon, scoop the jelly into a piping bag fitted with a rounded tip/nozzle. I don't break up the jelly too much before putting it into the piping bag because it is a soft product that will break down as I pipe it into the cake. Fill the core with jelly by inserting the tip as far as you can without putting pressure on the top of the cupcake and piping it in. Stop before the jelly protrudes from the top.

7 Trim the top off the removed cake core and stick it back into the cupcake to seal in the jelly.

MAKING DUCKS

1 Color up a small amount of gum paste in yellow and orange. For these ducks I have used 1 drop of gold and two drops of lemon yellow to make the duck color—gold provides an earthy base to the bright lemon yellow that provides depth of color and vibrancy.

2 Roll yellow gum paste into a ball, the size will depend on the size of your cupcake.

3 Place the ball on your work surface and roll each end with your finger so it becomes an oval shape. Pinch one end upwards to create tail.

4 Roll yellow gum paste into a smaller ball to make the head. Attach the round ball to the top of the end of your oval body shape using sugar glue to secure it.

TROUBLESHOOT: If you use too much sugar glue the head will slide off of the body. If you you are having trouble use a piece of raw spaghetti inserted into the body and head for support.

5 To make the beak: roll a very small ball of orange gum paste. Using your finger in a rolling motion over one end shape it into a teardrop shape on the work surface. Stand it up on its heavier end and use the work surface to flatten the base and your fingers to mould the teardrop into a triangle shape. Using sugar glue, stick the beak to the front of the yellow ball head.

If you would like the beak to be open in a quack, simply take small, sharp embroidery scissors and cut the beak at the halfway point, approximately two-thirds down the length of it, to open the beak further, use your fingers to bend the ends of the cut pieces up and back.

DECORATING THE CUPCAKES

1 Break up the blue chocolate and place it in a heatproof bowl set over a pot of hot water. Keep moving the chocolate until it is liquid then take it off the heat immediately. Do not overheat the chocolate and resist the temptation to melt it quicker by boiling the water in the pot. If your chocolate changes color or takes on a granule-like texture then you have overheated the chocolate and need to start again.

Note: if you are using couverture chocolate, follow the instructions for that product as it will perform differently). If you are coloring your chocolate blue see page 28 for details.

2 Dip the cupcakes, cake top first into the bowl of melted blue chocolate—I dip the cake so that the chocolate just starts to cover the top of the cupcake case, this gives a nice finish tot the edges and hold the paper in place.

3 Add your ducks to the top of each cupcake right after you dip it, that way the chocolate will secure the duck to the top of the cupcake and you will never risk them falling off in transit!

Green Tea and Pistachio Cupcakes

DIFFICULTY: ✐✐✐✐✐

TIME TO MAKE: ⧗⧗⧗⧗⧗

Want to make light, soft, decadent cupcakes for afternoon tea? Try these! A gentle infusion of green tea in a light, fluffy, sweet sponge cake batter with surprise centre of cold, delicious pistachio-flavored mascarpone cream, hidden away under a scalloped edged flat white fondant disc adorned with a small, sweet rose.

OPTION ALERT!

Add 1 teaspoon of rose water to your sponge cake batter instead of green tea and add cranberries to the mascarpone for a tart taste or raspberries/strawberries for a sweet taste (if you do this be sure to use pink gel food color in your batter instead of green).

YOU WILL NEED

1 batch sponge cake batter (page 37)
Mascarpone cream
Pistachio food flavor or paste
White fondant
Pastry cutter (circle with scalloped edges)
Small amount of green buttercream or ganache
Gum paste

Gel food coloring: soft pink for the rose, avocado and mint green for the batter
Cupcake cases
Cupcake tray
Piping bag
Round piping tip (medium sized)

MAKING THE CUPCAKES

1 Preheat the oven to 180°C/350°F for sponge cake batter. Line the cupcake tray with cupcake cases.

2 Make one batch of sponge cake batter. To infuse the green tea in the cake, put the green teabag in a pan with the milk required for the sponge batter. Heat the milk to 80°C/175°F, stirring constantly. Once it reaches this temperature, remove from the heat source and continue to stir. Allow to cool and use when cold.

3 Three-quarters fill the cupcake cases. Bake for 17–20 minutes, or until a skewer, when inserted into the cake centre, comes out clean.

4 Allow to cool, then refrigerate to chill.

5 Using an apple corer, remove out the centre of each cupcake carefully and set it aside for later. Repeat this for all of the cupcakes.

For the filling, flavor a small amount of mascarpone cream with pistachio paste/flavoring. Part-fill a piping bag and pipe the pistachio mascarpone cream into the core of the cupcake by inserting the tip as far as you can without putting pressure on the top of the cupcake. Stop before the mascarpone cream protrudes from the top.

6 Trim a small piece of the cake core from the top and use this to plug the top of the hole in the cake. (Optional step)

7 Place a dollop of green buttercream or ganache on top of the cupcake so that the rose decoration will be held securely. You will need to keep these cupcakes in the refrigerator before and after decorating.

DECORATING THE CUPCAKES

1 Roll out the white fondant quite thin, using the scalloped edge of the round pastry cutter, cut out one circle for each cupcake. Choose a scalloped circle cutter slightly smaller than the top if the cupcake. I do this step in advance so the circle has time to stiffen. If you are in a hot or humid climate, add a small amount of CMC powder.

2 Make the roses and allow them the same time to dry as the white fondant discs. I use gum paste for these.

Make a long thin sausage of gum paste and use your rolling pin to roll it out flat so you have one long thin flat elliptical shape. With your fingers, gently start to roll one end of the flat elliptical shape to create the start of a spiral; you want the inside of the spiral, or rose centre to be going downward not sticking out.

Once you have made a good start on the spiral, pick it up with clean, dry, cornflour-dusted fingers, holding it in one hand, then use your other hand to gently wrap the rest of the gum paste around the spiral, now working upward, not recessing the spiral.

When you hold the gum paste tail out away from the spiral, push and bend it back in and make waves in it, secure it with sugar glue at regular intervals and keep going all the way around—this will start to look like many rose petals. When you have run out of gum paste or reached the desired size, cut away the excess and finishing it by securing the tail end underneath the rose. Start to pull slightly on the peaks of the rose petals, bending them outward a little to make them more lifelike.

3 Place one white fondant disc on top of each cupcake. Apply a small amount of green butter cream or ganache to the centre of the disc. This will act as a glue to secure the rose and also give the impression of green leaves. Place one rose in the centre of each cupcake.

Monster Ball Cake

DIFFICULTY: ✎✎✎✎✎

TIME TO MAKE: ⏳⏳⏳⏳⏳

Monster-themed birthday parties are all the rage at the moment and they are just so fun and easy to cater for. The reason I love making kids' cakes so much is because they are just so darn happy when they receive them, the idea of adding additional excitement to their lives when they cut the cake to find a treasure trove of lollies inside is just too good to pass up! So I have designed this purple ball of monster sweetness, which conceals a fantastic surprise inside for the kids.

OPTION ALERT!

Simply change the gel food color you put in the buttercream to make your monster in the recipient's favorite color! Instant win!

YOU WILL NEED

1 batch chocolate mud cake batter (see page 34)

Ball tin (pan) 16 x 7 cm/6¼ x 2¾ inch

Small amount of chocolate ganache (or melted chocolate)

Gel food coloring: regal purple for the fur, royal blue for the eyes

Buttercream

233 Grass piping tip/nozzle

Coupler

Piping bag

Fondant white and black (small amount for eyes and fangs)

Sugar glue

Circle cutter

Oval cutter

Triangle (or square) cutter

Teaspoon

Lollies

Display board

MAKING THE CAKE

1 Preheat the oven to 130°C/265°F for chocolate mud cake. Grease both sides of the ball tin and place them in their ring holders on a baking sheet on a flat surface.

Note: If you are unable to get access to a ball tin, you can use oven safe soup bowls instead.

2 Pour an even amount of batter into each half of the ball. I like to fill the cake tins leaving only one thumb width of space between the batter and top of the tins. With the small rise expected of a mud cake, the cake should reach just above the tin, which will make trimming a lot easier (see step 3). Place the tray in the oven and bake for 40–60 minutes. Check the cake halves after 30 minutes to assess how well the cake is baking. Remember cooking time will vary based on recipe, size of your tin and your oven. To check if the cake is cooked through, insert a skewer into the cake centre. If it comes out clean, the cake is ready.

3 Once the cakes have been cooked and turned out onto a wire rack to cool, wrap each cake in cling film (plastic wrap) and refrigerate to chill.

4 To trim a ball cake, return the baked cake to its tin, securing it on the ring that held the cake level in the oven. Using a sharp bread knife and gentle sawing action, slice the top off of the cake using the top of the tin as a guide. This will help to achieve two halves of a perfect sphere to create a real 'ball' shape.

5 Using a circle cutter, mark the position of the hole in the cake—aim for the centre. Remember you don't want the hole to be so big it destabilises the structure.

6 Using a teaspoon, follow the cut made by the circle cutter and remove the centre of the mud cake. Repeat for each cake half.

HOT TIP: To make sure the holes are the same depth on both sides, I place my index finger in the centre of the hole and note where the depth comes to match at both sides. If you've made one significantly larger than the other, make that the bottom one.

7 Fill both halves with lollies. Apply a small amount of chocolate ganache to the cake surround the lolly holes on both sides. If you don't have any chocolate ganache to hand, don't make a batch just for this, melt a small amount of chocolate in a bowl over hot water and use the melted chocolate directly. Note: if you use this option you need to work fast.

8 Working quickly to avoid lollies falling out, stick the two halves together by holding one sphere in each hand and gently pushing them together, starting at the base.

DECORATING YOUR MONSTER

1 Make and color the buttercream.

2 Attach the grass tip/nozzle to the coupler in the piping bag and part fill the piping bag. Buttercream melts quickly so you don't want too much in the bag, in your hot hands.

3 Start at the bottom of your monster. Have him flipped upside down and work from the centre of the base out, you want to cover the bottom third with fur before flipping it over onto your display board. When you get to this point, simply start working from the centre of the top of the monster, outwards.

4 To achieve the 'fur' look, start working from the centre of the top of the monster outward. Hold the piping tip just above the cake and squeeze out the buttercream. With even pressure, move the piping bag slowly downward, following the line of the cake—this will create long lines of fur. When you have reached a natural stopping point continue the same pressure over one spot to anchor the long strands. Repeat over the entire cake.

IMPORTANT NOTE: The key to this is consistent pressure on your piping bag. If you find you are going well and all of a sudden it starts to look different or if the buttercream doesn't hold its shape, it is probably too hot. Squeeze it out of the piping bag back into the bowl and replace with cool buttercream. Squeeze out the excess stuck in the tip and when it runs clear, start piping again. You could decorate the cake in stages, returning the cake and buttercream to the refrigerator periodically, or, if you are working in very hot conditions consider a buttercream replacement based on vegetable fats.

CUTE EYES AND SOME CHEEKY FANGS

The fangs

1 To make the fangs roll out a thin layer of white fondant (it doesn't need to be gum paste), and using a triangle cutter, cut out two triangular shapes and attach them directly to the face. The buttercream will act as glue to secure them in place. In the absence of a triangle cutter you can cut a square cut in half or free hand triangles with a little knife.

 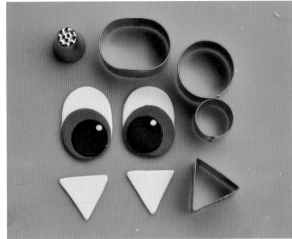

The eyes

2 To make the eyes, use two different size round cutters and an oval cutter. If you do not have cutters, follow the instructions for Daisy Cow on a larger scale, and to achieve the oval shape, simply start with an oval ball.

3 Roll out some white fondant and cut out two ovals.

4 Color a little fondant blue for the iris of the eyes and roll out as before. Using the larger circle cutter, cut out two circles and attach each to the lower half of an oval using sugar glue.

5 For the pupil roll out some black fondant. Using the smaller circle cutter cut out two circles and attach each to the centre of the blue-iris circles using sugar glue.

6 If you have edible white paint, white dust and rose spirit, or batter whitener, add white dots to the top right-hand corners of the pupils to appear as if light is reflecting from the eye. You can also use the tip of a Dresden or ball tool to add the paint or even very small balls of white fondant.

7 Once you have made the eyes, attach them directly to the face. The buttercream will act as glue to hold them securely in place.

i'm having a...

Gender Reveal Belly Cake

DIFFICULTY: ✏✏✏✏✏

TIME TO MAKE: ⧗⧗⧗⧗⧗

This cake is so exciting! I love the idea of baby-gender reveal and while there are some really cool photographic ways to share your news online, there is nothing quite like seeing the anticipation on someone's face!

These sort of cakes have been hugely popular for revealing a new baby's gender to grandparents and siblings—kids love surprises and you can keep them guessing. Be it siblings, grandparents or the wider family and friends; be sure to have the camera at the ready to record their reactions.

OPTION ALERT! If you don't want to color the cake, make a flavored cake and choose lollies/chocolate to place inside in an appropriate color for the reveal.

YOU WILL NEED

Hemisphere tin (pan), small 15 cm/6 round and
   7.5 cm/3 deep (or use an oven-safe soup bowl)
250–500 g/8½ oz–17½ oz ganache
1 kg/2lb 3⅓ oz fondant
Gel food coloring: skin tone*, blue, pink and
   yellow
½ quantity of white chocolate mud batter (see
   page 35)
Display board

CMC powder, to add to fondant
Letter cutters
Sugar glue
Rolling pin
Non-stick mat
Icing mix, for dusting
Fondant or kitchen knife
*see the techniques section on page 24 for advice
   on achieving skin color

MAKING THE CAKE

1 Preheat the oven to 120–130°C/250–265°F for mud cake, or 180°C/350°F for sponge cake batter. Grease the cake tin and dust it with flour. Stabilise the tin on a tray and egg ring, or rest it on a small round cake tin that is one-fifth filled with water (or less to ensure the water does not touch the hemisphere tin).

2 Make up a half quantity of white chocolate mud cake. Color and flavor the cake batter. For this cake, I used a small amount of royal blue food color to make a bright medium blue batter with no need to whiten the batter first. I find the pigment in the lighter blues is not dark enough to overtake the yellow base of the batter and will turn green. If you are coloring your soft baby pink color the batter with white food coloring first to avoid it turning orange. Tip the batter into the tin.

Flavor ALERT! I have used a white chocolate mud cake base and added coconut flavor to it and served it up with coconut biscuits and fruity tea. You can use whatever flavor suits you or the recipients of the cake best.

3 Bake for 40–60 minutes, or until a skewer, when inserted into the centre, comes out clean. Be sure to test your cake 10 minutes before the timer is due to go off to get an idea of how it is progressing and adjust the timing from there. Depending on your oven, the type of chocolate used and the size of your hemisphere tin/oven-safe soup bowl your cooking time may vary, so be flexible. Once cooked, turn out onto a wire rack to cool.

4 When the cake has cooled, wrap the cake in cling film and place in the refrigerator. The next step requires a cold cake for optimal results.

TROUBLESHOOT If the cake has risen into a dome in the oven—don't despair! The cake being cooked through is the most important thing. Once it refrigerator cold simply place the cake back in the tin and using the edges of the tin as a guide, carefully slice the dome off the cold cake.

5 Place the cold cake dome side up. Using a bread knife cut off the top one-third of the cake like a lid and set it aside. The straighter it is the easier it is to put back together with minimal seams.

6 Using a circle cutter, or an egg ring if you don't have cutters, line up the ring over the centre of the cake. Resist the temptation to make this a large circle, the closer to the edge you go the more you will compromise the cake's structural integrity and it needs to hold the heavy weight of fondant. Insert the circle cutter as far as it will go or to the required depth (depends on your cutter) and remove it. Using a teaspoon, spoon out the cake inside the circle you have just cut. I try to make a bowl or dish shape.

7 Fill the cake with chocolate or lollies, ensuring the sweets lay flush with the top of the cake, being careful not to over fill it. Apply ganache, like glue, to the top of the cake around the lollies and all the way to the edge—this will seal your lid in place. Replace the lid of the cake ensuring it sits flush with the cake beneath it. If it does not, remove some lollies to ensure it does otherwise your end look will be ruined. Return the cake to the refrigerator to harden. Once hardened, remove the cake from the refrigerator and apply a layer of ganache over the cake.

TIP: I find using a hemisphere tin gives me a perfect curve, ganaching it like a usual cake actually makes it less smooth. (For me anyway!) For a perfectly smooth hemisphere, I heat ganache until it is the consistency of pumpkin soup and pour it over the cake. The ganache is thin enough to coat the cake and take on the cake's shape rather than help to shape the cake. This seals the cake, gives the fondant something to stick to and retains the perfectly smooth belly curve.

DECORATING THE CAKE AND BOARD

1 Place the ganache-coated cake on a clean work surface. I like to cover this cake twice. This means rolling the fondant a bit thinner, but I find it's worth it. Roll out the white fondant thinner than usual, on a non-stick, dusted surface. Arrange it over the hemisphere cake and using your hands smooth it down over the cake immediately. Tuck it in at the bottom edge and cut away the excess with a fondant or kitchen knife. If this excess doesn't have any ganache or moisture on it, you can fold it into your remaining white and use it again. Set the cake aside for this layer of fondant set a little.

2 While you are waiting, cover the board. To make a pink and blue swirl to keep them guessing, color two equally sized balls of fondant pink and blue (each 200 g/7 oz) and roll both into fat sausage shapes. Twist these sausages together like a rope and on a non-stick, dusted surface. Start to roll out the 'rope' like a standard piece of fondant—as you roll and stretch it into a rectangle big enough to cover the board the colors will merge to make an attractive swirl.

TROUBLESHOOT: If you have trouble rolling out the fondant and need to gather it up and roll it out again your swirls might start to blend into each other too much and turn blue-grey. If this happens, start again. If you don't have enough fondant to start again from scratch, add another sausage shape of pink.

3 Place the belly cake onto the board, centring it on the last two-thirds of the board, leaving enough room above it for breasts, dress straps and lettering, while still allowing enough space at the base for a pretty bow. Secure the cake to the board by applying some ganache to the board OR directly to the base of the cake if it has been cut and is crumbly—this will help with the moisture retention.

4 To make the breasts, color some fondant skin tone (see page 25 for instructions on how to achieve this color) and roll two equal oval shapes. You will be tempted to make these round but when you place two round balls atop of the belly you will notice that it does not look visually balanced—make them predominantly round with light elliptical ends (a gentle oval shape)— these will sit nicely atop the belly and create a soft curve that, once the dress has been added, will travel the eye around and across the shape. This shape is also a lot easier to cover.

5 Using a small amount of water or sugar glue, lightly coat the fondant on the belly and the lower quarter of the boobs so the new piece of fondant will stick. Roll out the rest of white fondant long and wide enough to cover half of the breasts and the belly again. At the end of the fondant you intend to apply to the breasts, use a fondant or kitchen knife to give it a sharp clean edge.

Gently pick up the fondant and place it on the cake. Start at the breasts and place it over the belly. Smooth the fondant over the belly and work your way up to the breasts. Stretch the ends of the fondant to cover the breasts in the desired shape. I have gone for a straight across look. You may wish to stretch the fondant up higher on the sides by smoothing with your hands, to give a heart-shaped neckline.

Carefully trim away the excess fondant, being careful not to cut the fondant on the board.

6 For the dress straps, make two wide rectangular strips of white fondant. Cut one end straight and flat with a fondant or kitchen knife, then using sugar glue, attach this straight end to the top of the dress and place the strip down over the top of the breast and onto the board. Trim the excess at the edge of the board.

OPTION ALERT! If you have time and it suits your design, you can make buttons or flowers out of fondant or gum paste to put over the join of the strap and bodice of the dress.

7 For the bow, color some fondant yellow. If you would like the bow to sit up, add some CMC powder to the fondant. I prefer a bow with dimension for this so I have used CMC powder. Make the ribbons of the bow first by cutting two rectangular strips. Cut a triangle out of each end. Using sugar glue, apply these to the board as desired.

Then to make the two ears of the bow, cut out two fat rectangles, one at a time fold the two short ends together with a touch of sugar glue and then pinch them together. Then sit your bow ear up right on your dusted work surface and with your fingers pull the ear into a nice shape. Repeat for the second bow ear and join the ends together in the centre. Position the two bow ears at the base of the belly, covering the point where the ribbons are attached with a small rectangle of yellow gum paste, tucking each end behind them and under the joint of the bow ears.

VARIATION: If you want to model a summer dress, you'll need a longer board and a larger piece of white fondant for the last covering step. Follow the same instructions and instead of cutting away the excess at the bottom of the dress, manipulate it into folds or waves to indicate the skirt of a dress. Be sure the shape of the skirt flares out a little after the belly so you know it's a dress.

8 The lettering. You can make this say anything you like, personalise it to capture a family joke or pet names such as a "baby peanut is a ...." or "jacks new... (sister/brother)..." or "boy or girl?" or "It's a....." Secure your letters with sugar glue and you are done! Now on to the best part: cutting the cake, revealing the gender and sharing the joy!

Day of the Dead
(Dia De Los Muertos)

DIFFICULTY: ✏✏✏✏✏

TIME TO MAKE: ⏳⏳⏳⏳⏳

Living in Australia, there is not a huge celebration of the day of the dead, but it had always struck a chord with me. It wasn't until we happened to be in Mexico during this time that we got to understand it a bit better and it was a truly amazing experience. The day of the dead or Spanish 'Dia de los Muertos' is a celebration dating back to the time of Aztecs, held over two days, November 1st and 2nd, it focuses on gathering together family and friends to honour those who have passed on by remembering them in stories, preparing their favorite foods, lighting a candle in their honour and praying for them. Traditionally, alters called 'ofrendas' are made to honour the dead and decorated sugar skulls and marigolds adorn the altar. This is mainly celebrated in Mexico where it is a national holiday but is also practiced in pockets across the world. The sugar skulls and their colorful, happy designs took off as a fashion item a few years ago and in a reversed way caused interest in the origins and understanding of the celebration on a pop culture level. If you know about Day of the Dead, I hope you like this cake design. If you don't know about it and are interested I highly recommend reading up on it.

OPTION ALERT!

To make this design a lot simpler, hire a skull cake pan and follow the instructions.

YOU WILL NEED

1 batch chocolate mud cake batter (see page 34)

Ball tin (pan) 16 x 7 cm/6¼ x 2¾ inch

Chocolate ganache

Gel food coloring: regal purple, orange, red. royal blue, deep pink

Edible gold & pink paint

Gum paste

Modelling tools: Dresden tool

Edible black-ink pen

Sugar glue

Paintbrush

Cutters: heart, star and daisy

Lollies

Display board

Skull face (to use as a mould for the gum paste)

I have also used flexible lace moulds to create butterflies and dragonflies. This will not be covered off in this book, if you are interested in this I suggest it looking up!

FIRST MAKE THE FACE

1 The face will take a good amount of time to dry. First find a skull that is about the size of the ball tin you have, ideally you want the face to fit over the ball tin leaving space from the nose down to fill with lollies. Try your old Halloween decorations; it is around the same time of year so there should be lots of cheap, plastic options in the shops. I have a concrete skull that sits on our bookshelf that found itself reappropriated for the task.

2 Spray your clean, dry, skull with vegetable oil to stop the gum paste from sticking to it as it dries. Rollout your gum paste and lay it over the skull face, leaving excess all around. First mould the gum paste into the eyes and nose socket to make sure you have enough gum paste to stretch into these area, then smooth the rest of the gum paste over the face using your palms to smooth and

 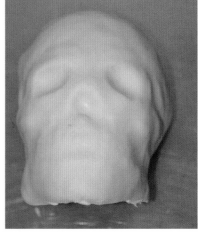

your fingers to press the gum paste to take the shape of the skull face. Tuck the gum paste under the jaw lines and chin and cut away the excess all around. You want to leave some gum paste over the head to give an anchor point when you add it to the ball cake.

Allow this to dry thoroughly—this may take a few days depending on how thick you rolled out the gum paste and the weather.

3 While you are waiting for the gum paste face mould to dry, do a little research and decide on your own unique design for the skull face. Trace these designs onto baking paper ready for step 4 in 'Attaching the face and decorating'.

MAKING THE CAKE

1 Preheat the oven to 130°C/265°F for chocolate mud cake. Grease both sides of the ball tin and place them in their ring holders on a baking sheet on a flat surface.

Note: If you are unable to get access to a ball tin, you can use oven safe soup bowls instead.

2 Pour an even amount of batter into each half of the ball. I like to fill the cake tins leaving only one thumb width of space between the batter and top of the tins—with the small rise expected of a mud cake, the cake should reach just above the tin, which will make trimming a lot easier (see step 3). Place the tray in the oven and bake for 40–60 minutes. Check the cake halves after 30 minutes to assess how well it's baking. Remember cooking time will vary based on recipe, size of your tin and your oven. To check if the cake is cooked through, insert a skewer into the cake centre. If it comes out clean, the cake is ready.

3 Once the cakes have been cooked and turned out onto a wire rack to cool, wrap each cake in cling film (plastic wrap) and refrigerate to chill

4 To trim the cake, return each half to its tin, securing it on the ring on which it was baked. Using the top of the tin as a guide, a sharp bread knife and gentle sawing action, slice the top off the cake.

5 Apply chocolate ganache to both halves of the cake and stick them together.

6 Apply ganache over the whole ball and allow to set. Apply ganache to the cake board and stick the cake to the ganache. Allow this to set so that it is secured to the board. I have used an embossed black cake display board to accentuate the skull.

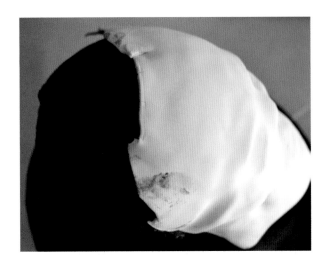

ATTACHING THE FACE

1 Gently remove the face from the skull mould and carefully slide it onto the ball cake to attach it. Apply some more chocolate ganache over the seam where the gum-paste face meets the cake and build it up a little so it becomes a smooth, curved surface, not an obvious ridge.

TROUBLESHOOT: Got skull bits that stick up? Oops! Just turn these bumps into the fissures that you see in skull bones and accentuate them with your edible black ink pen.

2 Fill the gap between the cake and the gum paste skull face with lollies, use lollies you can stack—this will take a long time and required a very gentle touch, enlist the use of someone with very thin fingers!

3 Lightly dampen the gum paste face. Roll out the white fondant and place it over the ball cake and skull. Smooth it into the grooves and holes of the skull face first and then smooth outward from there, and down the back of the cake. Cut away the excess fondant.

TROUBLESHOOT: Help! It looks messy! Don't worry, lightly dampen it and cover it with another thinner layer of fondant—this will cover your ugly wrinkles or cracks.

4 Place your baking paper over the cake. You can secure with tape or simply use one hand. Using a combination of your Dresden and ball tools, trace over your design to emboss it onto the front of your cake, you are going to want to work in good sunlight for this and the next step!

5 Once you have finished tracing, remove the baking paper and inspect your embossing, if you are happy with it, Allow the fondant to set, so that when you touch it, it feels a little firm.

6 Paint the face with your chosen pattern. For intense color I painted with undiluted gel food coloring, for a softer, brighter effect, dilute drops of edible color with rose spirit and paint with the paste it forms. You can also paint with dusts but you have to hand mix them with rose spirit the same way. Use the edible black ink pen to draw lines and detail on the face and across the skull.

7 Now to add the shapes. First I added yellow/gold daisies to the eye sockets because I was unable to replicate the marigolds with my cutters. To make the daisies, color some gum paste yellow. Roll out and cut out two daisies for each eye. To give them lift and curl, run the ball tool from the tip of each petal toward the centre and they will thin slightly and curl inwards. Attach the first daisy with sugar glue over the entire back of it and stick it down over the skull, with the centre embedded into the eye socket—this forms a base shadow for the second daisy, also attached with sugar glue on the back of the centre embedded into the eye socket, but still up and out to give dimension to the design. Color a small amount of orange gum paste, roll it out and cut out two stars to make the flower centres. Stick in place with sugar glue.

8 The nose and chin are also adorned with love hearts and a butterfly. To make these decorations, color some gum paste pink, roll it out and cut out some hearts. Paint with some edible gold paint, edible metallic pink paint or leave plain pink. I made the butterfly with pink gum paste in a silicon mould (see page 24).

9 The butterflies and dragonflies were made using the Claire Bowman Butterflies Silicon Mat and black Cake Lace powder.

Island of Treasure

DIFFICULTY: / / / / /

TIME TO MAKE: ⏳⏳⏳⏳⏳

Who doesn't love pirates, deserted islands and buried treasure. It's a theme at the heart of so many of our favorite childhood adventure stories. Here is a super basic, easy to master pirate on an island of treasure cake for you to try—add to it and make it your own … your imagination is the limit.

OPTION ALERT!

For this cake design I have used a hemisphere tin, the rounded shape gives the immediate impression of a small deserted island. If you don't have a hemisphere tin you can use an oven safe bowl or do a version of this in a round cake tin.

YOU WILL NEED

Hemisphere tin 20 x 20 cm (8 x 4 in) (or oven safe soup bowl)

1 batch white chocolate mud cake or sponge cake (see page 34)

Food flavoring, optional (I used marshmallow)

Buttercream

2 cups of white sugar granules (for the sand)

Gel food coloring: royal blue for the cake batter and chocolate water, gold and egg yellow for the sand and buttercream, ivory, brown and black for the pirate boy)

Red fondant

CMC powder and fondant to make gum paste

Embroidery scissors

Sugar glue

Wood grain embosser, or similar

Edible gold paint

Black edible ink pen

Chocolate gold coins for centre of the cake

Icing mix, for dusting

Plastic palm trees for the cake

Circle cutter

Ball tool

MAKING THE CAKE

1 Preheat oven to 120-130°C/250-265°F for mud cake or 180°C/350°F for a sponge cake batter. If you are using packet mix cakes, follow the instructions on the packet for temperature but be flexible with your cooking time, this tin is a different shape and make take a little longer than a standard round tin.

2 Grease the cake tin and dust it with flour, or alternatively line the tray with baking paper. Stabilise the tin on a tray and egg ring, or rest it on a small round cake tin that is one-fifth filled with water (or less to ensure the water does not touch the hemisphere tin).

3 Make the cake batter, adding the flavor before mixing and adding the color just as the ingredients combine, before beating on high for the set period of time.

4 Bake for 60–75 minutes for the mud cake or 30–40 minutes for a sponge cake, or until skewer comes out clean. Test the cake 10 minutes before the end of cooking time and reassess. Once cooked, turn out onto a wire rack to go cool.

5 When the cake has cooled, wrap the cake in cling film (plastic wrap) and place in the refrigerator. The next step requires a cold cake for optimal results.

TROUBLESHOOT: If the cake has risen into a dome in the oven, don't despair! The cake being cooked through is the most important thing. Once it is refrigerator-cold simply place the cake

back in the tin and using the edges of the tin as a guide, carefully slice the dome off the cold cake.

6 Once cold, place the cake dome side up. Using a bread knife cut off the top one-third of the cake like a lid and set aside. The straighter it is the easier it is to put together with minimal seams.

7 Using a circle cutter, or an egg ring if you don't have cutters, line up the ring over the centre of the cake. Resist the temptation to make this a large circle, the closer to the edge you go the more you will compromise the cake's structural integrity and have less cake to serve the guests!

Note: mud cake is denser and therefore more structurally stable than sponge cake and as such will cope better with a deeper/larger hole. Remember you will be adding decoration to the top of the cake so if you have opted for a sponge recipe; keep your hole for your lollies more conservative in size.

8 Insert the circle cutter as far as it will go or to the required depth (depends on your cutter) and remove it. Using a teaspoon, spoon out the cake inside the circle you have just cut. I try to make a bowl or dish shape.

9 Fill the cake with chocolate gold coins ensuring they lay flush with the top of the hole in the cake, being careful not to over fill it. Apply a small amount of melted chocolate, like glue, to the top of the cake around the lollies and all the way to the edge—this will seal your lid in place. If you do not have chocolate, buttercream will do. Replace the lid of the cake, ensuring it sits flush with the cake beneath it. If it does not, remove some lollies to ensure it sits flush otherwise your end look will be compromised.

TROUBLESHOOT! I have been too rough with my cake and it has cracked apart, what do I do? This depends on the size and location of the crack and whether or not you have lollies in it yet. The entire side of the cake coming off is harder to fix. First things first, I would put both pieces on the display board and using buttercream (surprisingly better than ganache for gluing cake back together) to stick the two pieces back together, refrigerate it. When it comes out, cover it completely in buttercream to create a thin protective shell and put it back in the refrigerator. If that works you may have saved the day.

10 Secure the cake to your display board using buttercream. I put the cake at the back of the board so there is plenty of 'water' at the front of it—this makes it more obvious that it is an island. It also gives you plenty of room to add sea creatures and birthday messages.

DECORATING THE CAKE

1 Color the buttercream for the cake and the sugar for the sand using one drop of gold gel food color to every two drops of egg yellow gel food color. For instructions on how to color buttercream see page 19. To color sand you simply add the drop of food coloring to a bowl of white sugar crystals and stir with a fork until the color is combined. If excessive clumping occurs, break apart color clumps with your fingers in a cake-crumbing motion.

2 Cover the cake with buttercream and extend the buttercream onto the board as far out as you want the 'beach' to extend.

3 Add the 'sand', this is messy. I place the display board over a baking tray to catch the excess sugar granules. Using a cupped hand, gently press the sugar-sand onto the side of the cake; repeat over the whole cake. If it looks patchy simply go over it again. Excess sugar will roll down the side of the cake and catch on the buttercream beach. Add additional sugar with your fingers to fill in the gaps on the beach. Brush away the excess sugar-sand from the non-beach areas of the board.

4 Gently melt blue cake pop chocolate or white compound chocolate and blue coloring over a pot of water that has been boiled but is not still boiling. Keep moving the chocolate around in the bowl with a spoon, turning it over, the heat from the base of the bowl will melt it gradually. (If you do this too quickly it will become dry and clump together—if this happens discard that batch and start again.)

A note on color: See page 24 before trying to color chocolate.

Use a big spoon to ladle melted chocolate onto the board. Using the back of the spoon, smooth the chocolate out using sideways swiping movements, this gives long ripples that look like waves. Be generous with the chocolate and don't spread it too thin, you want enough to

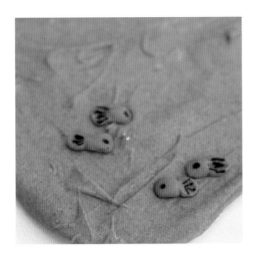 

make sure you get waves. The chocolate will set quite quickly to the touch, if you intend to secure anything in place within the melted chocolate have them ready to add and close to hand and insert them as soon as possible.

MAKING THE DECORATIONS

1 For the fish, make small oval balls of orange fondant, flatten them with your finger and squeeze at the one-third point causing the fondant to narrow—this creates the distinction between body and tail.

Using the edible black ink pen, draw a dot for the eye and line patterns for detail.

2 For the pirate boy, take three balls of gum paste, a small ivory one for the head, a red one for the shirt and a blue/grey one for the pants (or your chosen colors). On a non-stick surface, shape the smaller ivory ball of gum paste into a round ball with slightly elongated sides —you make this shape by squashing the ball ever so gently with even pressure.

3 Apply a very small amount of sugar glue to the ear and nose positions. Make 3 small balls of ivory gum paste for the ears and nose and attach each with your finger and secure it using a Dresden tool. For the ears, place the Dresden tool in the centre of the ball and push downward to create a dent to represent an ear canal and curl the top of the ear over slightly. For the nose, make two small indents at the base of the ball to represent nostrils.

4 To make a smile, take your circle cutter and insert it in and upwards at a 45-degree angle in lower the third of the face. Make dimples by inserting the large ball tool at each end of the cut made to represent the smile. You can do this by applying pressure directly down, or also at a 45-degree angle, applying pressure inward sand upwards to help shape cheeks.

5 Using the small ball tool, make shallow indents where the eyes will sit. This allows the small balls of fondant that make the eyes sit more flush with the face and also secures them in place better. You can start with small white balls of fondant and squash them down slightly. Take even smaller balls of blue fondant and positioning them over the top of the white balls of fondant, squash them into the bottom end of the white balls. Using a small amount of sugar glue in the eye sockets, attach the eye to the socket. Allow this to dry before drawing on the pupil with the edible black pen.

6 For the hair, mix brown and yellow gum paste lightly kneaded together to make sun streaked hair. Roll a small portion into a flat oval shape, you want some thickness to this because to make hair you will need to take sharp-pointed embroidery scissors held level to the gum paste and cut directly into it. This will create little triangles of gum paste that sit upwards like hair spikes. Start from the front and work backwards for two-thirds of the hair. For the last one-third, turn it around and cut back in the other way. This will make a gentle difference between the front and top of the head hair and back of the head hair. Affix with sugar glue and trim until you are happy with the shape.

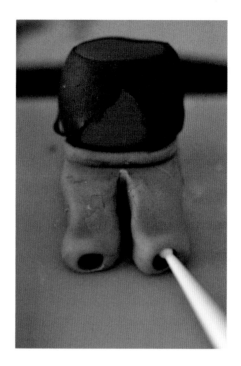

7 To make the body, shape the red shirt into a block shape.

8 Roll out a small amount of brown fondant very thinly into a rectangular shape and cut into the bottom of it with scissors to make it look ragged, using sugar glue wrap it around the body overlapping it at the top of the neck. Make a small brown ball of gum paste and attach at this overlap point to make a button on a coat.

9 Next, make little red cubes for the shirt sleeves, using your ball tool, hollow each out slightly to give your arms a place to join without being seen. Attach these with sugar glue and allow them time to dry.

10 To make the pants, make the same shape as the top only thinner and longer. Using scissors cut the last two-thirds of it in half and, using your fingers, gently round each leg a little. Using your ball tool, hollow out the ends to allow the legs to fit in.

11 Adjust the pants so that the top one-third is sitting upright and the last two-thirds are sitting flush with the top of the island. If you need to use a stick of raw spaghetti to secure the pant base into the cake do so.

12 Attach the head to the body with sugar glue and a raw spaghetti stick for support while the sugar glue dries.

13 Place the body onto the pants, affixing it with sugar glue and if you need to, another stick of raw spaghetti.

14 Now you can make arms and legs. To do so, simply roll sausages of ivory gum paste and bend and shape them with your fingers. To shape the ends of the limbs I have used a silicon mould, which allows me to simply insert the end of the limb into the relative hand/foot shape and it shapes it for me. There are many free tutorials for this on line, so a silicon mould is not required.

15 Attach the limbs by inserting small segments of raw spaghetti sticks into the end of the limb and inserting it into the body cavity, securing it in place with sugar glue.

I assembled this little guy directly onto my cake, if you need to make him in advance leave him somewhere safe to dry (and propped up) but be sure to dry his legs in the shape of the cake you want him to sit on! Using the upside down tin is the best approach.

16 Lastly, affix the pirate boy to the cake using a small amount of buttercream mixed with sand or if you plan to travel with the cake, be extra cautious and attach him with a small amount of melted white chocolate. Allow the chocolate to dry. Insert the palm trees and any candles or other island embellishments you may have created and you arrrrr ready to party like a pirate!

ACKNOWLEDGEMENTS

First thanks have to go to my husband Ben for being my rock, my sounding board, my unconditional support and chief of washing up and holding things. Thank you, my love, for all the late nights and sacrifice. Being with you makes everything worthwhile.

Thank you to Diane Ward of New Holland Publishing for giving me this opportunity; it's a dream come true.

With thanks to Mum, Debbie Clayton, my inspiration for this book. Your attention to detail at every event, no matter how large or small, gave me a passion for small surprises and details both in my cake design and in life. Every birthday, Christmas, Easter and milestone has been special because of your effort Mum; words cannot describe how special that is or how thankful I am.

With thanks to my dad Gary Clayton, who put off his own goal of finally owning a brand new bike to help me achieve my goal of writing this book. For your continued love and support and encouragement throughout my life, even when you don't really understand why I'm doing things! Words fail to describe how thankful I am for the continued and unconditional support and love of my parents.

And a huge thank you to my boss Tania Pantos, consummate professional and inspired decorator who has helped to keep it real, reminded me that inspiration comes from the most unlikely of places and has covered my shifts! I couldn't have done it without your support. Thank you to Kirstie Blain of Sweet Splash! a brilliant backdrop product made by a wonderful, talented lady, and to Carole Daniela of C for Cake, for your support and advice. Thank you to Luke and Alison of Cake Decorating Solutions for your support during the writing of this book and for the great products. Thanks to Chris Lane Photography and Make Up By Alexandra for the photoshoot and photograph-taking tips! I am blessed to work with such talented people. Thanks to Caitlin Foster, for her great work, editing my photos.

With thanks to The Northern Sydney Institute, part of TAFE NSW for allowing me to include some of their recipes, sometimes you just can't improve on a good recipe.

I have to thank my friend Sarah Timms, not only for her support but also for giving me the push I needed to make the hobby that made me happy into a business that makes me happy. Also to my friend Lynda Pallone, for her unconditional support, brave honesty and for turning up when I wanted to give up, giving me a new piping tool, a deadline and a much-needed kick in the butt! Also thanks to John R Phillips, artist, photographer and friend—thank you for your advice.

To Andrew, Alex and Jo, Sarah, Jim, Jenny, Maria and Nathan and all of my other friends and family—thank you for your continued friendship, support and offers of help despite my absence. I am sorry for all of the birthdays and social things I have missed, the late text message replies and forgotten things. This book is also for you.

Thank you to my Uncle Gary and Aunty Angela Emmerton, with their perfectly timed 'pop ins' for a cup of tea and random phone calls just when I needed encouragement to keep going. I am fortunate and ever thankful to have you as friends.

Thank you to Margaret Tessarino, my first cake decorating teacher, if it wasn't for your inspirational teaching and simplified techniques, I would never have found the love of cake decorating; you have infinite talent and a heart of gold.

A special mention to Rob Ryan for the inspiring beautiful silhouettes, your talent is beyond words, and to Jason Mraz, who provided the positive, sanity-keeping soundtrack to the many hours I put into this book. I continue to practise a mantra of grace and gratitude everyday and your music is a subtle reminder of this. I truly am—making it mine.

The last word is reserved for my Nan Betty Emmerton. The best Nan the world has ever known and my best friend always. You are where the love comes from and where unconditional support is known. I'm so lucky to have you in my corner. Love you Nanny-Possum-Face x.

ABOUT THE AUTHOR

Cake decorator and florist, Candice, is the owner, designer and decorator
behind the custom novelty cake business The Fairy Cake Mother, the freelance artist
behind The Cake-Florist and author of the nutrition and recipe blog The Candy-Apple
Bakery. Starting cake decorating as a hobby in her early twenties (before YouTube)
Candice found that information was limited and those who had it liked to hang onto it;
a decade on it is no surprise that she loves to share what she knows to help make cake
decorating easier and accessible for everyone who wants to give it go.
This is Candice's first book.

First published in 2015 by New Holland Publishers Pty Ltd

London • Sydney • Auckland

The Chandlery Unit 009 50 Westminster Bridge Road London SE1 7QY United Kingdom

1/66 Gibbes Street Chatswood NSW 2067 Australia

5/39 Woodside Ave Northcote, Auckland 0627

www.newhollandpublishers.com

ISBN: 9781742576237

Managing Director: Fiona Schultz

Publisher: Diane Ward

Project Editor: Jessica McNamara

Designer: Kathie Baxter Eastway

Production Director: Olga Dementiev

Printer: Toppan Leefung Printing Limited

10 9 8 7 6 5 4 3 2 1

Keep up with New Holland Publishers on Facebook
www.facebook.com/NewHollandPublishers

UK£ 16.99
US$ 19.99